SCHOOLCRAFT COLLEGE LIBRARY
W9-AFS-948

The Economics of Competitive Coexistence

Convergence Through Growth

CYRIL A. ZEBOT

FREDERICK A. PRAEGER, *Publisher*
New York • London

FREDERICK A. PRAEGER, *Publisher*
111 Fourth Avenue, New York 3, N.Y., U.S.A.
77-79 Charlotte Street, London W.1, England

Published in the United States of America in 1964
by Frederick A. Praeger, Inc., Publisher

Library of Congress Catalog Card Number: 64-16695

Printed in the United States of America

This book is dedicated
to the memory of

JOHN F. KENNEDY

FOREWORD

This book presents a comparative study of the root problems of economic growth in each of the three great subdivisions of the contemporary world: the newly developing countries, the Soviet orbit, and the West.

Economic development and growth dominate the thoughts and policies of the contemporary world. The Communist Party Program of November, 1961, based Soviet global designs on its expectations regarding economic development and growth in the newly developing countries, in the Soviet orbit, and in the West. To assess these designs correctly, and to counter them effectively, we must understand clearly the key problems of economic development in each of the three main segments of the world. This is the particular subject and purpose of this study.

The newly developing countries are struggling through the early stages of economic growth. Their economic development is guided typically by deliberate, sometimes arbitrary, political aspirations, which often produce irregular and precarious patterns of growth. The Soviet orbit has attained that stage of development where modern technology is broadly applied to production. Its productive capacity however, which is chiefly oriented toward technological superiority in support of Communist power, falls short of satisfactory levels of consumption. The advanced industrial countries of the West, on the other hand, have developed affluent societies of high mass consumption, even though they experience the pressures of pluralistic institutions and rigidities, relative deficiency of public services, and increasing requirements for defense, foreign aid, and space navigation.

The United States finds itself in a particularly intricate dilemma. Its rate of economic growth has been sluggish for years, with high rates of unemployment and idle industrial capacity. On the other hand, because of its world-wide commitments, the United States has experienced a chronic deficit in its total payments relations with the rest of the world, a situation which has resulted in systematic losses of monetary gold. It is not entirely clear how much of the sluggishness in the American economy is due to technological change and institutional rigidities and how much of it can be blamed directly on the deficiency of the total demand for goods and services. Because of the persistent difficulties concerning the balance of international payments, American monetary and fiscal policies have been cautious lest another upsurge of inflation further aggravate the country's international payments position.

Against the background of such differences, each of the world's three great subdivisions has a particular root problem of its own economic growth. For the newly developing countries, the key problem is not primarily the shortage of capital, but the vast and uneven lag of human skills in production and its organization. Examination of Soviet economic development reveals that the main obstacle is the widening and deepening contradiction between the autocratic management and the pretended socialist character of the Soviet economic system.

Faced with their pluralistic pressures and institutional rigidities, the increasing need for expanded public services, defense, foreign aid, and the space race, the advanced industrial economies of the West in general, and of the United States in particular, must view the constant danger of two-pronged inflation (from the cost and demand sides) as the main difficulty of economic growth. Since vigorous growth-oriented policies can generate inflation as their unintended by-product, fear of inflation may act as a basic obstacle to an otherwise desirable and possible higher rate of growth. If this dilemma, which is particularly acute in the United States, is to be overcome, inflationary pressures from the cost side must first be eliminated or effectively harnessed. This now appears an essential condition for a simultaneous solution to the dual root problem of the American economy.

But the phenomenon of inflation is not limited to the West. Although in the economies of the new nations and the Soviet orbit there are growth problems that are both more basic and more important than inflation, inflationary pressures are a common characteristic of all contemporary economies. Moreover, analysis shows that the key problems of economic growth in the newly developing countries (cultural lag and entrepreneurial lag) and in the Soviet orbit (increasing tension between autocratic management and socialist pressures in the Soviet economy) are closely associated with inflationary tendencies in their economies. Inflation thus assumes a broader significance in the framework of the global problems of economic growth. Inflation is a comprehensive indicator of the existing limitations and of specific obstacles to economic growth in all contemporary economies.

This book examines each of the three distinct root problems of economic growth and seeks ways to their solutions. It also explores the possibility that through solution of these problems the economies of the three main subdivisions may gradually develop increasing similarities.

To put it in more conventional terms, this book may be said to deal with the unresolved problems of interdependence and interplay between economic development and growth on the one hand, and the various social systems of economic organization on the other. That differences in economic systems are bound to influence processes and achievements of economic development and growth has, of course, been admitted all along. However, such differential influences have either been beclouded by ideological squabbles or simply dismissed as subjects unsuitable for economic analysis. This book makes an attempt at clarifying and specifying these influences.

In the course of exploring solutions to the specific problems of economic growth that are found to be inherent in the various economic systems of today, the inverse relationship emerges. When their inherent growth problems are recognized and attacked within each system, the corresponding processes of economic development and growth begin to generate significant "feedback" effects on the economic systems within which they evolve.

In spite of the still great differences among them, the various economic systems in the world today are already showing signs of converging toward greater similarities in their essential functions. This tendency has potential implications that reach far beyond the narrow limits of "economic" welfare alone.

Although organized systematically and presented analytically, the book is written in as nontechnical language as the overriding objective of dependable explanation permits. Some of the shortcomings of this approach are offset by including short appendixes on the more important technical aspects of the subject. It is felt that the potential usefulness of the book will thus be enhanced without impairing its readability. The appendixes may well serve to make the book suitable as a school text in a variety of courses.

I wish to thank all those who have offered assistance in the preparation of this book. Professor William Fellner of Yale read the manuscript and expressed critical evaluation of its several parts. My colleagues, Professors Goetz A. Briefs, Josef Solterer, Gunther Ruff, Henry Briefs, and Stanislas Wasowski read and discussed with me various sections of the manuscript. Special thanks go to Dr. S. Pejovich, who untiringly assisted me throughout the preparation of the book, particularly its many references and appendixes. But I alone am responsible for any shortcomings of the book.

A number of distinguished European economists were of great help to me when I was studying the European aspects of the subject. I am particularly grateful to Professor Erich Schneider and his able staff at the Institut für Weltwirtschaft of the University of Kiel, Professor François Perroux of the Collège de France, Professor Godfried Bombach of the University of Basel, Professor Friedrich Lutz of the University of Zurich, and Professor Francesco Vito, Rector of the Università del S. Cuore in Milan. A generous grant from the Relm Foundation made the research for the book, both here and in Europe, financially possible.

Mrs. Elinor Briefs, Mrs. Margaret McFadden, and my son Francis read the manuscript in its various drafts and made valuable editorial suggestions. Still others must be thanked for having been helpful in one way or another, particularly the graduate students at Georgetown University who attended my seminar in Advanced Economic Theory during 1961–62 when parts of the manuscript were under discussion. The unlimited support of my generous wife and helpful children sustained me throughout the labors that went into this book.

I owe this book to the opportunities given me at Georgetown University. May the book, published in the year of Georgetown's 175th anniversary, be a small contribution to the reality of the anniversary year's theme, "Wisdom and Discovery for a Dynamic World."

C. A. Zebot

Georgetown University
Washington, D.C.
March, 1964

CONTENTS

1. THE RACE IN ECONOMIC DEVELOPMENT AND GROWTH

When World War II ended in Europe, the Soviet Union terminated its wartime alliance with the Western Powers—an alliance that had been essential for its own survival between 1941 and 1945. The fateful Soviet decision was entirely unilateral. It had no foundation in the recorded actions or revealed intentions of the West, which by the end of the war was clearly determined not only to coexist peaceably with the Soviet Union but also to cooperate with it in the establishment and consolidation of the newly won peace.[1] Huge Allied armies were being disbanded and repatriated in a great hurry, and the new United Nations organization was being promptly set up with great enthusiasm.

In spite of its continuing monopoly in atomic weapons and its unchallenged superiority in the air and on the seas, the West did not present the Soviet Union with an ultimatum when the Soviet Government unmistakably defied the wartime agreement to permit political self-determination of the peoples of Eastern Europe. These peoples had fallen under what was claimed to be only a transitional Soviet military occupation.[2]

Other details and later events in the worsening of Soviet-Western relations since the war have virtually all followed from the fateful Soviet decision in 1945 to part company with the West and to turn its temporary military control over Eastern Europe into a permanent *fait accompli*.

The subsequent Communist conquest of the mainland of China created a similar geopolitical situation in Asia, but with two important differences. The new Communist China was not a great power, and the bordering countries in Southeast Asia possessed much less inner strength to resist further Communist penetration and expansion than did the areas along the new Iron Curtain in Europe. If West Berlin had been internally as weak as Indochina, for example, it would have been extremely difficult for the West to hold it from the very beginning. And no Marshall Plan could have saved Western Europe if Europe itself had not been determined to remain non-Communist. This inner strength of Western Europe made the Marshall Plan feasible and thus paved the way for the NATO alliance, which has prevented westward Communist expansion of the Asian type.

Meanwhile, the West not only lost its nuclear monopoly, but appears to have been matched if not overtaken by the Soviet Union in rocket power and space navigation. This has hardened the Soviet Government's post-1945 attitude and emboldened its global ambitions.

That Khrushchev shares the original Communist global ambitions can no longer be doubted. The Soviet Communist Party Program of 1961 has officially proclaimed this objective.[3] Because of the existing nuclear stalemate, Khrushchev may be sincere in his declared intention to avoid a new global war. But he is unwilling to renounce other means of aggression short of overt Soviet military invasion. Nor is the Soviet Government prepared to accept mutually controlled nuclear disarmament.

The Communist Party Program of 1961 reiterates the three public tenets of contemporary Communism: (1) Capitalism is dying; (2) the Soviet "socialist" economy will shortly surpass the United States in per capita production, the prerequisite for the subsequent final stage of a classless Communist society of unlimited abundance; (3) there is no need for another war since peaceful coexistence and competition between the two opposing systems will soon lead to the inevitable victory of Communism. However, if the "exploiting classes will use violence against the people," it will be "necessary to consider a nonpeaceful transition from capitalism to socialism."[4] This continued flexibility as to the means for world-wide Communist expansion was reaffirmed during Fidel Castro's long visit to the Soviet Union in May, 1963. A special investigating committee of the Organization of American States (OAS) concluded from the joint Soviet-Cuban communiqué of May 23 that "the Soviet Union in a major reversal of policy had endorsed Premier Castro's theory that Communism in Latin America should be achieved through violent revolution."[5]

Thus, whichever way it goes, it is now obvious that the Communist bloc, in spite of the differences between Moscow and Peking, does not intend to withdraw from its course of global expansion reinaugurated in 1945. This was publicly acknowledged by President Kennedy in June, 1963, when he stated that the "Communist drive to impose their political and economic system on others is the primary cause of world tensions today."[6]

In the underdeveloped areas of the world, a new tripartite formula, with different shadings in different countries and regions, has been in the making. It is concerned with the orientation of these countries in world affairs and with their problems of economic growth and development. These countries want to be "neutralist," "uncommitted," or "nonaligned" with respect to the Western-Soviet world tensions; "socialist" in regard to the methods of organizing their national production; and willing to accept foreign aid from either side or from both.[14]

IV

But appearances, even when logical, are sometimes deceptive. The neutralism of a new or weak country may be due less to its unwillingness to choose between two basic conceptions of human ends and means than to mere perplexity. What else can a relatively small and weak political entity do in a world overshadowed by two giants in nuclear stalemate? Actually, as revealed with laboratory precision in the Belgrade Conference of the "nonaligned" countries in September, 1961, it is the subconscious fear of Soviet terrorism that makes so many of the small countries seemingly pro-Soviet or even, in some cases, pro-Chinese.

Similarly, economic socialism in these same countries may not actually mean a convinced preference for a bureaucratic organization of production. In many of the underdeveloped countries, socialism may be a rationalization of the sociological fact that a small political elite is the only available pool of social leadership and economic management. Or the word "socialism" may simply denote the economic fact that in some of these countries the government is virtually the only accumulator of capital—capital which, moreover, may have to be used mainly for investment in fundamental social projects that by their very nature are governmental responsibilities. Finally, to some of these countries socialism may be only a matter of diplomacy, an inspired misnomer (to please or placate the Soviet bloc) for all kinds of normally public and cooperative arrangements. This, for example, would seem to be the case with India's repeated claims to economic socialism; actually, the percentage of the national product that falls to government in India is one of the lowest in the world.[15]

In assessing the early stages of economic development in the newly developing countries of today, one should compare conditions there with the specific conditions prevailing in Western E. rope on the eve of the first Industrial Revolution.

A new social philosophy of liberalism had developed. This philosophy was the product of a long sequence of postscholastic philosophical and religious currents, such as nominalism, the Protestant Reformation, secularism, rationalism, natural philosophy in England, and the development of natural science. The basic creed of the new philosophy was maximum freedom from the fetters of the past—freedom from guilds, from government, and even from the moral teachings of the churches. Liberalism stressed the combined powers of human reason and individual freedom which, together with the discovered laws of nature, would open the road to progressive mastery over the physical environment. New frontiers, which had been opened up in the fifteenth and sixteenth centuries, provided room for a bold application of these new ideas and concepts. As a result of mutual interaction of these philosophical and historical factors, there took place in Western Europe an upsurge of individualism accompanied by a gradual reduction of the role of government. Thus, a strong entrepreneurial spirit developed, and this channeled economic development along the lines of free private enterprise.

Now let us consider the conditions in the newly developing Asian, African, and, to some extent, Latin American nations today.

In modern times, most of these countries were colonies of Western powers. The recent upsurge of nationalism all over Africa and Asia, coupled with the withdrawal of the colonial powers, has led to sudden political independence for most of the former colonies. These newly established countries are extremely sensitive and jealous of their political independence. They consider their new governments as *the* symbol of their independent existence. The basic creed of liberalism, freedom from the fetters of government, is still an alien concept to them, associated with their former colonial masters. They feel that a strong national government is the best protector of their newly won independence.

Therefore, it is "society," not the individual person, that is stressed in Africa and Asia today. The behavior of these countries is the result of their specific historical development, very different from that of Western Europe and the United States. It must be added that the newly developing countries suffer from a basic shortage of entrepreneurial aptitudes and technical skills. Governments and their bureaucratic apparatus appear to be the main source of economic management as well as of public administration. Under the slogan of "socialism," a sort of neomercantilism is taking hold of non-Communist Asia and Africa. How long will it last? What will it lead to? These are the truly significant questions to which we shall return.

As for the seemingly cynical attitude of the newly developing countries toward foreign aid, the explanation is not difficult. Since any underdeveloped country feels that it can use much more capital than it can possibly accumulate itself and receive from abroad,[16] why not take all the foreign aid within reach, no matter where it comes from, as long as this does not irrevocably entail open political and military commitments to either world bloc? It is rather for the givers of foreign aid to exercise such restraints in their disbursement of it as are indicated by political judgment and economic analysis.

V

These are the basic impressions that arise from an observation of economic development in the light of Soviet-Western tensions and the psychology of underdeveloped countries. Now the whole subject should be submitted to a more detached and systematic examination.

2. THE HISTORICAL PATTERN OF ECONOMIC GROWTH

Perhaps the most influential view of the complex problem of economic growth and development today is that of Professor W. W. Rostow,[1] formerly Deputy Special Assistant to President Kennedy for National Security Affairs and now Chairman of the Policy Planning Board in the Department of State. Combining historical description with analytical insights, Rostow draws a general pattern of the sequential stages of economic development and growth.[2] According to him, human societies pass through five such stages: traditional society, the preconditions period, the take-off period, the stage of economic maturity, and the period of diffusion on a mass basis of durable consumers' goods and services.

Rostow's "traditional society" denotes a primitive society—primitive in the ways of scientific knowledge, organization, and technology, in which the prevailing attitudes toward nature and its human use for production of goods and services are pre-Newtonian and in which methods are correspondingly simple, of low efficiency, and accepted fatalistically, hence with few significant innovations. This traditional society gives way to a "society in the process of transition," when the explanations and findings of modern science begin to be accepted and applied. As more efficient techniques are gradually understood and introduced, the traditional fatalism begins to yield to a new outlook that regards nature as susceptible to an increasing measure of human mastery, resulting in more efficient and abundant means of human existence. This transition in man's view of, and control over, nature is accompanied by a transformation of the political organization of society in the direction of broader national interests. Presumably, this transformation is rooted in the realization that men themselves can also be more efficiently organized and that a better organization and administration of society will enlarge the newly perceived possibilities of control over nature.

Before such a transitional society can set the final stage for the take-off into a systematically increasing economic growth and development, it must fulfill two important specific economic tasks.

Agricultural production must become efficient enough to free an increasing part of the population for other industrial pursuits. In addition, the transitional society must also build a great deal of "social overhead" capital, such as modern means of mass transportation as well as a minimum of other collectively required public services. Only then will further savings and new technological possibilities be in a position to be more massively directed toward the production of a greater diversity and abundance of goods and services for increasing industrial and individual use.

Once the transitional society has irrevocably transformed the traditional society, improvements in production become more and more visible and regular. Now the society is ready for its historical take-off toward a more general, faster, systematic, and self-sustaining economic growth. At this stage, the society already understands the economic meaning, and develops habits, of substantial saving (on consumption) for the purpose of investment (in capital). Saving and investment reach 10 per cent or more of the society's production and income, which permits economic growth to be self-sustaining. In conjunction with increasing technological and organizational advances, such a rate of investment starts yielding an increasing rate of growth in production, which depends largely on the evolving capital-output ratio, that is, on the average amount of capital per unit of product.[3] But the crucial take-off is centered in one or a few particular industries (such as railroads) from which other industries, both closely and more remotely related, then evolve.

II

After such a take-off in saving, investment, modern technology, and in their massive application to some key industry, there follows a relatively protracted period during which technological advancement and corresponding capital investment are being gradually spread throughout the various old and new branches of production. In most of the Western nations, this spreading-out process, after the initial take-off, went mainly from railroads to steel, which was needed for better rails, and from steel to machine tools, machinery, and equipment whose construction steel had made possible. Regional and historical variations in the pattern of industrial spread-out are determined by the characteristics of the take-off industry, by the technological requirements and potentialities it unfolds, and by the natural resources on hand or conveniently imported.

When the evolving modern technology has been applied to the bulk of a country's resources, the society has reached the stage of economic or technological maturity. Now, with real income growing faster, the mature society can choose from among several further alternatives. It can continue, or initiate, a more individualistic course of further economic growth and development toward more abundant and diversified consumer goods and services; or it can turn toward more leisure time, culture-building, and increasing social welfare and social security; finally, such a society can choose to use its developing industrial potential to assert its national power in the world. One reason why there have been considerable differences in the economic make-up of the various Western nations in their postmaturity stages is that these various alternatives have been used by them in various combinations, depending on historical circumstances and the political orientation of individual nations.

Rostow nevertheless lists the typical fifth stage in the historical pattern of economic growth and development following the maturity stage as the "period of diffusion on a mass basis of durable consumer goods and services" or "the age of high mass consumption." This classification seems to indicate that no matter what the initial postmaturity direction of economic growth and development may be, high mass consumption sooner or later asserts itself in such a society. In Europe, this outcome had been politically delayed until after the post-World War II reconstruction, and in the Soviet Union it is still being held back by the totalitarian designs and global power orientation of Communism. But one can already discern growing pressures toward higher mass consumption, even in the Soviet Union and its European satellites. This interesting question will be taken up later when the special case of Soviet economic growth is examined.

The high mass consumption stage in the sequential pattern of economic development is characterized by an increasing diversification of consumer goods and services. Where the distribution of consumer goods is carried through by means of voluntary purchases in corresponding markets, as has been the case in the West, the pattern of diversification of consumer goods is ultimately determined by the market-revealed price- and income-elasticities of demand; that is, by the people's buying responses to changes in commodity prices and in their own incomes. Thus, an article of consumption, in relation to which consumers are either price- or income-conscious, or both, will be mass produced and distributed only when technology permits and when competition brings about cheaper production. In this manner, durable consumer goods have entered mass production and consumption in Western countries. As real income per person continues to increase, this process of gradual diffusion of new consumer goods both deepens and widens.

III

The question now arises as to whether the fifth, or high mass consumption, stage of economic development is to go on indefinitely or whether it is to be followed by yet another and different sequential stage. Rostow raises this question, but realizes that if it is of any foreseeable practical significance at all, it is so primarily for the United States. And here he shares J. K. Galbraith's vision of the "affluent society," although with caution and some reservations. It will be convenient to take up this question when we come to examine the special case of economic growth and development in the United States and in other advanced industrial countries in the West.

3. THE NEWLY DEVELOPING COUNTRIES: MAN VERSUS TECHNOLOGY

Rostow's theory of economic growth and development is composed of a set of generalizations derived primarily from the historical experiences of the leading Western countries. Although this theory is well-articulated and flexible enough to accommodate a variety of differences in the economic development patterns of various nations, one basic question remains. How dependably can such a pattern, set up as it is largely against a background of Western history, measure the early stages of economic development in the countries outside the Western cultural orbit? As yet, few of these countries have reached Rostow's take-off stage.[1] Most of them are still struggling to break out of their traditional societies into the transitional phase.

Rostow himself asked this question and answered it. He found but few real dissimilarities. Some of these render the problem of economic growth in the newly developing countries more difficult, but others make it easier than it was for the West during parallel periods of development.

According to Rostow, the newly developing countries of today have two comparative drawbacks and two advantages. On the positive side, there is incalculable advantage in the fact that economically infant countries today can freely tap the inexhaustible supply of scientific inventions and technological possibilities that the advanced industrial countries have accumulated. The other advantage is that the modern pioneer countries can benefit from extensive and still expanding, even competitive, foreign aid in technical assistance and capital, whereas the Western countries had to lift themselves by their own cultural, technological, and entrepreneurial achievements.

The two comparative disadvantages that the newly developing countries of today have to face, according to Rostow, are their higher rates of population increase[2] and the inroads of international Communism on the minds and emotions of important segments of their population. The higher rates of population increase make their economic growth relatively less effective since more new investment is required merely to maintain a given level of consumption, while Communist influence in non-Communist countries systematically obstructs their national development efforts.

Nevertheless, it would seem, according to Rostow, that on the whole it should be easier today for newly developing countries to advance economically than it was for the pioneering countries of the West. This is, of course, the general hope. But one must beware of wishful thinking. Hopes, policies, and efforts based on deficient analysis can mislead gravely. Rostow's generalizations and comparisons should be carefully scrutinized.

II

One basic shortcoming in Rostow's explanation of Western economic growth and development is his lumping together of all pre-Newtonian Western history (that period before Newton's physics was widely accepted and gradually applied) into an undifferentiated concept of "traditional" society. This is too gross an oversimplification. Newton was indeed the father of modern mechanics, and accordingly his contribution marks an essential dividing line in history. But Newton did not appear like a spaceman from another planet. He was the product of long centuries of painstakingly accumulated knowledge, culture, and civilization. Would Newton have been possible at all had there not been, long before him, such intellectual giants as Plato, Aristotle, Euclid, St. Augustine, St. Thomas, Francis Bacon, Descartes, and many others, with their cumulative sequence of intellectual achievements? The fact is that there has been an often interrupted but always re-established continuity in human progress from the Egyptians, Israelites, and Babylonians, through the Greeks and the Romans into the early Christian era, on to the Middle Ages and across the Renaissance straight to Newton and beyond.

These are but a few of the major contributors to the comprehensive and steadily rising culture that molded Western man, from the towering university centers to the humblest mountain villages. He was aptly schooled to use the subsequent Newtonian gift as a powerful means to enrich the human liberties that Western culture has systematically evolved and spread. Thus, the twin products of modern capitalism and democracy emerged. From its rough beginnings, it has since been shaped into an immeasurably more valuable good.

It is not possible to leave out of any meaningful explanation of the historical processes of Western economic development the many tangible and intangible *human* qualities and potentialities that the West had cultivated long before the various take-off dates on Rostow's illuminating calendar. These human characteristics affected deeply the recorded Western sequences of economic development. And how many students of these problems seem to forget that the economic achievement of the Soviet Union is also rooted in centuries of active participation in the cultural efforts of the West on the part of a sizable stratum of the Russian population.

III

It is unlikely, to say the least, that the newly developing countries of today could duplicate the Western economic achievement, shortening the course of their development in the process, without very determined efforts to duplicate also, in one way or another, the West's preparation of the human agents of the development. It was perhaps presumptuous of the Western colonial powers to assume that they should "Westernize" the colonial peoples under their rule and influence. Actually, they have done comparatively little to accomplish this. What they should have done, and what should not be glossed over now that most of these countries are politically independent, is to realize that the human mind *anywhere* must be developed before a country's resources can be properly developed. It takes educated and experienced men to visualize, conceive, plan, build, run, operate, and man efficient farms, mines, factories, schools, and a host of other private and public services, and to coordinate them into an effective social system, without which there can be no true economic development to project and no economic growth to measure.[3]

This basically important human dimension, relegated to an unexamined background in Rostow's theory of economic growth, bears fundamental policy implications for the newly developing countries. No matter how much capital they can raise or others can provide for them, their primary concern, for which above all they need our aid, should be to build the cultural foundations of all progress, including economic development. The mainspring of economic growth is rising productivity, which, in its turn, depends on the increase and spread of the human know-what and know-how.[4]

In the West, deep and broad cultural preparation for the economic take-off and technological progress since the end of the eighteenth century had long been under way before its full economic application and use. The newly developing countries of today, outside the traditional Western cultural orbit, cannot possibly be expected to duplicate such a systematic sequence of cultural preparation and economic development. There is no time for anything like this. In a sense, their cultural preparation must be reversed. Instead of beginning with a systematic and gradual liberal education of their people, these countries must first provide for a more direct training of selected groups in specific technical skills. Much of such training must come by way of technical assistance as the basic, and probably the most immediately important, form of foreign aid. Without such a training in applied technical knowledge for various productive skills, modern technology, as embodied in and required by contemporary mechanical tools and equipment, is of little use to them. The pace of their economic development depends on the availability of the relatively scarcest resources. In most of the newly developing countries, the scarcest resource is the many human skills that are needed if modern technology is to be used at all.

But this would still be only a stopgap solution of the human problem of economic development of new countries. Over a longer pull, more than this is needed. The whole population must gradually share in a systematic cultural progress if their economy is to develop toward the hoped-for take-off and beyond. To this end, the newly developing countries need a twofold system of education—formal schools for the rising generations and parallel efforts in adult education covering an elemental understanding of the laws of nature and of the meaning of man and of unfolding society. They need, above all, qualified teachers, educational films, technical assistants, and many excellent libraries and bookstores.[5]

IV

If Rostow's theory of economic growth grossly underplays man, the product of a long cultural history, other approaches to economic development overrate the role of the *political* factor in economic growth. This trend is being fostered by Communist influences in particular.

Thus, we are being given the impression that the potential economic growth and development of the newly developing countries is virtually unlimited, or that such limits as might exist could be freely extended by the determined and aggressive political effort of a national elite, however small. And since the totalitarian system of government as practiced in Communist-dominated countries is capable of more intensive and aggressive political action, loud claims are made that Communist methods per se are conducive to a faster economic development. Political action is held up as a kind of magic wand capable of dispensing with the broad human foundations and other requirements of economic development.

When the cultural basis of economic development, with its various limitations and obstacles, is duly considered, and political action is cast in its proper role, there emerges a simple general pattern by which the economic growth and development of underdeveloped countries may be assessed and guided. This pattern reveals the following set of limits to economic growth—limits which the process of economic development must systematically overcome.

First, there are, as we have seen, *basic human limitations* to economic growth. These reveal themselves in a society's culture, in the degree of its scientific achievements, in the skills of its people, and in their ability and willingness to work together. Political effort should help strengthen these human prerequisites of economic advance, but it can also hamper their development, and it certainly cannot create them from scratch.

Then, there are *natural limits* of production, such as climate, geography, and natural resources. That climatic conditions, for example, are an important determinant of human existence in all its manifestations, including economic development, is amply proved by the fact that the yet underdeveloped countries, China excepted, are situated almost exclusively in tropical and subtropical regions. From the very beginning of his existence, man was capable of reducing the obstacles of a cold climate by means of heat generated from simple fire. But only a very expensive, massive system of recently developed air conditioning can reduce the great obstacle to human performance presented by hot and humid southern climates. Here, too, improvement may be encouraged by political efforts, but clearly it will be a slow process, the success of which will depend on the realization that political efforts can be helpful mainly as an additional source of human motivation and as a means to better social cooperation on the local, national, and international levels, but not as a substitute for personal wills, abilities, and efforts.

There are *technological* limits to economic expansion, as expressed by the degree to which a society's production processes are mechanized and "automated." Political voluntarism may be required in extending these limits, but in the newly developing economies a careful selection of priorities is essential if political efforts are to help the social process of mechanization rather than hamper its logical sequence. Many developmental efforts have been wasted on projects that had no priority justification in the order of human needs and corresponding production requirements.[6] Furthermore, a dictatorial political elite often stifles the creative freedom of scientists and innovators, particularly of those outside its own narrow ranks.

Another set of limits to economic growth is inherent in the *economic system* as the sum total of institutions and organizations of a society's production and the disposition of its income and output results. The only human purpose of production is to serve the needs and aspirations of the people that make up a society. It therefore follows that whether the existing social organization of production itself is primarily "private," "socialized," or "mixed" (such as ours is claimed to be), the people can be truly served by it only when there is a balanced system of personal, voluntarily associated, and politically collective dispositions for the composition and distribution of output and income. There is no scientific formula for the exact proportions among the various personal and social constituents of a balanced system of economic dispositions. It must be surmised, therefore, that the proper answer to this question can come only from the self-determination of the people composing a given society.

For an underdeveloped country, a *dictatorial* solution may seem the simplest solution. But it is no solution at all. Clearly, there is much need and room for *leadership* in every human society, particularly in the newly developing countries. But if one accepts the proposition deriving from the most common human experience that freedom of choice (within intellectually and physically available alternatives) constitutes the essential difference between the actual or desired behavior of human beings, on the one hand, and the rest of nature, on the other, then leadership of men and nations must assert itself within some framework of genuine social self-determination.

The facts of contemporary experience in underdeveloped countries concur with this timeless philosophical insight. Given its enormous limitations, democratic India has made more basic progress in the few years since its political independence than many politically older underdeveloped countries, where a small landed class holds back the clock of history, or than countries where brutal

Communist autocracies exploit the people for their power-oriented technological applications.[7]

An emerging society's choice of system for the allocation of resources and the disposition of the resulting income and output sets the immediate limit to its economic development. There is only a limited quantity of resources to be allocated to different branches of production, and there is only a limited quantity of resulting products to be distributed. If a country's system of allocation and distribution does not reflect the will of its people, their individual and social aspirations will be treated arbitrarily. If, on the other hand, investment in education and technology is neglected or ill-placed, economic development will be slow.

When allocation and distribution are in the hands of leaders who respect the evolving sequence of their people's aspirations because they are truly responsible to the people, and when those leaders are also informed about the input-output implications of educational and technological progress—only then will the process of economic development be both what it *should* be and what it *can* be.

Thus, the rate of overcoming the various interrelated limits to economic development ultimately hinges on a people's basic understanding of the true ends and appropriate means of life, on the people's political awareness and participation, on the resulting legislative and administrative institutions (including the economic system), and on the leaders selected. In other words, it all comes back to the basic human element.[8]

V

So much for the main national conditions of economic development. But efficient economic development depends on still another important factor—the extent of international economic cooperation.

If contemporary political and economic systems allowed unhampered freedom of international trade on the basis of comparative production and transportation costs and corresponding market prices in different countries, and if international migration of human skills and capital in search of their most advantageous employment were also encouraged, economic growth of the newly developing countries would then be as efficient and fast as it could be. Products, skills, and resources of all countries would cater to wide international markets, thus realizing their productive po-

countries of Eastern Europe. This Communist bloc is intent on using its total political and economic power in the pursuit of Communist global expansionism. Communism has thus become a unique world-wide aggressor in a combined ideological, political, and military sense.

In spite of the Sino-Soviet ideological squabbles, the bloc as an effective world power and world-wide aggressor is militarily, technologically, and economically dependent on the Soviet Union, at least for the foreseeable future. "As goes the Soviet Union, so willy-nilly, goes the Communist bloc"—in any strategically serious global respect. This is ultimately true also with respect to the subversion by the Communist parties outside the bloc, even though some may appear to be taking orders from Peking rather than Moscow.

III

The Soviet Government is a constitutionally unlimited, essentially totalitarian government, selected and controlled by the exclusive and hierarchically constituted Communist Party. When, during World War II, Stalin combined in his own person his original position of General Secretary of the Communist Party with that of Prime Minister of the Soviet Government, the monolithic, autocratic nature of the Soviet totalitarian system was complete.[5] Since Stalin's death, Khrushchev has been attempting to establish a combined single leadership of his own. Khrushchev, too, is both the top secretary of the Party and the prime minister.

So constituted, with unlimited administrative jurisdiction, the Soviet Government controls the entire visible activity of Soviet society and its economy. Arbitrarily, the Communist Government selects the objectives for the Soviet society and allocates the economic means for the implementation of these objectives. In the Soviet system, the government is in the hands of a self-perpetuating Party leadership now personified in Premier Khrushchev.[6] It is the Western system upside down.

To understand the functioning of the Soviet economy, one must keep firmly in mind that the totalitarian and autocratic Soviet Government administers all natural resources and other means of production. There are no independent nongovernmental enterprises. The Soviet Government decides what to produce and disposes of all the economic goods produced.[7] The amount of consumer goods permitted the people is regulated by means of a flexible, over-all system of sales taxes (the so-called turnover taxes), which constitute on the average, roughly one-half of the sales price.[8]

In addition to regulating total consumption and the various amounts of particular consumer goods to be sold, the turnover taxes on consumer goods are also one of the main sources from which the Soviet Government finances investment in capital and expansion of its own power.[9] This means that the masses of the people must shoulder, out of their low incomes, a heavier burden of taxation than the minority of privileged members of the ruling Communist class, whose incomes are high. Thus, in regard to its economic and financial structure also, the Soviet system is an inverted reflection of that commonly found in the West.

In such a system, how is high mass consumption attainable? Unless the Soviet Government shifts in a much more democratic direction, the level of civilian consumption will remain at the mercy of the autocratic Communist regime, committed to its own self-perpetuation and to its demonstrated objectives of global influence and expansion. The Soviet Communist Party Program of 1961 makes this unmistakably clear.[10]

Thus, there is no reason to expect from the *Soviet Government itself* a democratic political reform, which would naturally lead to a high mass consumption economy, or a direct authoritarian reorientation of the Soviet economy toward high mass consumption. Even if the Soviet Government sincerely desired to establish an "affluent society," it clearly is not yet in a position to have at the same time both the largest power establishment in the world and high mass consumption. Even the United States is feeling the pinch of increasing defense and space expenditures, plus a high mass consumption economy,[11] although it can be presumed that the United States uses a smaller percentage of its much larger total and per capita output for the combined purposes of defense, space, and foreign aid than do the Soviets with their more far-reaching power establishment and much smaller total and still smaller per capita output.[12]

Rostow hopes that the Soviet Government may be persuaded in favor of high mass consumption at home and "diffusion of political power in the world"[13] by the specter of the approaching danger when China reaches technological maturity, and under the pressure of the newly awakening individualism and pluralism in the Soviet society. But these are imponderables far too speculative for reliable prediction or policy formulation. Presumably, the Soviet Government has sufficient means at its disposal to contain any undesirable economic developments in China and to control the masses of the Soviet people, who are without any effective non-Communist organization.

IV

A deeper analysis of the problem of Soviet economic "maturity" was indicated by Milovan Djilas in his famous book on contemporary Communism.[14] Djilas' views may be briefly summarized as follows.

According to Marx, developed capitalism was to be a social and economic system with two irreconcilably opposed classes: the progressively shrinking class of capitalists systematically exploiting the ever-increasing class of proletarians,[15] who would eventually overthrow the capitalists and establish the "dictatorship of the proletariat."[16] Once the capitalist class was eliminated, society would eventually become and forever remain a classless and stateless Communist society. This final utopia would spring from such a degree of economic development (accomplished by means of a transitional socialist system of production) that scarcity would disappear, sweeping away all class distinctions. Such a society, rooted in material abundance and having neither exploiting nor exploited classes, would be entirely self-sufficient. Its natural spontaneity would even make superfluous the compulsory institution of government.[17]

Communist propaganda is still reiterating this Marxist dogma of heaven on earth. The Communist Party Program of 1961 almost dates its beginning. But the facts of history have played a strange game with this fundamental Communist article of faith. It is the advanced capitalist societies of the West that are gradually becoming classless. The actual development of Communist-dominated societies has moved in the opposite direction. Instead of becoming classless, they have developed new and deeper class divisions. On the one hand, there is a privileged new class of political, economic, military, and cultural dictators; on the other, the subjected masses. The new class, consisting of Party leaders and carefully selected Party favorites, dominates completely. It disposes of all the national resources and enjoys wide social and economic privileges.

Djilas revealed the abyss that separates the reality of the Communist system not only from its utopian promises, but also from the proclaimed terms of its own legal status. In Communist states, Djilas reminds us, "property is legally considered social and national property. But in actuality a single group manages it in its own interest. . . . The words of the leading group do not correspond to its actions. . . . All actions result in strengthening its property holdings and its political position."[18] Djilas distinguishes between Soviet "socialism" as it is on paper and in unredeemed promises, and as it is in actuality, perverted into a private monopoly of the Communist leaders. Djilas was not the discoverer of this contradiction, but he certainly has elucidated its dynamic implications:

> The new class is not immune to every type of opposition. . . . Demands to return to the old pre-revolutionary relations seem unrealistic, if not ridiculous. Material and social bases no longer exist for the maintenance of such relations. The Communists meet such demands as if they were jests. . . . The new class is most sensitive to demands . . . for freedom of thought and criticism . . . *within the limits of "socialism."* . . . Criticism of the new class's monopolistic administration of property generates [in Communist leadership] the fear of a possible loss of power. . . . This contradiction cannot be resolved without jeopardizing the class's position. . . . The contradiction between the new class's real ownership and its legal position . . . has within it the ability not only to incite others, but also to corrode the class's own ranks. . . . This contradiction, when intensified, holds prospects of real change. . . .

Every word of this significant passage from Djilas's book is rich in meaning. It should be read and reread with deep reflection.

V

To appreciate the dynamic implications of the basic contradiction within the Communist system as Djilas singles it out, one must compare his insight with the standard predictions about the future of the Communist system. There are three typical varieties of "predictions" about the future of Communism in power.

The Communists themselves continue to insist that they will in due time transform their present "socialism" into a classless and stateless society of universal abundance (communism).[19] Since, by any historical test or rational standard, a purely spontaneous civic society without conflicts and without government is an outright impossibility, this persistent claim can be explained only as a needed opiate under the indefinite continuation of the harsh Communist reality.

Some Western optimists, subscribing to the semideterministic evolutionism of the Rostowian "stages" theory,[20] hopefully expect the Communist system to "evolve" toward an unspecified but acceptable social and political reality.[21] Having no dependable empirical support or convincing rational meaning within the totalitarian Soviet system, such wishful predictions cannot serve as the basis for a workable foreign policy.

The Rostowian view is not a valid generalization from history, and given the unique nature of the Communist aggressor, is even less reliable as a projection of history. Not every expansionist system in history actually evolved toward a peaceful, not to say democratic, outcome. In recent history, Hitler plunged the world into a global war. So could Communism, suddenly or piecemeal. There is no deterministic guarantee against such a possibility, especially not against a totalitarian power system based on such a pseudo-religious ideology as Communism.

Finally, there are anti-Communists who will admit of no solution other than a violent overthrow and total liquidation of everything that is associated with Communism. Since this view is implicitly predicated on the need of war as a means to peace in a time of nuclear warheads and space missiles, it is both a logical contradiction and a political illusion.

Djilas' insight leads to a different outcome. The fundamental contradiction between the pretended transitional Communist system ("socialism") and the actually existing arrangements (a complete political and economic monopoly by the Communist leadership) is generating, widening, and intensifying internal pressures. These growing tensions tend to force the Communist reality both toward that which it is supposed to be, but is not, and further and further away from it. Thus, Djilas visualizes a solution other than utopian transformation, mysterious evolution, or violent intervention. He implies that inherent pressures within the Communist system can be systematically encouraged. If so, there may develop a serious clash between two alternatives. Either the formal Soviet socialism, now suppressed and dormant, may start coming to life and mark the beginning of the end of Communist global expansionism; or growing domestic pressures for genuine socialism will progressively weaken Communist influences and expansion in the world.

Are these implications of Djilas' analysis any more realistic than their standard counterparts? Obviously, it is impossible to make a reliable prediction about the future of such an arbitrary social reality as the existing Soviet system. However, it is much more practical to encourage an acceptable outcome—genuine socialism—that in principle is constitutionally sanctioned and psychologically fostered in the Communist system itself, than to hope for changes that are plainly utopian, mysteriously vague, or totally unthinkable.

The implications of Djilas' central insight suggest a development that is sociologically and psychologically feasible. Once utopian and war-type solutions are discarded, there remain only two alternatives. One is to expect and encourage internal uprisings and revolts entirely outside the constitutional framework of the Soviet system. After the experiences in East Germany in 1953 and in Hungary in 1956, there is for the time being little psychological and sociological basis for an effective revival of such liberation attempts in the satellite countries and virtually none in the Soviet Union itself. It is clearly more fruitful to expect and encourage the deep internal contradiction within the Soviet system to come more and more into the open. The ensuing manifold pressures and conflicts would then evolve within the constitutional, sociological, and psychological framework of the Soviet system, avoiding easy accusations and suppressions as plain treason. That is why the implications of Djilas' proposition must be taken seriously. There is no acceptable alternative that would be as realistic.

VI

Many examples can be given to illustrate the implied potentialities of Djilas' proposition and to expand its seminal insight. One is very broad and obvious. To be able to run the machinery of a huge and ambitious totalitarian state in a technological age, the Soviet regime was forced to greatly expand basic and technical education. In the process, new generations of scientists and semi-intellectual technicians have come into being. Having been permitted to develop their reasoning powers in fields more or less neutral ideologically, they now unavoidably grow increasingly curious about the philosophical, cultural, and even political aspects of life. Here, then, within the Communist system is a potentially disruptive force of more than one dimension.[22]

Nonideological influences reach further still. In spite of the pseudo-religious, dogmatic character of official Communist ideology, the observable attitudes and, even more, the aggressive capabilities of the Communist leadership are necessarily codetermined by a variety of extraideological factors, partly originating from within their own system[23] and partly from without.[24] These two sets of extraideological factors are subject to historical processes that do not of necessity obey the dogmatic Communist dialectics. Furthermore, and most important, both sets of extraideological factors are susceptible in various degrees to manipulation by the free world's strategy. The dogmatic Marxian dialectics in Communist-dominated countries finds itself in daily conflict with the non-Marxist logic of the physical sciences, as well as with the nondialectical (in the Marxist sense) realities of religion, psychology, sociology, military strategy, economics, and even politics. The actual and potential dimensions of this increasing conflict must be systematically explored.

As Communist regimes pass through the actions, reactions, and accidents of history, Communist ideology unavoidably loses its initial, seemingly all-determining influence on events, attitudes, and behavior. Increasingly, the dialectic Communist ideology must share influence with the nondialectically (in the Marxist sense) operating extraideological factors. In the light of this insight, the vaguely recognized notion of "erosion" can now be analytically sharpened. Erosion of the Communist power system may result from the impact of the two sets of extraideological influences on the Communist will and/or ability for world-wide conquest through subversive or aggressive violence. The crucible of history even has some feedback effect on the Communist ideology itself. In the course of development of Communist-dominated societies, ideology comes under the growing pressure of succeeding revisionist tendencies. These pressures are being resisted by a combination of the dogmatic status and dialectical flexibility of Communist ideology. But the growing generations of Soviet citizens (scientists, technicians, administrators, managers, artists, students, etc.) who, by virtue of their assigned work and study, cannot help becoming better informed extraideologically, surely must be tempted to doubt the credibility of such a decreasingly meaningful ideology.

Communist leadership therefore tries to adapt the dogmatic Communist ideology to unavoidable extraideological developments through official reinterpretations. Khrushchev's version of "peaceful coexistence," for example, amounts to a reinterpretation of Stalin's proposition on "capitalist encirclement" (which was itself a reinterpretation of the Lenin-Trotsky view of world revolution). Although Stalin preached (and Chinese Communists continue to assert) that this encirclement must be violently eliminated by means of Soviet military power, Khrushchev now pretends that the "circle" will collapse through its own decay. Thus, Khrushchev gives the appearance of reverting to the evolutionary determinism of Karl Marx.

The self-eroding aspect of such ideological adaptations should not be exaggerated, however. The method of dialectical twisting imparts to Communist ideology a unique verbal adaptability and resilience. In the logic of Communist dialectic, Khrushchev's concept of peaceful coexistence is perfectly capable of "explaining" any turns that outside events or Communist strategy and tactics may take in the course of their "implementation." The ideology, of course, continues to be subject to further reinterpretations at any time. But no matter how resilient and adaptable the dialectical Communist ideology may be, it has not been able to pre-empt the inexorable influence of extraideological factors.

Rigid anti-Communist identification of the nature of Communist regimes and societies with Communist ideology may stem from an inadvertent mental transference to Communists *inside* the bloc of the attitudes and behavior of convinced Communist activists *outside* the bloc. The outside-the-bloc Communists are bent on *weakening* and eventually *destroying* the system (non-Communist) within which they operate, because such subversion is the very precondition for the "forces of history" to start working in favor of Communism. In this *destructive* performance, Communist ideology is, in fact, their only motivation and guide. The inside-the-bloc Communists, however, are in exactly the opposite position. They must first of all *build* and *strengthen* the system (Communist-dominated) within which they operate. And it is precisely in this *constructive* endeavor that inside-the-bloc Communists, whether ideologically "convinced" or not, are faced with the unavoidable extraideological influences.

The difference between the Djilas approach and the rigid ideological approach is self-evident. But the Djilas approach also differs from Rostow's in the following two important respects. First, instead of conveniently assuming a more or less automatic, only containment-supported evolution away from Communism, the indicated third view based on Djilas' original insight calls for careful analytical search for and empirical identification of specific extraideological factors of actual and potential erosion. Second, this view posits that extraideological eroding factors are susceptible, and must be subjected to, active influence by the free world. This third view is an expression of historical realism, supported by a most searching and active strategic voluntarism of various dimensions.

VII

Let us now turn to examples of more specific tensions within the Soviet system concerning its pretended socialist character.

One such tension is related to the Soviet workers' influence on the plant and industry levels of Communist economies. A growing tendency toward union self-government, collective bargaining, grievance procedures, and other phases of labor's participation in social and economic management is no doubt in the minds of the more thoughtful workers in the Soviet Union and other Communist-dominated countries.[25] The statesmanship of Western labor leaders must find a way to break out of the inactive rigidity of their present policy of having no contact with labor in Communist-dominated countries.

Similar, or even more pronounced, is the managerial aspect of the basic internal contradiction within the Soviet system. Political planning of production and distribution in the Soviet Union imposes upon the managers of Soviet firms and plants heavy penalties for not fulfilling the requirements and directives of the plan.[26] Soviet managers are, in general, loyal Party members and belong to the lower echelons of the new class. But they live in constant fear of losing their lucrative positions as members of that class. This unavoidable undercurrent of fear has turned the Soviet managers, albeit unwillingly, into another important element of the system's internal contradiction.

Granick gives us the following picture of the Soviet manager's social and economic status:

> The red executive has come far since the days of the revolution. . . . He is a college-educated engineer with a sound technical and administrative background, and he bears little resemblance to the flamboyant party director of the early days whose credentials were years in prison. . . . Never in his life will he have any certainty of tenure in his post. The Russian manager is a man with power, but he is no independent decision-maker. . . . His production goals, his costs and even his industrial research objectives are set for him. . . . No excuse exists for failure. Often the drive to meet quotas will force him into illegal activities. . . . In this sense, the red executive is very much an independent businessman.[27]

H. S. Levine also acknowledges that the Soviet manager often finds himself in a position from which the only escape is to procure the badly needed supply of inputs through "informal activities." Levine blames this situation on the tight centralized planning of production, which is causing too many shortcomings.[28] On the other hand, according to Berliner, the Soviet manager enjoys a much higher living standard than that enjoyed by ordinary citizens in the Soviet Union.[29]

Constant pressure exercised on the Soviet manager by the laws, government commands, and Party controls, on the one hand, and relatively good financial rewards on the other, have given birth to a managerial class "which is capable of functioning reasonably effectively under Soviet conditions."[30] The most recent appraisal of the ability of the Soviet manager came from Galbraith, who commented that a visitor in Russia today sees Soviet managers as a remarkable group of people, able and willing to perform their tasks as satisfactorily as possible.[31]

The Soviet managerial elite has grown out of the process of Soviet economic development and growth. The more the Soviet Union develops economically, the more significant will be the role of Soviet managers and the more weight this important aspect of the basic contradiction within the Soviet system will have. In the broader context of the contradiction between constitutional and psychological socialism, on the one hand, and the autocratic Soviet reality, on the other, the Soviet managerial problem is bound to find an effective outlet for its growing dissatisfaction.

Another more specific but typical example of the same inherent contradiction is related to Khrushchev's proposal of January 22, 1958,[32] that the traditional Soviet Machine Tractor Stations be abolished and individual collective farms supplied with their own equipment.[33] Taken alone, this proposal looked like a "liberalization" and "decentralization" measure; for the Machine Tractor Stations were once an important means of tightly centralized control over the collective farms. In the same speech, however, Khrushchev also mentioned that Soviet collective farmers would be "invited" to surrender their present family gardens and cattle. Considered in this connection, the Khrushchev proposal concerning the Machine Tractor Stations clearly loses its seemingly liberalizing aspect. What the measure was aiming at was reduction of long-range overhead costs. In addition, such technically self-sufficient farms would increase Soviet military security in the event of a nuclear war. Beyond these technical and military objectives, the change was a step in the direction of implementing Khrushchev's long-standing desire, reconfirmed in the 1961 Party Program, to transform all Soviet collective farms (Kolkhozi) into state farms (Sovkhozi). Such a transformation would eliminate the legal character of Soviet collective farms as formal cooperatives.[34]

Thus, this agricultural change was a good example of Djilas' insight. Djilas understood clearly that Khrushchev's liberalization and decentralization measures are only a "new method . . . for the further strengthening and consolidation of monopolistic ownership and totalitarian authority of the new class."[35] Here, then, is another opportunity to widen the breach between the pretended socialist character of Soviet economy and society, on the one hand, and its actual subversion and exploitation by dictatorial Communist leadership, on the other.

Recent attempts at regional reorganization of the administration of the Soviet economy form a prime example of the growing manifestations of this basic contradiction that Djilas has indicated. The traditional rigid centralization and administration of Soviet economic planning had two opposing weaknesses. It was more and more resented by the people, and it was less and less effective in controlling increasing local deviations. To placate the people while at the same time reducing deviations, Khrushchev first resorted to the device of "regional decentralization" of industry,[36] followed by an analogous "decentralization of agriculture."

From the standpoint of the people, regional decentralization created the impression of a concession to pretended socialism. From the viewpoint of the Soviet Government, however, this decentralization actually strengthened the grip of the Communist Party over the economy. Totalitarian control was brought closer to the operating production centers than it had been before. But the Party remained as strictly centralized as it had been.

Decentralization of the Soviet economy formally began in 1957, when the administration of Soviet industry was subdivided into seventeen regions. The declared purpose was to provide a greater scope for decision-making on the managerial level. What is the outcome of these measures?

Oleg Hoeffding, an American expert on the Soviet economy, reported:

> What was done in 1957 at both the top and bottom levels of Soviet Industrial Administration was intended to remedy weaknesses in the system of central direction of industry and not in any sense to weaken central direction itself. . . . Although in public the need for administrative reform was justified mainly in terms of shortcomings of the old chain of command, there has been ample implicit admission that the quality of the high level decisions and orders passing

down this chain had often been defective. The outstanding and grossest case was the party directives for the Sixth Five Year Plan which evidently had badly failed to match the planners' target with the real production possibilities of the economy.[37]

Herbert Levine of the Russian Research Center, Harvard University, in a paper submitted to the Joint Economic Committee, came to a similar conclusion:

> Before the 1957 reorganization of industrial administration, the planning hierarchy ran along vertical branch lines. At the top stood Gosplan. . . . Below Gosplan were individual ministries. . . . Each ministry had a supply board and a sales board, which handled the planning of supply. Under the ministry there were normally a number of branch administrations and at the bottom, the individual enterprises. The reorganization has changed industrial administration from branch lines to geographic lines. The planning hierarchy is now at the top, still Gosplan, below it the planning commissions of the 15 Union Republics, below them the national economic councils which administer individual economic regions within the Republics and, at the bottom, the individual enterprises.[38]

The decentralization of 1957 was thus little more than an attempt by the Soviet Government to correct some of the most glaring deficiencies of the centralized command economy without really distributing economic power and without increasing the freedom to innovate on the part of the managers of Soviet enterprises. Furthermore, on July 23, 1961, special control commissions were established to deal with false reporting by managers. One commission was established at the national level, headed by Mr. Khrushchev himself, and fifteen others on the Republics level. The reason given for this further tightening of political control was the tendency of the managers and local officials to falsify the reports concerning production.[39]

The reorganization of the Soviet industry in seventeen major economic regions was completed, according to the Soviet sources, on February 23, 1962. The Soviets expressed their hope that this reorganization, which began in 1957, would increase economic efficiency and encourage better planning and coordination.[40]

In March, 1962, Soviet agriculture was similarly decentralized. The new regional administration was put under rigid control by the Communist Party. In a dispatch from London, Drew Middleton commented that, according to British experts, Khrushchev was "trying to remedy the situation by bureaucratic reorganization and stricter party control when the facts call for a much greater investment and higher incentives."[41]

Later in 1962, revelations of a large-scale, underground private-enterprise system of production and marketing were reported, and massive misinvestments in plants and equipment were discovered.[42] Proverbial Soviet shortages of food, especially meat, led to further increases in food prices.

It was against this background that the Soviet Communist Party Central Committee, meeting in November, 1962, decided to embark on yet another "reorganization" of the Soviet economy. This newest organizational pattern of the Soviet economy is set up as follows: The economy is divided into four separate segments. Foreign trade and all construction are to be centralized in Moscow, each under one deputy premier. Agriculture and industry were to be organized into a smaller number of regions, but each under strict discretional control of separate Party groups. There would also be mergers of basic production units into still larger enterprises. The entire new structure is under the centralized Council of the National Economy, with more power than the previous State Planning Committee (Gosplan). Furthermore, a new joint Party-government control agency was instituted "to ferret out persons guilty of mismanagement, embezzlement and other economic practices."[43]

It is interesting to note that the new reorganization of the Soviet economy resembles very closely the organizational structure of the Chinese economy. "Thus the Russians, like the Chinese, have centralized 'decentralizations' at party headquarters," said a *New York Times* editorial on November 28, 1962.

At the same session of the Soviet Communist Party Central Committee, there was some talk about the need for the Soviet economy to rely more on profit incentives and on a more genuine price system. But it is hard to see how such true liberalization of economic management could possibly develop within the new system of "centralized decentralization."

At the meeting of the Central Committee of the Soviet Communist Party and the subsequent session of the Supreme Soviet in December, 1963, Khrushchev revealed the staggering proportions of the unresolved Soviet agricultural problem. But again, the proposed solution missed the obvious core of the problem. For Khrushchev is again seeking solutions outside the human and organizational base of Soviet agriculture. Once he triumphantly introduced massive plowing of virgin steppe lands. No solution came of that. Now he proposes massive resort to chemical fertilizers. This will require huge and lengthy investment in chemical industry. If it is carried out, it will help Soviet agricultural yields with the additional side-promise of more chemical products for future consumption.

It has not yet occurred to Khrushchev, however, that despite all their natural and historical differences, all Communist-dominated countries share a similar agricultural crisis which must therefore have similar basic causes—collectivization of agricultural ownership, organization, and operation; or, as in the cases of Yugoslavia and Poland, where much of agriculture has not yet been collectivized, other Communist forms of political and financial harassment of the farmers. As this root problem of Communist agriculture becomes clearer every day, it is certain that grass-root pressures for a genuine social reorganization of agriculture will build up with increasing insistence. Communist-dominated countries have on their hands an "agrarian reform" problem in reverse that is at least as serious and acute as is the need for agrarian reforms in the developing nations.

The Djilas-diagnosed basic contradictions in the Soviet system between the autocratic rule of the Communist new class, and "socialism" is coming to a head. As an editorial in *The New York Times* of November 23, 1962, pointed out, "the enlarged party pressure and supervision may well tend to create intensified frictions and antagonisms between the managers directly charged with controlling production and the party bureaucrats who will now sit above them." Here, then, is a crucial contradiction within the Soviet system, with far-reaching disintegrating possibilities.

VIII

What about the Soviet successes in space navigation? The Soviet Government exploits these successes as if they represented the most convincing proof of the superiority of the Soviet economic system. This is a false claim. It confuses a one-sided development of technology with the general performance of the economy. That the Soviet space flights constituted a great technological accomplishment, no one could deny. Nor is the scientific significance of space exploration being contested.

But this is still a world of harsh scarcities—in the Soviet Union much more so than in the West. From the viewpoint of the allocation of the resources of the Soviet Union, the hurried and massive Soviet space effort is a crying testimony to the systematic misuse of the limited economic possibilities of the Soviet system. Even the "affluent society" of the United States could not with clear conscience start allocating such a disproportionate share of its resources to space navigation. It has to be done now because the Soviet Union initiated this massive race whose dangerous military implications cannot be ignored.[44]

On the priority list of human needs and aspirations, however, there are many more important things that should be done first. In the Soviet Union, most of the people are still without decent housing. Who can doubt that if they had any say about the use of their own national resources, they would vote overwhelmingly in favor of systematic housing development? If the extolled Soviet socialism were truly "social," this is what would happen. But the Soviet Government wants power, prestige, and global expansion. It has to disguise these aims in pleasant-sounding "socialist" oratory. That is why the Soviet space flights are propagandized as a proof of the superiority of the Soviet economy. In reality, the Soviet space program is another manifestation of the deep contradiction within the Soviet system.

A comprehensive picture of this contradiction and of the deceitful ways in which the Soviet leadership tries to cope with it is presented in the new 1961 Program of the Soviet Communist Party. This "new" program for the Soviet Union and the whole world is a sequence of specific contradictions, all stemming from the basic contradiction within the Soviet system. Here are a few striking examples, taken from the text of the Program.

"The great objective of the working class can be realized without world war. . . . The Marxist-Leninist parties prefer to achieve transfer of power from the bourgeoisie to the proletariat by peaceful means, without civil war." Of course, "when the exploiting classes resort to violence against the people, the possibility of nonpeaceful transition to socialism should be borne in mind." This would justify the Laos-Vietnam type of Communist violence anywhere in the world.

"In the current decade (1961–70) the Soviet Union . . . will surpass . . . the U.S.A. in production per head of population. . . . Everyone will live in easy circumstances. . . . The U.S.S.R. will become the country with the shortest working day." But, "complications in the international situation and a necessary increase in the strength of the armed forces can delay realization of the plans for improving the people's material welfare." Since the first is impossible to accomplish unless the United States deliberately stops growing, the Soviet people will have to accept the delay.[45]

Even the exclusive leadership of the Communist Party is to be reformed. According to the 1961 Program, members of the Presidium of the Central Committee of the Communist Party, as well as other "elective" Party and government offices, will in the future be limited to three two-year terms. However, members of "recognized authority, organizational abilities and other qualities can be elected to the leading governmental bodies for longer periods of time."[46]

This newest comprehensive document of the official Soviet policy on the entire range of Communist activity in the Soviet Union and in the world furnishes a truly striking verification of Djilas' important conclusion that Khrushchev's "liberalization" measures and promises are only a "new method for the further strengthening and consolidation of monopolistic ownership and totalitarian authority of the new class."[47]

There are other examples. The subject is so important that it clearly requires systematic exploration by specialists in the various areas of its potential applicability. In general, any significant Soviet domestic policy, administrative decision, or official pronouncement ought to be concretely analyzed in terms of its specific deviations from its pretended socialist framework; and the results of such comparative examination should be widely publicized, both within and without the Communist orbit.

IX

One immediate advantage of a broadened Djilas approach to the strategy for world peace is that it could greatly weaken the existing Communist propaganda line. Both offensively and defensively, at home and abroad, the Communist propaganda runs under the label of "socialism" as a cleverly employed disguise for the indefensible Communist reality. Indiscriminate anti-Communism, lumping together in one compounded negation the autocratic Communist reality and its rationalizing socialist underpinnings, has made the traditional and continuous Communist propaganda line much easier to use and that much more effective. By carefully distinguishing between the Communist reality and genuine socialism, and by singling out the former for persistent and detailed criticism of its perversion of socialism, the West could make Communist propaganda much more difficult and less effective.

If promoted wisely, such an approach to the Soviet economic development would also demonstrate to the world, particularly to the suspicious nations of Asia, Africa, and Latin America, that the predominant purpose of American and Western foreign policy is to work for peace and not to impose the Western economic and political system on others. It would make them realize that the West is indeed not pursuing an irresponsible policy of violent "liberation," but that it wants the people of each country to play a decisive role in the management of their own production and its use, because such is the requirement of peace in a world and an age in which another global war is unthinkable. Only if the people themselves control a nation's production and its disposition—either through the market mechanism in combination with complementary democratic political controls, as we do it, or through direct social democratic management of the economy, as genuine socialism proposes to do it—can it be safely turned away from the costly means of war into the channels of civilian consumption and human welfare.

In other words, a Western foreign policy that would include the Djilas approach would demonstrate convincingly to the world the essential connection that exists at this juncture in history between social and national self-determination and world peace.[48] And it would be much easier to convince the world of this functional interdependence between freedom from totalitarian dictatorship and world peace if we admitted openly that, even under the conditions of a most propitious development of the fundamental contradiction in the Communist system, the people of the Communist-dominated countries would have no wider choice than to substitute a sort of democratic socialism for the present subversion of it by the Communist dictatorship. There can be no doubt, for example, that even if the extreme case of the Hungarian uprising in October, 1956, had been successful, the people of Hungary could by way of transition have done no more than to replace dictatorial Communist ownership and management with a system of democratic controls over a socialized economy. Even such a change by them would have required much time and effort.

X

There is still more to the impact that such an approach to peace could have on the neutralist segments of Asia, Africa, and Latin America. The growing Soviet propaganda successes among the people of the emerging nations have been largely due to the ingrained aversion of many of them to capitalism, on the one hand, and, on the other, to their erroneous belief that the Communist system is at least economically, if not politically, socialist. They do not like capitalism, primarily because they associate it with colonialism. Very few of them have had contact with the highly efficient and humanistic contemporary capitalism in the United States and other Western nations. Furthermore, many of their leaders do not consider capitalism the most suitable system for the hasty and selective economic development that they feel to be needed by new countries starting almost from scratch. In a statement of January 18, 1958, to the annual session of India's governing Congress Party, Mr. Nehru reaffirmed this conviction when he bluntly declared that "socialism suits India."[49] President Nasser has inaugurated a brand of "Arab socialism."[50] Similar "socialist" declarations have come from many other Asian and African countries.

In a sense, the inclination of underdeveloped countries toward socialism is a modern parallel, under very different cultural and political circumstances, to historical European mercantilism. Had not the policies of European mercantilism laid the foundations for effective government administration, developed national markets and international trade, and encouraged the formation of a large, new business class, the subsequent evolution toward modern industrial capitalism and political democracy would most likely have been historically delayed. Socialist tendencies in underdeveloped countries today could play a similar although, hopefully, much shorter transitional role.

By accepting socialism—not as its own social philosophy and public policy, but as a legitimate and necessary element of a realistic world peace policy—the West would remove an important psychological factor that now favors Communist influences and impairs those of the West in both the neutralist and friendly world of newly developing countries.

In conclusion, Djilas' approach to the related problems of economic development and peace, if consistently and persistently pursued and applied to ever newly evolving situations, could greatly accentuate the hopeful process of internal disintegration of the Communist system in favor of a potential socialist transition to a high mass consumption economy. Under the circumstances, this is the world's most promising road to peace, as well as the only way to better living conditions for the people of the Soviet Union and its foreign dependencies.

If promoted wisely and accompanied by disinterested foreign aid programs to needy countries, this approach would also open the eyes of the people in the neutralist world to the evils of Communism as a perverter of socialism and the greatest obstacle to world peace. It would thus act not only as an effective deterrent to further Soviet psychological and political gains in the neutralist world, but could actually "roll back" the already accumulated inroads of Communist influence in Asia, Africa, and Latin America.

There is a wealth of policy implications to be derived from the central insight of Djilas' analysis of the Communist system. These implications must be systematically explored. Their practical potentialities for economic development and world peace must be carefully established and implemented. This project should be given the same priority that the West has assigned to new military and space technology. This method might well be the key to world peace. The Djilas approach to turning the Soviet economic growth toward high mass consumption, and thereby toward world peace, appears particularly suitable and promising since the Soviet regime has become increasingly sensitive to world opinion.[51]

XI

The preceding analysis was concerned with socialism from the viewpoints of the economic development in the Soviet orbit and its repercussions in the newly developing countries, and of world peace. But a word should also be said on the subject of socialism from the standpoint of social philosophy, to which it primarily belongs.

As far as Communist-dominated countries are concerned, any kind or degree of genuine socialism would be, from the viewpoint of the Western social philosophy of personalism and pluralism, as well as from that of world peace, an essential improvement for the people of those countries. This is so obvious that no more need be said. With respect to the politically noncommitted and economically undeveloped countries of Asia and Africa and for the development-conscious nations of Latin America, a Western foreign policy pressing for *real* socialist developments in the Soviet Union would have an indirect psychological effect. Admittedly, from the standpoint of the prevailing Western social philosophy, this indirect effect might not be wholly desirable. It might unintentionally encourage socialist inclinations in the newly developing countries. But one should keep in mind that "socialism," as an ideological catchword, has been spreading in Asia, Africa, and even Latin America, in spite of our active opposition to it. On the other hand, it has been shown earlier that in non-Communist new nations the word "socialism" is often only an emotional or foreign-policy contrived slogan which, in terms of actual domestic policies and objectives, means something much less ambitious than complete socialization of all production. There is more effective socialization in parts of non-Communist Europe, perhaps even in the United States, than there is in neutralist Asia and Africa or in Latin America.[52]

Finally, there is a most hopeful reason why the West need not fear a trend toward socialism even if it should spread, as it already has to some extent, over much of non-Communist Asia and Africa. From long and direct experience, we know—and for this reason firmly believe in—the superiority of a personalistic and pluralistic society and an essentially nongovernmental market economy. We may and must remain confident that when and so long as the people of even an integral socialist country are in a position *democratically* to manage their own national resources and to decide on their use, they will come to see and eventually to adopt what experience will undoubtedly have indicated to them to be better. They will discover in due time, as most of the European and even some non-European socialists already have done, that integral socialism, no matter how democratic, must be a very clumsy and unfair way to serve the well-being of the people who not only want to break out of their centuries-old condition of squalor and poverty, but also to aspire to higher regions of human freedom and progress. If, as abundant evidence indicates, ever-new elements of nongovernmental business undertakings and devices continue to emerge illegally even in the totalitarian Communist-controlled countries, it is not difficult to imagine the irresistible pressures for gradual desocialization of a growing variety of production in democratically governed socialist countries.

One can rest assured that a democratic socialism would gradually but systematically evolve toward a pluralistic economic organization, including real markets and progressively more private enterprises.

We have examined, in Chapter 3, the requirements for a promising economic development in the new nations. We have explored, in this chapter, the outlook for the Soviet economic growth toward high mass consumption in the light of the fundamental contradiction between its declared socialist character and its autocratic reality. Now we can focus our attention on the economic growth of the American and other economies in the West, which are our first concern.

5. *BEYOND HIGH MASS CONSUMPTION IN THE WEST: PRIVATE WANTS VERSUS PUBLIC NEEDS*

Rostow's systematic examination of the historical sequence of the various stages of economic development stops at the fifth stage, which he calls the stage of high mass consumption. This stage has been reached, if not completed, in the United States and, to lesser degrees, in other Western countries and Japan.

At this point, Rostow speculatively asks: What lies beyond? What will happen to high mass consumption societies when real income rises to the point of making good food, housing, clothing, and automobiles available to all? "This stage has not yet been fully attained; but it has been attained by enough of the American and Northern European population to pose, as a serious and meaningful problem, the nature of the next stage. . . . What will happen when . . . diminishing relative marginal utility sets in, on a mass basis, for real income itself?"[1]

Then, as if realizing that the dialectics of this approach to an understanding of economic development carried his thought a bit beyond legitimate inferences from the facts of history, Rostow stops again and qualifies: "For this generation and probably the next, there is a quite substantial pair of lions in the path. First, the existence of modern weapons of mass destruction. Second, the fact that the whole southern half of the globe plus China is caught up actively in the stage of preconditions for take-off or in the take-off itself."[2] What he is saying is that the defense requirements imposed on the high mass consumption economies of the West by Soviet global expansionism plus the growing danger of Red China as it drives toward economic maturity, and the related need for increasing aid to the new nations, will be such an added burden to the West that they will check its tendency to move "beyond high mass consumption" toward the next stage of their economic development.

This "next stage" has been foreshadowed in J. K. Galbraith's view of the "affluent society." While Rostow only intimates that "diminishing relative marginal utility on a mass basis, for real income itself"[3] (that is, of *total* consumption plus savings and not only of particular consumer goods) may appear in the not too distant future, Galbraith argues that, with respect to private consumption at least, this has already happened. According to Galbraith, "it must be assumed that the importance of marginal increments of all production is low and declining. The effect of increasing affluence is to minimize the importance of economic goals."[4]

In spite of this sweeping statement, Galbraith not only recognizes but laments the relative neglect of "public goods" in Western affluent societies. He does not minimize the defense burden and fully recognizes the increasing need for foreign aid. He differs with Rostow in that he feels that there is plenty of room within the existing economies of Western affluent societies for an adequate provision for all the varieties of public goods, including defense and foreign aid, if only the excess production and consumption of private goods were eliminated. This could be achieved by means of a much more extensive use of the sales tax, for example.

If excess production of private goods is eliminated, a satisfactory balance between the production of private and public goods can be established, without straining the economy by trying to impose on it an unnecessarily high rate of economic growth. We could afford not only more straight leisure time, but also a more leisurely pace of work and a higher rate of unemployment with more generous unemployment benefits. Thus, the next stage in the development of the advanced Western economies, as visualized by Galbraith, would be characterized by a new social balance between public and private goods, work and leisure, production and its "true" human purpose, technology and culture, market and society, private enterprise and government.

Rostow has no similar outline of the characteristics of the next stage, which he visualizes within one or two generations. He can think only of "boredom" as a general sequence to high mass consumption. This one can take as a kind of negative supplement to Galbraith's positive characterization of the postaffluent society. Common to both is the implied absence of further major economic challenges. This similarity in projecting the next stage reveals a similarity in their underlying social philosophy.

How meaningful is this philosophy? There is nothing in history which would justify serious expectations of a problemless or challengeless future. Only extreme philosophical rationalism or dialectic progressivism can lead to carefree utopian outcomes, whether Marxian or non-Marxian. Any degree of philosophical realism or logical pragmatism should suffice to prevent postulating a terrestrial finality of universal satisfaction. As more elemental needs are more or less satisfied, more sophisticated human aspirations, whether virtuous or vicious, individual or social, keep people "poor." Varying degrees of poverty depend on different gaps between the rates at which aspirations grow and the rate at which productivity improves, on the one hand, and on psychological, cultural, and moral differences among different people, on the other. As old problems are being met, new ones already are taking their place. Thus, relative scarcities are ever present and challenges never missing. Such, at least, has been the course of human history so far.

Rostow and Galbraith seem to differ in their dating of the "next stage." For Galbraith, the new stage of economic development in the West has virtually, or at least potentially, arrived. Its full implementation is being held back only by our failure to understand its meaning and possibility. For Rostow, the next stage is about two generations away. But this difference can be reconciled readily in Rostow's favor by the recent experience that our defense needs, including space navigation and foreign aid requirements, can readily absorb all the expansion that the increase in the Western rates of economic growth would permit. Therefore, Galbraith and Rostow can compose their difference in dating the next stage by agreeing on a continued need for a high rate of economic growth, at least for the time being.

A higher rate of economic growth is indeed still very desirable. The reason for it, however, is not to be sought only in increasing defense needs and foreign aid requirements. Even in the United States, the alleged affluence of individual persons and families is by no means accomplished, as Galbraith put it, nor even around the corner, as Rostow predicted. To clarify this proposition, it will be useful to re-examine the reasoning that led Galbraith to his concept of the "affluent society."

II

The principal significance for economic analysis of J. K. Galbraith's *The Affluent Society* is in its new theory of demand based on substantive inferences concerning the generation and nature of human wants. Most of the remainder of Galbraith's analysis proceeds from this base.

From an incisive introductory review of the historical development of economic reality and its analysis since Adam Smith, Galbraith comes to the sweeping conclusion that in their central propositions contemporary economic theory and policy are still based on conditions and ideas that, for the United States and much of the West in general, have long been outgrown and outdated.

Economics emerged as a separate science at a time (the last quarter of the eighteenth century) when concomitant technological and political developments began to indicate the possibility that production might eventually be expanded beyond the traditional limits of general poverty. Thus, historically, emphasis was on production and productivity. This period, which occurred in England earlier than on the Continent, was Rostow's "transitional" stage, approaching the "take-off." There was no point in speculating about the origin and nature of wants. In a world of so obviously urgent needs and corresponding aspirations, no ingenious theory of demand was required to justify all the productive effort that could be mustered. Maximum productive efficiency was the self-evident organizing principle and welfare criterion of the new science.

But poverty in its historical meaning and as a general characteristic of life has since been conquered in the West. According to Galbraith, production in the West is no longer guided by urgent needs, as it was in the days of mass poverty. Still, we go right on striving for ever-increasing productive efficiency and growth. Economic production, which at one time had a pressing priority in man's thinking and acting, continues to be the idol of our ossified economic attitudes.

Galbraith thinks that most of the wants that now underlie increasing production in the West are of little or no real urgency. The prevailing economic theory of demand throws no light on this basic point, because it avoids the question of what generates wants and, furthermore, excludes the possibility of comparing the various states (or changes) of the utility of different products as between different persons and different points of time. However, behind this formalistic façade of sterile theoretical neutrality, there is an informal tacit assumption that expansion of human wants over time has no significant limits or that, to put it in traditional marginal utility terms, the utility of additional (real) income in general, as distinguished from the utility of additional quantities of particular goods, is not diminishing. It is this informal assumption behind the inconclusive formal theory of demand that Galbraith is attacking. He is thereby indicating the need for a theory of demand that would deal with the *origin* and *nature* of wants and not only with the *expression* of *given* wants in particular demands or in some aggregate consumption function.

III

Galbraith's reasoning, which leads him to this broader concept of demand theory, can best be summarized in the following quotation from his book:

> However, there is a flaw [in the formal theory of demand and in the informal assumption behind it]. If the individual's wants are to be urgent they must be original with himself. They cannot be urgent if they must be contrived for him. And above all they must not be contrived by the process of production by which they are satisfied. For this means that the whole case of wants [as guides to production] falls to the ground. One cannot defend production as satisfying wants if that production creates the wants.[5]

Production influences consumption in two ways. It does so directly through the medium of advertising and indirectly through emulation among the consumers. But Galbraith provides no systematic historical examination or psychological analysis of emulation and advertising. He makes wants and demand depend on production by inferentially assuming that emulation and advertising, in pushing an ever-growing and changing variety of *products* (means), actually create in this process the underlying *wants* (and implied human ends) themselves. It is this assumed dependence of wants on production, which Galbraith calls the "dependence effect," that serves as the key concept of his analysis. Galbraith examines the workings of the affluent society's economy in the light of the implications of the dependence effect.

The prevailing theory of demand treats wants as given—that is, it considers them as originating and behaving independently of the economic system, and therefore leaves this basic question *outside* the scope of economic analysis. Wants enter into economic analysis only to the extent that they are vaguely assumed to underlie individual demands as expressions of the willingness and ability of various consumers to buy varying quantities of an economic good at different prices. But Galbraith believes that in the affluent society wants are so significantly generated by forces that operate *within* the economic system itself that economic theory must take this dependence into its own analytical account. The treatment of wants as *dependent* variables of economic analysis is the most important single element in Galbraith's thinking.

Galbraith's new vision of wants has significant implications for other parts of economic analysis, beyond the theory of demand, and also for public policy. Within his analytical framework, the dependence effect leads to the concept of social imbalance between marketable goods for private consumption and government-financed public goods for collective use. This imbalance is viewed as one of the central economic problems of the affluent society. In addition, the dependence effect is also seen as sharing the responsibility for the inherent inflationary tendency in the affluent society, as well as for recurring recessions. In a sense, all the economic ills of the affluent society appear to stem, directly or indirectly, from the dependence effect.

Galbraith arrives at the dependence effect by means of a direct inference from the empirical facts of consumers' emulation and producers' advertising. By propagating specific *goods*, emulation and advertising *thereby* "contrive" or "create" the corresponding wants.

Now, to postulate such a radical influence of economic emulation and advertising is to view the Western consumer as a psychological and intellectual vacuum to be filled from the outside in a purely accidental manner. Obviously, even the most casual consumer is more than a psychologically empty, passively receptive shopping bag, haphazardly stuffed by entirely unreflective responses to two extraneous factors: emulation (a kind of monkey effect) and advertising (a kind of Simple Simon effect). Although every man is subject to influences from his environment, such influences, particularly those stemming from emulation and advertising, have no meaningful explanation unless they are related to some pattern of pre-existing human aspirations.

IV

A more realistic approach reveals economic emulation and advertising not as basic generators of new wants in an elemental sense, but rather as social propagators of specific ways and means for the attainment of human ends. The ways and means reflect a given and changing level of technology and a specific but varying structure of relative scarcities of various resources and productive services. The ends or aspirations, on the other hand, stem from human nature operating within the social setting of a particular civilization and culture. The various competitive and selective aspects of economic emulation and advertising, which Galbraith relegates to a footnote,[6] actually confirm the existence of such a complementary relationship between economic goods and human ends.

If it were true, as Galbraith claims, that emulation and advertising create wants from scratch, so to speak, it might be possible to treat such extraneous wants as *ipso facto* unimportant, with all the ethical and policy implications that such a conclusion would entail. If, however, in accordance with a more realistically human interpretation, economic emulation and advertising are viewed as operating primarily on the level of *specific* ways and means for the attainment of *inherent* human ends, rather than as a sort of substitute for the ends themselves, then no such sweeping conclusion is warranted. In appraising the effects of emulation and advertising so understood, one is of course bound to use the twin *logical-ethical* principle that in a world of scarcities there must be both a workable and a socially acceptable scale of priorities. But one cannot automatically dismiss as *psychologically* unimportant an end itself, for the sole reason that the specific means by which the end happens to be served passes through the conventional channels of emulation and advertising.

Whatever its interpretation, emulation is certainly not an invention of the affluent society. It is as old as mankind itself. In its broader meaning, as distinct from the narrower emulation of specific economic goods, emulation is almost synonymous with society. It is the very life of society, the medium of culture, the engine of civilization. There is no society without emulation. Beyond this generalization, it is even possible to argue that the impact of emulation is comparatively greater in nonaffluent societies where rigid social customs and habits shape life and where the scope of personal choice and originality is correspondingly circumscribed. The affluent society inherited emulation from history, but actually relaxed and diversified its social impact. In the affluent society, emulation tends to become *less rigid* in its structure and *less enforcing* in its effects than it is in less developed societies.

Advertising, another vehicle for social influencing, is more characteristic of the affluent society, especially in the ubiquity and intensity of its use. Perhaps this is precisely because of the general loosening and lessening of emulation in the affluent society. More specifically, advertising appears to be an unavoidable corollary of the technological complexity and diversity of modern products. No matter what the extent of its exaggeration or misuse, there is an irreducible informative core in advertising which cannot be eliminated as long as the technology of products and the diversity of the conditions of their availability continue to grow more, rather than less, complex.[7] Even in Communist economies, characteristically devoid of any need to sell, increased advertising seems to be an unavoidable appendage to technological advance, although much of it may simply serve as a pusher of shoddy, substandard products.

Since the days of Veblen, economic emulation and advertising have been subjected to strong criticism.[8] This is to be expected. For emulation and advertising are as legitimate objects of social scrutiny as any other socially relevant human act or institution. Constructive criticism would naturally aim at progressive improvement in emulation as the medium of the most general social process of learning, which, like all education, is presumed to lead to more and more discerning individual and social choosing. As to advertising, the obvious policy objective would seem to be to strengthen its informative function by progressively reducing its misleading and wasteful exaggerations. Commercial interindustry advertising could well serve as a guide to consumer advertising. There is still much to be done in this direction.[9]

Thus, the valid purpose of criticizing emulation and of policing advertising is to improve their social performance in terms of human choice. This, however, is very different from a summary condemnation of emulation and advertising on Galbraith's assumption that they *create* wants that are therefore *ipso facto* unimportant.

V

Following his elemental interpretation of the dependence effect, Galbraith blames this effect for the existence, in the affluent society, of what he calls the social imbalance, denoting a chronic excess of private goods accompanied by a systematic shortage of public goods. Galbraith's opinion that the influence of emulation and advertising is predominantly in the direction of private consumption goods may or may not agree with the facts. Undoubtedly, however, there is emulation also with respect to public goods for collective use. By their very purpose, such goods can hardly be original with every individual citizen or community. Similarly, the multitude of written and spoken words on public issues may be construed as representing, to a large extent, competitive advertising for public goods. In pluralistic Western societies, both kinds of emulation and advertising, for public as well as private goods, are *strongly competitive* and therefore do not eliminate choice but *demand* it. Thus, the question of whether a particular want or aspiration would

huge backlog in public goods and services. In another category are such items as educational institutions and facilities of all kinds, and whatever other public services our growing cultural levels will require as common supplements to individual and family provisions for them. In some of these respects, the United States clearly trails Western Europe. In others, Europe has been left behind.

Fourth, the West will not easily escape its growing defense burden, will undoubtedly more and more have to increase its space efforts, and will have no choice but to continue to assist the newly developing countries in the advancement of their human, technological, and financial requirements for a speedier and more efficient economic development.

Continued pressure for antinuclear shelters is a special case. If *real* protection is to be provided without intolerable discrimination, it becomes obvious that we are facing an entirely new category of public need of staggering proportions. The tremendous cost of effective protection plus the overwhelming hope in the ultimate success of the Western policy for preventing nuclear war make a rational decision on the problem of shelters very difficult. Decision would be rendered much easier if an effective shelter program could be functionally combined with some major peacetime use of the required facilities.

Congested metropolitan areas, particularly in the United States, have desperately unresolved transportation problems. It may well be that the two sets of problems can be resolved simultaneously. Extensive new subway networks and underground garages may perhaps be so constructed as to serve at the same time as the best possible antinuclear shelters. If such double-purpose structures are technically feasible, they would provide the needed psychological relief of antinuclear protection while at the same time securing high peacetime productivity of the corresponding public investment. Western political leadership and technological effort should seriously explore the possibility of such a solution.

VII

Thus, Western production in the next stage of economic development will have to grow as much as our understanding of our own needs, and as best as our scientific and technological progress and will to work will allow it to grow. There will be no shortage of demands on the production of goods in Western societies.[14]

In consequence of these multiform and expanding aspirations and corresponding production requirements, it is impossible not to sense that there will continue to be the danger of systematic inflationary pressures on Western economies from the demand side. The more we are aware of our expanding private and public needs and aspirations, the greater will be the ensuing danger of inflationary pressures from demands running ahead of corresponding output.

But this is not all. In addition to the inflationary pressures associated with the potentially excessive demands on production, the economies of Western countries have yet another source of inflationary pressures—this one on the production side. Common experience and evidence accumulated over the postwar period show that there are on the production and selling side of the contemporary economies of industrially advanced countries large institutions and strongly organized groups. Both possess varying degrees of power to influence prices of goods and productive services, and they have been using this power to push up prices, with a view to improving their respective income shares; but the result has been lower output and increasing unemployment, except where (as recently in Western Europe) these results have been counteracted by further inflationary pressures from an excessive aggregate demand.

Fortunately, we have lately become inflation-conscious. Unfortunately, however, in the United States the awareness of inflationary evils has firmed into an overcautious attitude toward economic growth. Our public policies have not always fostered economic growth as much as they could because of the fear of two-pronged (demand-and-cost) inflation.[15] Such an attitude would be justified if our growth requirements were not as great as they are, or if it were impossible to promote economic growth without generating inflation in the process. But we do need as much growth as we can get without inflation, and our knowledge of the effects and causes of inflation has recently increased to the point where suitable anti-inflationary policies need not retard any real economic growth that is humanly and technologically feasible.

Thus, control of inflation is the key to policy toward the "next stage" in the economic growth of the West. We will attack this subject systematically in the next three chapters. Then we will examine the problem of inflation in relation to each of the two key problems of economic growth in the newly developing countries and in the Soviet orbit, respectively.

6. *INFLATION AS A LIMIT TO ECONOMIC GROWTH IN THE WEST: THE FACT AND FEAR OF INFLATION*

The inherited cultural-technical-entrepreneurial lag in the newly developing countries is the crucial limiting factor in the early stages of their economic growth. In the Soviet orbit, with an almost complete absence of decentralized private enterprise, the suppression and perversion of democratic socialism as the directing force of nationalized production constitutes the main obstacle to high mass consumption, which, according to Rostow's analysis, the Soviet Union should already have attained. In the industrially advanced economies of the West, on the other hand, inflationary pressures appear to be the key difficulty in extending or surpassing the stage of high mass consumption.

What is inflation? What are its direct manifestations? What are its economic effects? Why is it a limiting factor of economic growth and development? What are its basic causes? What are its remedies? These are the questions that must be answered if inflation is to be properly understood and its impact on Western economic growth and development reliably assessed.

Inflation usually manifests itself in the rise of all prices taken together. Rising prices are the visible symptom of the underlying inflationary pressures, whether these pressures come from the demand side of various markets or from the production side of various goods and services. When such inflationary pressures prevail on the demand side of the markets for goods and services, product prices tend to rise because more goods are demanded at the existing prices than production can readily turn out to match increasing demand. Rising prices tend to absorb the excess amount of money expenditures. And when inflationary pressures gather on the production side, prices tend to increase, because excessive money incomes, relative to productive performance (output per unit of resources used), are demanded. Rising prices tend to cover such increased money costs of production.[1]

From this introductory description of the comprehensive working of inflationary pressures, a preliminary characterization of inflation may be attempted. When the two sets of its basic pressures are delineated, *inflation* comes to signify that a nation's *economic system has been financially overstrained* either because of *excessive demands for* the *output* of its production, *or* because of excessive demands for *incomes* from its production, or *both*.

This preliminary insight into the fundamental economic meaning of inflation points to the immediate conclusion that inflation is first of all a comprehensive indicator that real economic growth has hit an obstacle to its expansion; general price increases have substituted themselves for the attempted expansion of real output and real income.

It should be noted, immediately, however, that even when inflationary pressures are active, price rises may be prevented or checked without first removing the inflationary pressures and their basic causes. This is the case of so-called *repressed* inflation.[2] It is an exception and should be disposed of first. Inflation is "repressed" when, in the face of inflationary pressures, a government imposes and rigorously enforces a comprehensive system of price and allocation controls, usually during major wars when military and related demands on production are exceptionally great and immediate, and when at the same time the growth of production is hampered by conscription and military operations.

But not every inflation can be repressed, and no inflation can be repressed indefinitely. If inflationary pressures consist of effective increases in the money costs of producing a unit of output, price increases can be held back only within the margin of "excessive" profits, if they exist. In industrially advanced Western economies, gross profits (before taxes) make up 10 to 15 per cent of the total value of the national production of all goods and services and therefore of the average price. Since in the long run some return in excess of mere interest rate must be paid to firms if they are to continue to produce, and therefore to invest, there is obviously little room left for the absorption of inflated production costs per unit of output without price increases.

II

Most people are directly concerned with what happens to the prices of the *consumer* goods they buy. It is characteristic of inflation, however, that the price increases it brings are not limited to any single category of products. All the individual prices need not rise, of course, in any particular inflation, but price increases do occur for all kinds of goods and services on all levels of sales and purchases. If inflation is permitted to develop, only a deliberate repressing of price increases can exempt from it, and even then only temporarily, a broad category of goods or services. The unchecked impact of inflationary pressures on prices is general, because prices of various economic goods and services are interrelated into one economy-wide price system.

The interrelationship of all prices stems from four causes. First, prices of productive services (wages, interest, rents, and profits) constitute production costs and thereby affect the prices of corresponding products. Second, in an advanced economy, where production of any particular product is usually broken up into a number of separate stages, from raw materials through a variety of parts to ultimate products and their widely scattered outlets, the price of an unfinished item becomes part of the production costs of all the products that incorporate it in one way or another. Third, people's incomes, past savings, and newly extended bank credit (which increases the total amount of money in the economy) are translated, partly or entirely, directly or indirectly, into demands for all the goods and services—thus again interrelating and influencing the price system as a whole.

There is a fourth integrating influence at work in the Western price system today. Individual price increases, whatever their immediate causes, may provoke, under certain circumstances, similar price increases elsewhere by the social process of emulation. This may happen in regard to product prices within particular industries in the form of price leadership by one firm, or it may be an economy-wide occurrence when inflationary pressures from the demand side are generally anticipated. Such emulation as a form of the general interrelationship of prices is particularly significant as a vehicle of that inflation that comes from the production side. This will be further discussed when we examine systematically the working of inflationary pressures through the costs of production.

One cannot overstress the point that inflation is a phenomenon of the entire price system. The idea that special attention should be given to the prices of consumer goods is rooted in the limited economic interest and outlook of the average consumer, who is not an independent producer. From the limited interest and point of view of an individual consumer, it is not even the prices of *all* consumer goods that matter, but only the prices of the kinds of consumer goods *he* buys. From the point of view of the society, from that of the government and its policies, and for the performance of the economy as a whole, however, it is the change in the general level of all prices that indicates the presence of inflation or its absence. A limited price index could be on the rise even if the general price level were stable, and vice versa. At the very least, there will be some significant time lags in the comparative behavior of selected consumer prices and that of the other segments of the general price system. Hence, where a comprehensive, general price index is not available, a variety of partial price indexes should be examined and compared in order to ascertain whether or not the economy is in the grip of inflation and to what extent.

There is another difficulty associated with price indexes. In advanced Western economies, new products keep piling up on the existing ones, or replacing them, and the existing ones undergo constant quality changes. Some price increases may therefore be due to the higher costs of better quality products.[3] Now it has been contended that price increases, as reflected in price indexes, are due partly to product quality improvements, which involve additional production costs. The argument is not fully convincing, however. As a broad historical phenomenon, quality improvements should be viewed as one aspect of *productivity* improvements, which should obviate cost and price increases. Nor should costlier quality improvements lead to price-*level* increases, if prices of other goods were responsive to offsetting demand decreases elsewhere in the system. The blame for such price-level increases should therefore be on the insufficient flexibility of prices, not on the costs of quality improvements.

A rising general level of prices is the direct manifestation of inflationary pressures. But what are the *effects* of rising prices—that is, of inflation itself?[4] As a first approximation, these effects can conveniently be classified into two groups, the *direct* and *indirect* effects of inflation.

The direct effects of inflation are those that are inherent in the concept of the rising general level of prices itself. Since a rising price level means that one dollar will now on the average buy less than before, we say that inflation lowers the purchasing power of money. This first direct effect of inflation is automatic in the sense that its coming into existence, as distinct from its growing extent, does not depend on anybody's reactions to inflation. By definition, the purchasing power of money in general changes inversely and in exact proportion to the changes in the general level of prices. Nonetheless, the range of this effect differs greatly as soon as we decompose the general price index into its various subcategories and into individual prices. Then we see that the purchasing power of money for some categories of goods and their individual items may be much higher or lower than it is in relation to other groups of goods and their individual components.

Thus, for example, for the United States since 1947, the decomposition of the consumer price index shows that medical care and transportation services have led in price increases considerably above the average. Similarly, among the wholesale prices, those of finished steel have increased three times the average increase of the wholesale price index as a whole.[5]

The first direct effect of inflation (lowering the purchasing power of money) also varies for different persons, groups of people, and organizations. Since different persons, groups, and organizations have differing patterns of individual and associated purchases, the extent to which inflation has impaired the purchasing power of money for each of them will differ in accordance with the behavior of the prices of the various goods they buy.

There is another direct effect of inflation that is seldom, if ever, mentioned, but is in a sense the most detrimental one. When the general level of prices is rising and the purchasing power of money is correspondingly falling, money as the *yardstick* for measuring economic value of goods and services, and for calculating the plans for future buying and selling, loses its stability, and its reliability is thereby impaired. There is no self-evident reason why such impairment of the standard of economic value should be viewed with less concern than would arise were some unit of physical measurement to be subjected to similar instability. What would happen to the various sciences and corresponding practical arts if this were the case? Moreover, the third function of money, that of the store of value for liquidity purposes, may be entirely destroyed by inflation and replaced by well-selling shares of corporate stock or even by stockpiling of price-leading materials and products. However, such an impairment of the store-of-value function of money happens by way of reactive behavior of moneyholders. It is thus an indirect rather than direct effect of inflation.

In summary, one may say that the two direct effects of inflation have a considerable but differentiated impact on the immediate welfare of the people and on the working of the economy. Money is worth less and becomes an unreliable yardstick by which to make plans for future production and consumption. From this point of view, inflation impairs the immediate well-being of individual persons and of the community, and is also detrimental to economic growth.

Before we turn to the indirect effects of inflation, yet another direct effect of inflation must be noted, although it is direct only in part.

Since the prices of productive services (wages, rents, interest, and profit) form part of the interrelated system of all prices, they too participate, though in varying degrees, in the inflationary upward movement of the price system as a whole. To the extent that they do, the money income of various individuals, groups, and organizations will increase accordingly. But only some of such money-income increases are *directly* effected by inflation, namely, those which emerge even without deliberate reactive (inflation-prompted) behavior of the income receivers themselves. For anything that occurs within the framework of inflation as a consequence of *reactive* behavior of producers or consumers is an *indirect* effect of inflation, since it involves people's responses to inflation. Strictly speaking, therefore, one should count among the direct effects of inflation only those money-income increases which accrue to firms through higher *profits* resulting from rising product prices, *provided* the respective product price was not increased by deliberate reactive decisions on the part of the firm.[6]

All other inflationary money-income increases belong to the category of indirect effects of inflation. This is true not only of all increases of contractual incomes (wages, rents, and interest) but also of profit increases resulting from deliberately reactive price increases. Furthermore, money-income increases resulting from the reactive behavior of producers and consumers must be considered both as indirect effects of inflation and among the causes of its continuation and propagation. In other words, we have here a phenomenon that is both an indirect effect of inflation and a cause of further inflation.

This brings us to the *indirect* effects of inflation, which we have described as the effects of inflation on the *reactive* behavior of producers and consumers. As inflation evolves from its initial causes and gradually spreads throughout the price system, it directly affects the purchasing power of the existing incomes in relation to their existing buying and selling patterns. Then, as part of its process of propagation or extinction, inflation induces *changes* in people's buying and selling patterns as well as in their incomes.[7]

Almost all money-income increases during an inflation result from reactive behavior of the various income receivers, including firms as profit recipients when their prices are "administered."[8] But the bargaining power of various income recipients and the market power of various firms vary greatly, from the social security beneficiaries with zero bargaining power (except for whatever indirect political influence they may have) to a strategically located union with great direct bargaining strength; from a small competitive firm with an extremely price-sensitive demand for its product to a very large multiple-products firm, which may enjoy a combined demand that is fairly insensitive to price changes. Thus, it is easy to see that the money-income effect of inflation may differ greatly from person to person, from group to group, from organization to organization, depending on their bargaining strength and market power or political influence.

If we combine the differentiated *money*-income effect of inflation (an indirect effect) with the differentiated money-purchasing power effect (a direct effect) discussed previously, we get an even more differentiated *total redistribution effect* of inflation. In the subsequent discussion of the causes and propagation of inflation, it will be seen, however, that in the institutional framework of a pluralistic economy composed of large units and organized groups, reactive and emulative behavior tends to re-establish the prevailing pattern of *real* income distribution as such pluralistic blocks become engaged in a race to keep abreast or ahead of the general pace of inflation.[9] It is the professionally unorganized and politically uninfluential who are the chief victims of the combined redistribution effect of inflation.

Inflation also generates *expectations* as to its own future course. In conjunction with the total redistribution effect of inflation, these expectations tend to make the behavior of consumers and producers more and more speculative. If inflation is expected to continue, money savings will dwindle. Purchases and production will increasingly tend toward products where relatively greater inflationary price increases are expected. Inflationary expectations weaken the constraining influence of prices on wants of inherently lower priorities. To this extent, inflation weakens the primary function of the market as the coordinator of production with the genuine structure of human wants. Differentiated price increases assume an excessive influence on demand and supply.

There is no need to dwell on the effects of inflation on a country's exports and imports. Any degree of inflation will impair exports relative to imports and thus negatively affect the country's balance of international payments. The actual effect of inflation on the balance of payments will depend on comparative degrees of inflation in various trading countries. To this must be added the tendency toward capital flights from countries with comparatively higher rates of inflation.

III

The direct and indirect effects of inflation discussed so far are more or less recognized as undesirable in their impact on general well-being. Inflation arbitrarily changes the distribution of income and the composition of output. It may ultimately benefit some, but always at the expense of others and in a largely unpredictable and even undetectable manner, without regard to merit or guilt. Efforts at redressing the money-income and output balance can never be fully successful, and such efforts may lead to more inflation unless it is checked at its roots.

Were it only for the effects of inflation discussed so far, there would be nothing to recommend it or even to tolerate it. And yet inflation goes on virtually everywhere. This is due partly to mere negligence or to difficulties in preventing or stopping it. But there is another reason why inflation is tolerated or sometimes even fostered. There still exist differences of opinion as to inflation's net impact on economic growth and development, which is the primary concern of this study.

We have already noted three negative aspects of the relationship of inflation to economic development. First, the very appearance of inflation indicates that economic growth has been checked to the extent that general price increases take the place of desired increases in the real output of goods and services. In addition to inflation's significance for the existing economic growth, there are its influences on the course of further economic growth and development. The two direct effects of inflation (impairing the purchasing power of money and money's role as the yardstick of economic value) may seriously hamper the motivation and planning for future economic growth, especially if it requires large savings and very risky or long-term investments. The third growth-impairing aspect of inflation was implied in the conclusion that the total redistribution effect of inflation, together with further inflationary expectations, makes the behavior of demand and supply excessively speculative—that is, more responsive to expected price increases and less so to the genuine structure of wants, thereby impairing saving and distorting the qualitative aspect of economic growth and development.[10]

Those who see some positive relationship between inflation and economic growth have two arguments. Thus, the late Sumner Slichter argued that a degree of inflation is a necessary price for sufficient economic growth, primarily because union pressures for excessive wages must come in the face of stepped-up production.[11] But there is a much older argument, to the effect that inflation positively promotes economic growth and development because of the "forced saving" it generates in consequence of the tendency of contractual incomes to increase slower than product prices.[12] The ensuing higher profits are invested or used for repaying the credit by means of which investment in excess of voluntary savings was originally financed. Thus, forced saving was said to have increased real investment at the expense of consumption. This is why inflation was viewed as promoting economic growth rather than just being a necessary price of it, as Slichter had maintained.

There are two flaws in this argument. First, with the rise in the bargaining power and political influence of organized groups, contractual incomes have been closing in on the gap that supposedly separated them from inflationary increases in product prices. Thus, forced saving from inflation is now smaller or nonexistent. Second, the argument conveniently ignores inflationary increases in replacement costs of depreciated facilities. This loss may easily outweigh the amount of forced saving, if there is any. Sir Roy Harrod formalized this double fallacy of the old argument, which has since been adapted for contemporary development purposes.[13] Harrod calculated that for Western countries, on any realistic assumption about inflationary increases in contractual incomes, inflation reduces the value of depreciation allowances by more than the amount it provides in forced saving.[14]

Harrod made the calculation on the basis of purposely conservative estimates in order to prove his proposition beyond empirical doubt. Assume an excess investment demand amounting to 1 per cent of GNP. In order to account for consumers' dissavings (to supplement lagging incomes) and for the accompanying inflationary increases in contractual incomes, Harrod assumed that an approximately 3 per cent annual price increase would be necessary to secure net "forced saving" of 1 per cent of GNP to cover the assumed 1 per cent excess in investment demand. He further assumed a very low average length of life of physical capital (4 years), and the corresponding replacement to amount to 10 per cent of GNP.

The formula then yields the result that "amortization would be deficient to the extent of 1.1 per cent of GNP [to mean that] the loss of saving through deficient amortization more than wipes out the gain from forced saving."[15]

It should be noted that Harrod's formula may still yield a growth-favoring result for an *underdeveloped* country. This would provide a rigorous proof of Hansen's contention[16] that inflation may help economic growth in underdeveloped countries through forced saving. However, Harrod's equation will yield this result only on the assumption that in a particular developing economy consumers cannot significantly supplement their purchases by drawing on past savings; that contractual incomes do not rise with the rising product prices; and that the replacement backlog is insignificant because of the small extent of pre-existing capital facilities. Whether any of the existing newly developing economies actually experience these assumptions is a question that only empirical case studies could answer. Given the very exceptional character of the assumption above, it would not be surprising if such empirical studies would refute Hansen's hypothesis.

On a net basis, inflation thus actually curtails real gross saving and investment and thereby slows down economic development in countries where institutional and political conditions keep contractual incomes abreast, or even ahead, of product prices, and where replacement of the existing capital equipment is considerable. Both these conditions are present in the advanced industrial economies of the West. This is an added reason why inflation is the key obstacle to their economic growth.

It is thus necessary to conclude that the various effects of inflation seriously damage the well-being of persons and society, as well as the operation of the economic system, *including* the growth and development of production and its real income.

One final observation about the effects of inflation on economic growth will reinforce this conclusion. Because inflation has so many undesirable effects, and because deliberate promotion of economic growth may add to inflationary pressures, the fear of inflation has itself become a basic obstacle to economic growth.[17] This may be the case in particular in countries with a precarious balance of international payments. The United States is a case in point. In examining the causes of inflation and its remedies, it will therefore be necessary to pay special attention to the crucial question, whether inflation can be so controlled that a nation can achieve all the economic growth its potentialities and institutions will permit.

But to control inflation, we must attack it at its roots. Hence, in the following two chapters, we will examine the causes of inflation—those that operate on the demand side of the markets for goods and services and those that work through the costs of production.

7. *SOURCES OF INFLATION IN THE WEST: TWIN MONEY ILLUSION*

To answer the question of how *demand* can generate inflation, it will be helpful first to clarify the economic meaning of demand and then to recall the important characteristics of the price system within which demand operates.

Demand for an economic good is the financial expression of some want deemed urgent enough to be satisfied through the purchase of the corresponding products. Each case of demand must be viewed within the framework of all the other wants of the buyer. The buyer may be a personal consumer, a family, an organization (for associated production or consumption), or a government agency. The relative position of a particular want within the structure of all the wants of the buyer, the price of the corresponding product, the prices of other relevant products, and the total financial position of the buyer (his money income plus previously accumulated savings or newly created credit)—each of these has some influence on any particular demand.

In noninflationary conditions, it is the ranking of wants that is the strongest influence on demand. Income and prices act as economic constraints on wants, forcing these to be ranked and rationed according to their relative significance to the buyer. Scarcity, as manifested in prices and incomes, does not allow all human aspirations to be satisfied. A want that ranks highly will so influence the demand for the corresponding good that the demand for it will display a relatively low sensitivity to changes in the price of the good in question and in the prices of other goods, as well as to changes in the financial position of the buyer. The lower the relative rank of a want, the higher will be the sensitivity of the corresponding demand to changes in the economic constraints that influence it.[1] Higher prices of the good in question or of other goods in the consumer's buying pattern, lower income, lower previous savings, and higher cost of credit will all reduce such demand appreciably. In inverse cases, the demand will increase significantly.[2]

In inflation, the demand pattern undergoes the change already described as an indirect effect of inflation.[3] Demands for various goods, particularly those related to inventories, then tend to depend less on the basic ranking of underlying wants and more on differential increases in various prices. Expectations about the future course of inflation reinforce this tendency. The basic pattern of wants tends to lose its primary influence on demand. All buyers become speculators.

Now let us recall the major characteristics of the price system within which demand operates in order to see how demand can influence prices. That all prices are interrelated in an economy-wide price system, we have already seen. We also know the four integrating influences on the price system.[4] Of these four, *income* (together with the supplementary financial means: accumulated past savings and newly created credit) belongs to the demand side. Demand can therefore generate inflation in the price system only if money income or *its supplements* increase.

Money income can increase in three ways: if income recipients produce more, or if they receive more pay for the same amount of production, or through a combination of the two.[5] When people or institutions receive additional income, they may or may not use it all for purchases of additional goods and services.[6] They may save some part or all of it in a variety of forms, from cash in their own vaults to buying securities of various kinds and duration. Such savings may lie idle or they may be borrowed, directly or indirectly, by other individuals or organizations that want to use them for their own purchases of consumer or capital goods.[7] Only that part of additional income that continues to lie idle does not affect any current demand for goods and services. The rest of it goes to increase various demands. This raises the possibility of inflation.

Inflation may be triggered from the demand side if additional output of specific goods and services first gives rise to increased income, but then finds few or no takers.[8] Additional incomes may swell instead the demand for other products whose output has not been increased, thus possibly increasing their prices. But inflation will still not be triggered if lack of demand for the originally increased output reduces its price, thus offsetting price increases elsewhere. If production costs of the additional output are rigid, however, and therefore resist attempts to lower them, and if the firms producing these products have sufficient market power to prevent their prices from falling, prices will not be reduced. Then inflation will be triggered because the whole price system will now be higher, with some prices up and none down.

Inflation that results from increases in prices of some goods whose demand has increased and from the failure to fall of prices of the goods whose demand has decreased, in relation to other products, may conveniently be called "demand shift inflation."[9] In such cases, inflation has been triggered by the relative *shift* of demand away from some products toward other products, not from an excessive increase in the aggregate demand itself.

What about increases in money incomes without corresponding increases in production? These result from excessive claims and from the corresponding bargaining or market power of the recipients of such incomes.[10] But in such cases, inflation will have been triggered on the *production* side even *before* it could be generated by higher incomes as a *demand*-influencing factor. Then, just as in the case of strained capacity, inflation starts on the production side. This will be examined later.

As mentioned above, incomes as a demand-influencing factor can be supplemented by accumulated past savings and by newly created bank credit. If there are large, unused past savings or if the banking system has the ability to create appreciable sums of new credit that has not come from previous savings, inflationary pressures may originate in demand increases financed by these supplementary financial sources of demand. In fact, demand-caused inflations usually start this way.

Furthermore, people and organizations that for reasons of foreseeable future payments or speculative purchases in securities or commodities markets need or wish to have cash readily available can, in advanced Western economies, satisfy this desire for liquidity by holding instead of money a variety of securities that can be readily turned into cash when needed without much risk or delay.[11] The use of money for liquidity purposes is thereby reduced; more of the existing money can thus be used for purchasing goods.[12] Examples of securities that act as possible substitutes for money for liquidity purposes are short-term government securities, or even easily marketable long-term government securities, as well as savings and loan shares and time deposits.[13] In summary, the monetary and the financial system of an advanced contemporary economy is flexible enough to permit, at any one time, sizable increases in the aggregate demand for goods and services *beyond* the limits of current incomes and taxes.

When all the particular demands for final goods and services by all the persons, firms, organizations, and government agencies are added together, we get the financial measure of the total demand for all the currently produced goods and services in the economy, usually called "effective aggregate demand." Because of the flexibility of the contemporary monetary and financial system, it is easy to see why the effective aggregate demand *can* add up to more than the value of all the currently produced goods and services measured in their *existing* prices. When this happens, inflationary pressures are generated in the economy as a whole.

The first question one may ask in relation to the effects of excessive aggregate demand on the course of the economy is why it does not induce additional *production* instead of pressing for higher *prices*. The answer is that increased aggregate demand *can* result in increased production if there is room within the existing productive capacity for larger outputs of various goods and services for which the demand has increased. There may be, as in a recession, considerable amounts of unused capacity, unemployed labor, and other resources. Or the existing facilities may be capable of a more intensive use if more labor or labor hours are still available, if additional materials and parts can be obtained, or if the resources already employed can be used in a more effective combination through improved organization and coordination.

On the other hand, *major* technological and organizational improvements require large-scale investments and preparation and are therefore both costly and time-consuming. They cannot be resorted to at will just to satisfy the sudden outbreak of an increased aggregate demand. Even such additional labor, other resources, and organizational changes as are readily available to make possible a more intensive use of the existing productive capacity, will often cause additional production to be less efficient or more costly, resulting in a smaller increase in output per unit of resources used or higher costs per unit of output. In these cases, an apparently demand-triggered inflation gives rise to inflationary pressures on the cost-of-production side. This will be the consequence of an overstrained productive capacity coupled with the unwillingness of associated producers (labor and management, representing all nonlabor participants) to accept lower returns for their less efficient additional production.

II

It need not be repeated here at length why prices of various products will tend to respond differently to the inflationary pressures from an increased total demand.[14] Furthermore, only in a few almost perfectly organized markets, such as commodity exchanges where standardized staple materials are being traded, will price changes occur automatically or *mechanically* in response to the moment-to-moment interaction between continually changing demand-and-supply conditions in that market. In all other markets, price changes, when they occur, do not respond automatically to changes in the market demand and supply. It is individual firms that must make the price change by their own *deliberate* decision. Thus there will be time lags and incomplete adjustments of prices to the underlying changes in demand and supply.[15] It has recently become customary to call prices whose changes result from deliberate decisions by the affected firms "administered prices," as distinguished from automatic changes in the prices of goods traded in organized commodity and securities exchanges. These latter, the traditional "market prices," could, by comparison, be called "spontaneous prices."

Administered prices are not, however, all of a kind. The behavior of some of them may be very similar to those of spontaneous prices, except that their changes technically result from deliberate decisions by individual firms and are therefore likely to trail (or anticipate) the underlying changes in demand or supply. Here we are concerned with firms that are able to "administer" their prices with some real independence from changes in the underlying demand-and-supply conditions. Before we consider such "administered prices," it will be useful to clarify the related concepts of market power and bargaining power.

"Market power" is the traditional term denoting the ability of the supplier of a product or of a productive service to increase or at least to maintain his sales revenue by increasing the price of his product or service. Market power thus depends on the relative insensitivity of demand to price, which, in turn, depends on the relative urgency of the product or productive service and the commanding competitive position of the seller.

The concept of "bargaining power," as customarily used in economic analysis, denotes the ability of an organization (a firm or group of firms or a labor union) to press for, or resist, a contractual money-income increase. Such bargaining power depends on the degree of control of the supply of or demand for the type of service in question, on the ability to withstand transitional loss in earnings, on the presence or absence of public pressure, on the degree of political influence, and, to some extent, on the ability to foresee the ultimate *real*-income effect of a given *money*-income increase (that is, on the understanding and awareness of cost-generated inflation, its causes, propagation, and its interrelated effects).

The term "administered prices" was introduced[16] in 1935 by Gardiner Means, who defined it in the following words. "For administered prices the price is rigid, at least for a period of time, and sales (and usually production) fluctuate with the demand at the rigid price."[17]

Means conceived of administered pricing as a widespread phenomenon not limited to monopolistic situations. Traditional theory was wrong, according to Means, in its basic assumption of a uniquely determined *point* of profit maximization. He argued that there was no unique point of profit maximization but a "zone of relative indifference" (determined by the position of the total revenue and the total cost curves) within which it does not matter, from the point of view of the total profit of the firm, whether the price is set a bit lower or a bit higher. The total profits will be about the same anywhere within the zone. The existence of this zone of relative indifference supplies the management of each firm with the corresponding degree of discretionary power to administer its price. But the question as to *why* a firm selects any particular point within the zone was left unexplained.

In the postwar period, especially since the Korean War, the analytical and policy interest in administered prices has greatly increased. In 1957–59, the Subcommittee on Antitrust and Monopoly of the Senate Judiciary Committee staged extensive hearings on administered prices. At the same time, economic theory slowly came to recognize administered prices as a "phenomenon in search of a theory."[18]

A number of prominent economists engaged in the analysis of administered prices, but the trend has been to discard Means's "zone of relative indifference" and correlate administered prices with oligopolistic industries characterized by relatively few but consciously interdependent firms. J. K. Galbraith advanced the notion of "unliquidated monopoly gain," meaning that oligopolistic firms do not try to maximize their profits in the short run but usually set their prices below the profit-maximizing price, thus leaving room for a subsequent price increase if and when needed in response to increased wages, interest rates, or taxes.

G. Ackley[19] and T. Blair[20] maintain that administered prices are cost-oriented, with a predetermined markup added to the average costs of production. This treatment of administered prices found some empirical confirmation in Lanzillotti's findings[21] that the main objective of the oligopolistic pricing policies is some specific "target return on investment." A fuller analytical treatment of this approach to administered prices was attempted by Baumol.[22] Baumol's thesis is that sales maximization subject to planned (minimum) profit restraint, rather than a simple profit maximization, is the main objective pursued by big firms.

What is the conclusion about administered prices? First, there can be no doubt that most prices are calculated and set by management. Secondly, Baumol's hypothesis injects into the theory of administered prices a new concept, a new business objective quite different from the traditional notion of profit maximization, which originated within the mental construct of pure competition that had little or no counterpart in reality.

However, it would be absurd to assume that administered prices are completely independent of market demand-and-supply changes. Market demand and supply are essential factors that no firm can ignore if it wants to sell and continue to produce. For reasons of competitive uncertainty due to the relatively large size of oligopolistically competitive firms and to their product differentiation, as well as for reasons of convenience in accounting and production planning, there is an obvious reluctance to change the price in response to the daily fluctuations in demand. Furthermore, because of the resulting rigidity of costs reinforced by a steady upward trend of wages, administered prices are seldom cut, if ever. Administered prices are revised upward when increased costs, such as wages, press on all the competitors or when appreciable increase in demand, as in an inflation, has occurred or is generally expected.

Price administrators have but a narrow degree of freedom in relation to cost-of-production increases and may also be exposed to great temptations and pressures to make their prices follow or anticipate demand *increases* rather closely. It should be stressed, however, that such firms may be under less compulsion to make their price changes similarly conform to demand *reductions*, especially when their production costs are rigid. Even when production costs are reduced, price administrators with appreciable market power may be able to maintain their existing prices if their competitors are not likely to reduce theirs. One strong reason for such reluctance to lower prices seems to be rooted in the experience that it is less odious and risky to maintain a given price, even when lower costs would make price reduction feasible, than to increase the price again in the face of newly increased costs.[23] And production costs may always increase at the time of the next wage bargaining.

In conclusion, one may say that the prevailing tendency of administered prices seems to be to disregard smaller and temporary changes in demand as well as minor cost reductions, but to be rather sensitive to cost-of-production increases.[24] Furthermore, when appreciable increases in product demand occur, price administrators will be tempted or pressured into demand-induced price increases.[25] This is what generally happened in the United States during the demand-caused inflation in the early period of the Korean War, and again in 1955–57 with respect to capital goods which were then in very strong demand because of the investment boom at that time.[26]

A tentative definition of administered prices may now be formulated as follows: Administered prices are all those prices that are set and changed by individual *firms* pursuing business objectives *other* than straight profit maximization, either because the firm cannot or does not want to maximize profits. So understood, administered prices permit a larger scope for price rigidity or price increases.

III

Aggregate demand as a total is only a statistical concept. To understand its meaning as a cause of inflation, the aggregate demand must be broken down into its real components. Ultimately, one would have to go all the way back to the particular demands for individual goods and services by individual buyers. However, because of common culture and corresponding conventions, because of emulation of novelties, and because of public regulations, people in an organized political society tend to behave with considerable similarity. It is therefore both possible and useful to deal with large component categories of aggregate demand when trying to explain its impact on the economy. The broadest subdivision of the aggregate demand is that which views it as composed of consumer demand (expenditures), investment demand (expenditures), government purchases of goods and services,[27] and net demand from abroad for a country's goods and services.[28]

Although there are significant differences in the behavior of the various components of each of these four broad categories of aggregate demand, there are nevertheless sufficient similarities in the behavior of each of these large subaggregates to warrant their use for explaining the behavior of the aggregate demand. When viewed in relation to income, past savings, and new credit, all consumer demand displays certain regularities. Similarly, the demand for capital goods by business displays common characteristics in its relations to the expectations of future product demand, to technological innovations, to prospective profits, and to interest rates. Government demand for goods and services, in its turn, is determined primarily by the country's political objectives, by political pressures from the grass roots, by the level and effectiveness of political leadership, and by the international situation, as the chief determinants of collective wants.

If one looks back on the postwar experience, it would seem that inflationary pressures from the demand side tend to come particularly from two sources—from business investment booms and from sporadic major upsurges in government purchases of goods and services, particularly those associated with national defense. However, the sizable inflation in the United States in the early stages of the Korean War was caused largely by a sudden outburst of speculative buying by consumers as well as by producers prompted by the uncertainty as to the future extent and length of the new war.[29] But excessive demand for durable consumer goods also contributed to the early postwar inflation.

In countries such as Great Britain, where exports and imports represent a large part of the nation's total supply and demand, the demand for exports and imports must also be considered as a potential source of inflation on the demand side.[30] An increased demand for either imports or exports can generate an inflation at home. Higher prices of imported goods may act as higher living costs on wages or as higher production costs on other prices. On the other hand, higher prices of export goods may also, in addition to the analogous two domestic cost effects, result in significant domestic income and demand effects from higher sales revenues of export industries.

If we turn to the future, we can readily see the possibility that aggregate demand will tend to expand rapidly under the impact of the great variety of pressing needs and growing wants, as discussed earlier in conjunction with the question of the "next stage" in economic growth and development in the West.[31] Government expenditures on national defense, space navigation, foreign aid, and many needed domestic programs will be rising. And so will business expenditures for investment if Western economic growth is to be sufficient to meet these rising demands. Dangers of inflationary pressures from the demand side cannot yet be relegated to the files of economic history. They may turn out to be greater in the future than they have been in the postwar period thus far.

IV

Such are the ways by which inflationary pressures from demand can trigger cumulative price increases. An inflation "*trigger,*" in this case an increase in aggregate demand, sets the inflationary process in motion. But it is the ensuing process of cumulative *propagation* of price increases that produce the full fact of inflation.

Essentially, the propagation of inflation involves the spreading out of individual price increases that together lift the average of some meaningful statistical aggregate of individual prices. There are close similarities in the inflation propagation processes that are set in motion by inflationary pressures from the demand side.

We saw that an inflation may be triggered by a shift in demand away from some and toward other products when the prices of the products in increased demand go up but the prices of other goods do not fall (the steady price level of some goods may be due to the presence of rigid costs and/or appreciable market power of the firms that produce or sell those products). When such demand shifts occur, the ensuing inflation spreads out in the following ways. Shifts in particular demands cause the corresponding prices to rise. If other prices do not fall,[32] a measure of inflation immediately comes into existence. Now these increased prices will act as higher *cost* elements for firms using the corresponding products, whether in further production or for resale. Since most product prices are of necessity sensitive to cost-of-production increases,[33] these demand-induced cost effects tend to push up additional sets of product prices. Now the spreading inflationary process of cumulative price increases tends to grow larger and faster.[34] This phenomenon is the consequence of the role of cost of production, and of separation of various production stages, as two related price-system-integrating factors that were discussed in connection with the fact and effects of inflation.[35]

Furthermore, demand-shift-triggered inflation also spreads cumulatively throughout the price system as soon as the prices of important *consumer* goods are raised. Price increases of important consumer goods, if registered by the prevailing consumer-price index, are likely to set in motion wage increases induced by cost of living, either through the various escalator clauses built into collective and individual wage or salary agreements or by means of revised collective and individual wage contracts.[36] Such wage increases then act as further cost-pushers on still other prices, and so on cumulatively throughout the price system. There is also likely to be direct emulation of higher wages.

The firms that benefit from the initial demand shift, or from the subsequent demand increases stemming from inflation-induced income increases or from inflation-induced emergence of speculative buying, may now step up their own demand for labor and materials, thereby possibly causing further wage and price increases. This would accentuate the cumulative character of the inflation-propagating process.

Such, briefly, is the process through which an inflation that is triggered by some significant shift in demand spreads throughout the price system. It should be kept in mind, however, that this type of inflation-triggering and its subsequent propagation is based on two specific assumptions. The first is that most prices are sensitive to cost increases, a realistic enough assumption.[37] The second assumption, on which the possibility of demand-shift inflation is based, is that prices tend to be sensitive to demand increases but insensitive to demand decreases, both when costs are rigid and also when they are not—fear of rising costs being tantamount to actual rise in costs.[38] If this second assumption were rigorously true, it would then logically follow that inflation would be continuous and permanent. For then any appreciable demand shift, even without an increase in the aggregate demand as a whole, would *always* trigger an inflationary pressure, which would be further transmitted through the described channels of its propagation. In an economy where both consumers and producers shape their demands freely, demand shifts are one of its most regular characteristics. Only a comprehensive and rigid regimentation of all particular demands could prevent their changes. But this would mean the cruelest suppression of human freedom. It would destroy the adjustment of means to the changes in human wants, which are the expression of human liberties within an evolving culture that has characterized Western history for centuries. It can safely be said that the people in the West would tolerate such an encroachment on their individual freedom of action only in a major social emergency.

Not even the Communist system goes that far. In the Soviet Union consumers are free to change their particular demands. The difference is in the *effects* of demand changes on future *production*. Only the Soviet Government decides whether and to what an extent such changes in consumer demand will be permitted to influence the production of corresponding goods.[39] On the other hand, it is in the nature of an essentially nongovernmental system of production, such as the West has come to develop, that demand changes are effective in changing production accordingly. But in so doing, demand changes tend to generate inflation if prices are inflexible downward.[40]

When inflation results from an overstrained *aggregate* demand, as distinct from a mere demand shift within a given total demand, the process through which such inflationary pressures are transmitted through the entire price system is essentially the same as the one just described in relation to demand shift as the initial trigger of inflation. The only difference is that when an increased aggregate demand is the trigger of inflation, the ensuing process of its propagation is likely to work on a larger scale and therefore with more speed and impact.[41] If downward inflexibility of prices is considerable, an inflation triggered by aggregate demand will also bear the stamp of permanency. This is so because demand shifts will occur within a larger aggregate demand as much or more than within a given aggregate demand. Although demand shifts can occur independently from changes in aggregate demand, these latter always involve demand shifts also.

If prices were equally flexible both upward and downward, there would be no demand-shift inflation, and an inflation triggered by an increased aggregate demand would come to an end when its propagation through the price system was accomplished, provided further increases in aggregate demand in excess of production possibilities were halted. Aggregate demand goes up because in some of its major sectors an expansion or intensification of the underlying wants has occurred or is expected. If the monetary and financial system is flexible, financial means for translating the initial upsurge of wants into increased demands will be forthcoming in the ways which were described earlier.[42] When the initial upsurge of wants subsides, the inflation tends to stop as soon as it has spread throughout the price system.

But subsequent complications will occur. In the process of inflationary propagation, the combined direct and indirect effects of inflation will grow in size and in their relative differentials. Thus, feedback effects on wants and demands will be set in motion, further complicated by various degrees of inflationary expectations.[43] When and how such an inflation will come to a halt it is impossible to say until we systematically examine the various remedies for inflation. The important question is whether an inflation can be tamed without resorting to drastic direct controls over particular prices, individual income increases, and special categories of credit.

V

In the course of considering how inflation can be generated and propagated from the demand side, we have noticed some elements of inflationary pressures from the production side.[44] Thus, the real culprit in an inflation triggered by a demand shift may lurk in the background in the form of resistance to reduction of costs of the goods whose demands have declined. Similarly, cost pressures on prices play a role in an inflation that originates in an expansion of aggregate demand before the full use of facilities and labor have been achieved. Such inflation is at least partly due to the tendency of production costs to increase when production is approaching full capacity, because of increasing shortages or lesser availability of some labor skills, materials, or facilities.[45] Finally, the process of cumulative propagation of demand-generated inflation throughout the price system invariably involves subsequent inflationary pressures from cumulatively increasing costs of production. This happens because higher prices of one set of goods become higher costs in the production of other goods, and because wages and other incomes become engaged in a race to keep ahead of the general pace of inflation.

But all these instances of increased inflationary pressures from the cost-of-production side in the course of a demand-triggered inflation are themselves a consequence of an *initial* change on the demand side. They do not *trigger* inflation independently of demand. Our concern now is to consider the ways and circumstances in which inflation is *triggered,* not just reinforced and propagated, by the inflationary pressures that originate on the *cost*-of-production side.

J. M. Keynes, the originator of the theory of aggregate demand, himself acknowledged the possibility of cost-push inflation.[46] However, the cost-push idea has evolved into an explicit cost-push theory of inflation only in the last few years, under the impetus of the rising price level since 1955.[47] In fact, a variety of cost-push theories have been developed. F. D. Holzman[48] analyzed, among other varieties of cost push, a kind of "dependent" cost push (higher wages leading to higher prices via demand effect). Some other economists went the whole distance away from the traditional demand approach to inflation and have held cost push as an exclusive explanation of all inflation.[49] Others have treated the cost push on an alternative or supplementary basis.[50] Only a few economists of the "Chicago School" have simply rejected cost push as an independent trigger of inflation.[51]

Within a firm, cost of production of any particular good is made up of two sets of costs. First, there are the costs of the facilities, materials, and parts used in production. Second, there are the incomes to be paid to the various kinds of directly used labor, from unskilled workers to top management, and to the suppliers of borrowed and equity capital.[52] As we consider the behavior of the various elements in the cost of production as possible triggers of inflation, the distinction between the two categories of production costs is useful.

An increase in a component of the cost of production becomes a trigger of inflation, that is, an autonomous cause of inflation only if it has increased *independently* of or *beyond* the scope of previous increases in demand. Otherwise, it would be demand that acted as the inflation trigger. This distinction immediately eliminates the first category of production costs (costs of facilities, materials, and parts) as triggers of inflation whenever their prices have increased in consequence of a stepped-up demand for them. Also, when prices of facilities or materials have increased as a result of cost increase in the production of these facilities and materials themselves, the resulting inflationary pressure on product prices of the goods produced with such facilities and materials cannot properly be viewed as an additional trigger of inflation but can be viewed only as a further step in its propagation. For a product price increase from such cost increases of facilities and materials is either entirely or partly beyond the discretion of the *users* of these facilities and materials.

One special case must now be considered. Corporate and personal income-tax laws limit a firm's depreciation write-offs to the original (historical) cost of the facilities and generally lead to a straight-line depreciation accounting over the estimated lifetime of the facilities involved.[53] Consequently, any degree of inflation reduces by that much the replacement value of accumulated depreciation funds.[54] Then, even the mere replacement of the existing production facilities must be partly financed out of additional savings or new bank credit. That is one reason why, as we have seen, inflation is inimical to economic growth.[55] This problem can be resolved only if inflation is effectively prevented or, when inflation is not checked, if depreciation accounting is permitted to be geared closer to the increasing current replacement costs of the facilities involved.

If the second solution of the problem of depreciation and replacement is adopted, it may act as an additional trigger of inflation or at least as an additional wheel in the inflation-propagating mechanism.[56] If in any one year firms can write off a *higher* (than the preceding) percentage of the original cost of their facilities and do not reduce their pre-established profit margins accordingly, their *current* production costs are thereby increased and will therefore act as an additional inflationary pressure on the prices of corresponding products. If no other inflationary pressures were in existence before, such increased depreciation charges could act as a true initiating trigger of inflation.

With the cost of facilities and materials out of the way, we can now turn to the potential that direct productive *incomes* (wages, rents, interest, and profits) have as triggers and propagators of inflation.[57] By way of introduction to the cost aspect of incomes, it may be mentioned that when all the production costs for the *economy as a whole* are added up, the costs of materials and facilities resolve themselves in the income shares of the various labor and nonlabor participants in production. It is only within a *particular firm* that the costs of production appear divided between the costs of facilities and materials and those for productive incomes.

In the pluralistic Western economies, particularly the United States, the analysis of the behavior of productive incomes may be simplified by dividing them into two broad categories—wages of all kinds of labor, and other productive incomes (managerial salaries and related supplements, interest payments, rents, firms' profits). Directly or indirectly, the behavior of money wages is, to a large extent, influenced by policies of labor unions. Productive incomes other than wages are similarly represented by business management.[58] In the end, both categories of productive incomes are jointly determined by collective bargaining[59] and the price-output policies of individual firms.

Labor unions came into existence as a protesting and defensive movement of industrial workers in the earlier stages of Western capitalism. Until it had reached technological maturity in the Rostowian sense,[60] Western capitalism, particularly in Europe, was characterized by a still low over-all productivity, by high and increasing rates of new investment in plant and equipment, and by persistently great disparity between the low wages paid to abundant low-skilled labor, on the one hand, and high monetary returns to relatively scarce productive property and entrepreneurship, on the other.[61] It was against the combination of these three interrelated characteristics of earlier capitalism that the workers' movement began its opposition and revolt.

Under the influence of both pre-Marxian and Marxist socialism, most of the early European labor organizations were psychologically and ideologically anticapitalist. However, as Western capitalism grew more and more productive, and as the influence of the fast-spreading labor movement and of other social-reform developments[62] increased, conditions of work and wages began systematically to improve. This development gradually modified the attitudes and policies of the labor unions in the West,[63] they became adjusted, particularly in the United States, to the developing capitalist system and tried to improve the social status of workers from *within* the system.[64]

American labor unions adopted this approach to capitalism from their very beginnings. For the well-known reasons inherent in the political foundations, population, and economic geography of the new continent, the American version of the newer, progressive capitalism was more productive and expansive than its older European counterparts. It is this difference that shaped Samuel Gompers' pragmatic slogan of American unionism: "More, more, and more."[65]

VI

Gompers' simple union philosophy became a deeply rooted habit of American labor unions, and has also begun to shape labor attitudes elsewhere in the West. No major problem need arise from the practice of this philosophy so long as the over-all productive efficiency keeps improving at the rate of labor's claims for higher wages and for concomitant improvements in labor's conditions. On the contrary, wage increases in close step with the real improvements in over-all productive efficiency may even act as a useful stimulus for all to keep improving their productive performance.

A word about the meaning of "productive efficiency" is necessary. The term is usually employed as synonymous with "productivity." In official statistical calculations, productivity is taken to mean *output per man hour*. But this is clearly a deficient concept. If productivity statistics are to provide correct quantitative indications about the changes in productive efficiency within a firm, an industry, or a nation's economy, output changes must be related not only to the input of *one* productive factor (labor) *alone*, but to the *combined* input changes. It is easy to see, for example, that if changes in capital inputs or in their prices are simply ignored, an alleged productivity improvement from a given increase in output per man hour may in reality be partly or entirely offset by an unrevealed increase in capital costs per unit of product. To remedy this conceptual shortcoming in the currently used productivity-measuring methods (output per man hour), the National Bureau of Economic Research in New York has been working on a more comprehensive, *multiple-input productivity formula.* The result so far has been a combined labor-capital yardstick of productivity improvements.[66]

Such a broadening of the productivity concept is essential when productivity is used as an element in explaining how inflation can be generated and propagated from the production side.

The relationships between wage increases, other income increases, productivity improvements, and product prices are complex. Productivity may be improving in every branch of production, but it never does so at the same pace everywhere. In fact, there are great differences in the behavior of productive efficiency in various firms and industries. As a broad rule, productive efficiency will tend to improve more in industries where there is much scope for increasing mechanization and improving coordination of productive methods than in those branches of production where human skill and effort can receive but limited help from further specialization, mechanization, and organization. Some services are still being produced under such conditions.[67]

On the other hand, Gompers' philosophy of "more, more, and more" is not similarly differentiated. It is not even explicitly geared to productivity improvements, whatever their measure and differentials may be.[68] One persisting aspect of this philosophy is the idea that labor's income share could be further improved at the expense of business profits.[69] Labor everywhere in the West now tends to follow this attractive road to self-improvement through expecting and demanding "more" with eagerness and determination. And in doing so there is also a tendency to "follow the leader," that is, to bring relative wage demands everywhere closer to those of labor in the most productive and prosperous industries or in other key industries[70] such as steel, where labor unions are strong and firms used to possess considerable market power. The differentiated behavior of productivity improvements in various industries, on the one hand, and the tendency toward generally increasing but less differentiated demands for wage increases, on the other, are at the bottom of one of the persistent inflationary pressures on the cost-of-production side. The tendency to emulate higher wage demands in higher productivity conditions may be observed also in interregional or even international comparisons. These emulating tendencies result from the basic "more, more, and more" attitude of labor unions —an attitude that has never been explicitly related to productivity improvements and still less to their differentials.[71]

The term "key industry" is important for the analysis of cost push. It is a term that is much in use without ever having been analytically clarified. Significant analytical elements of a "key industry" appear to be its product and price as well as its wages. The product of a "key industry" is either a significant ingredient (such as steel) of a large number of other products, or dependent (such as automobiles) on a number of quantitatively important complementary products and services.

In both cases, a change in the price of the product of the key industry will have very wide repercussions. In the case of steel, a price change will directly affect production costs, and, through them, prices in related industries. In the case of automobiles, a price change will directly affect the output and employment of complementary industries, *provided* the demand for automobiles is sensitive to price and income changes. In either case, a price increase in a key industry may entail a tendency toward emulation in related industries.

As to wages, an industry is a key industry from this point of view when its wages are relatively higher either because of strong demand for its labor, or because of a strong union, or both. Such wages have a tendency to be emulated in other industries.[72]

If cost-generated inflation is to be avoided, the average rate of periodic increases of all monetary earnings from production must not exceed the average rate of national improvements in productive efficiency[73] that results from better cooperative performance of technology, management, labor, and other contributors to the productive process of the nation. When the rate of total money-income increases in the economy exceeds the rate of total productivity increments calculated at existing prices, such an excess can come only from inflated prices.

Difficulties arise because there is no formula commonly agreed upon for the distribution of the additional real income that is generated by productivity improvements. As a result, the sum total of increases in money-income shares tends to *exceed* the increase in real income from a given productivity improvement; that is, all the money-income increases taken together tend to exceed the sales value of productivity-increased output measured at existing market prices. The measure of the excess of *money*-income increases over the real-income accruals is a higher product price or, in periods of slack demand, dwindling profits.

VII

But wage increases must be agreed upon through collective bargaining. If a firm is willing to face a possible strike, it cannot be forced to accept a wage demand it deems excessive in relation to its own real productivity gains. If such an excessive wage increase is agreed upon, it can only mean that the individual firm or the group of firms that bargain together expect to be able to recover the difference, one way or another.[74]

A wage increase that exceeds the rate of the *realized* average productivity improvement may be recovered through better productivity during the *ensuing* period of the new collective contract. But if such expected productivity improvements are to come through improved mechanization or organization, the excessive wage is likely to reduce employment. In this case, it is precisely the *substitution* of additional mechanization or organization for excessively expensive labor that constitutes the source of the needed and expected productivity improvement. Thus, the higher hourly wage, resulting in increased labor cost per unit of output, will have been bought at the price of reduced employment. Automation represents a very intensive substitution of mechanization for labor.

Only if sufficient improvement in productivity is expected from subsequent better productive performance of *labor* itself does the possibility exist that the firm may recover the loss from the initially excessive wage increase without reducing employment. However, this possibility is not based on the expected larger output of more efficient labor performance alone; the firm must also be able to *sell* the incremental output at the existing price or sufficiently close to it to pay for the increased wage and to yield a profitable return to the firm itself.

If this second condition is actually fulfilled, it will be an indication that the firm either failed to tap the potentialities of its market before the wage increase[75] or that a demand shift in the firm's favor has since occurred or, finally, that the firm expected a general increase in the aggregate demand to increase the demand for the firm's products. Such an increase in aggregate demand could be expected either from an expansive monetary and fiscal policy or from economy-wide emulation of wage increases to be translated in increased demand, or from both. But in all these cases, assuming that they materialize, aggregate-demand effects will be likely to *trail* the initial and subsequent wage increases. Furthermore, specific impacts of such a delayed aggregate-demand increase on particular demands will be *differentiated,* depending on the various degrees of sensitivity of particular demands to increases in incomes and in credit opportunities in conjunction with the existing prices.

In all other cases, a wage increase in excess of the realized productivity improvement will cause a more or less proportional increase in the product price or prices of the firm or firms involved, or else it will result in an immediate profit "squeeze." The ultimate outcome, in terms of output and employment, will again depend on the underlying or anticipated demand for the firm's product or products. If the products involved are such that the demand for them is not very sensitive to their prices (urgently demanded goods), the market may absorb a higher price without a major reduction in the quantity of the product that will be purchased at the higher price. Then the firm may be able to recover the excessive wage increase without a considerable reduction in employment. In any other product-demand situation, however, a price increase caused by a productivity-exceeding wage increase cannot but result in appreciable unemployment. If an elastic demand precludes price increase, the resulting profit squeeze may still lead to unemployment via reduced output and/or reduced investment. Again, the excessive wage increase will be paid for in terms of reduced employment.

It is now possible to conclude that relative wage increases in excess of the percentage increase in output per unit of labor and capital combined will, as a rule, tend to lead to higher product prices or to profit squeeze or both, *coupled with lower output and employment.*[76] Only systematic inflationary monetary and fiscal policies can offset the unemployment effect of such cost push. Thus, inflationary pressures caused by excessive wage increases are more damaging to economic growth than inflation triggered from the demand side. Wage inflation directly generates unemployment as an additional negative effect which calls for more demand inflation to bail it out. It is therefore particularly inimical to economic growth.[77]

VIII

If the negative effects of wage increases in excess of productivity improvements are so obvious, why do unions continue to demand,

and employers to agree to, such wages? The answer is threefold.

In key industries, such as steel or automobiles, three factors conspire to permit the continuation of the wage-price spiral. First, the unions in these industries are strong and therefore have great bargaining power as well as political influence.[78] Second, the demand for the products of these industries is largely insensitive to changes in the prices of these goods, although the demand for passenger automobiles, for example, may be temporarily postponed and both steel and automobiles may be partly imported. Finally, by their size and the relative importance of their products, these industries are regarded as being of special public interest; this tends to bring government pressure to bear for a quick and peaceful solution to their wage disputes.[79] Such solutions usually result in excessive wage increases and higher product prices.[80] And as long as excessive wage bargains continue to be the practice in the key industries, their emulation in other industries will also continue.[81] Thus, the wage-push inflation will continue.[82]

Two additional factors reinforce the inherent tendency of wage increases to exceed the limits of productivity improvements. Labor unions, particularly in the United States, have come increasingly to use the institution of collective bargaining as a vehicle for the introduction of group welfare measures beyond increasing money wages and improving working conditions. Pension plans, medical services, life insurance, supplementary unemployment benefits, provisions of recreational services and facilities, and demands for other "fringe benefits" now press on collective bargaining over and above the demands for increased take-home pay itself. It therefore must be made clear that unless the *combined* increases in money wage *and* in fringe benefits remain within the limits of productivity improvements costs per unit of product will increase.

An additional remark about fringe benefits may be in order. If group welfare measures take the form of inflationary fringe benefits, the public at large has to pay for arrangements in the making of which it had no say, and the cost in this case is higher than it would be if such welfare provisions were paid for in voluntary contributions or in taxes rather than in cost inflation, which has a host of negative effects.

The third complicating factor in wage-caused inflation is the legal responsibility of, and political necessity for, the government to maintain a level of aggregate demand sufficient to support full employment.[83] The very concept of "full employment" is ambiguous.[84] It does not mean that everybody able and willing to work should actually be employed at any one time. There are types of unemployment that do not depend simply on the level of aggregate demand. People change jobs and places of work and may be unemployed in between. Changes in particular demands and in technology of individual firms and industries carry with them temporary displacements and require industrial and geographical mobility of labor. These forms of unemployment are not always self-correcting; "depressed areas" are extreme examples of a persistent lack of mobility.[85] Nevertheless, the required government help in such cases is specific rather than by way of general increase of the aggregate demand.

But there are further complications. If, say, about 4 per cent of unemployment is not due simply to the deficiency of aggregate demand but may be due to more specific causes[86] and the government automatically ensured an aggregate demand sufficient to finance a 96 per cent "full employment" *irrespective of wage push,* such a policy would in fact support an excessive aggregate demand. Such a blunt full-employment policy would directly encourage wage push in two ways; first, by tending to eliminate or to prevent direct unemployment effects of wage push, and second, by permitting the illusion that all price increases, actually co-triggered by excessive costs, were due exclusively to demand shifts or demand pull. And when excessive wage increases were translated into delayed demand increases, such an indiscriminate monetary policy would result in adding a measure of net demand inflation over and above the cost-triggered one.[87]

In the United States, such a crude full-employment policy was the rule in the early postwar period until 1951. Until then, the Federal Reserve was willing and ready to buy government bonds from the public at stable prices, thereby systematically keeping interest rates low and monetizing the Federal war debt. A change occurred in March, 1951, when the Federal Reserve system regained its independence in purchases of government securities and inaugurated a tighter monetary policy to combat inflationary pressures.[88] As a consequence of this basic change in monetary policy, the public gradually became aware of the possibility of cost-push inflation and its unemployment effects.

But in the process, the tables were turned. Instead of the Federal Reserve's bailing out inflated production costs, as before 1951, the new policy was to combat *all* inflation by tightening up the financial basis of aggregate demand, regardless of whether inflation was caused by excessive demand or excessive costs. To the extent that wage increases *continue* to exceed the limits of productivity improvements in spite of a demand-restricting monetary policy, such a monetary policy aggravates the unemployment effects of wage push instead of eliminating its cause. If its lesson is ignored by the cost-pushers, a restrictive monetary policy worsens the unemployment effects of wage-caused or wage-prompted price increases. It curtails further an aggregate demand already too small to absorb (at the higher cost-pushed prices) all the output that production at full employment can turn out.[89]

IX

If wage increases in excess of productivity improvements can trigger inflation from the production side, is not the same true in regard to the *nonwage* incomes from production (rents, profits, interest rates)? Yes, but with a difference. Interest rates are in a separate category because they are partly subject to regulation by the Federal Reserve system and by other central banks for purposes of monetary policy. The Federal Reserve can influence interest rates in several ways, primarily through its purchases of government securities[90] and through direct changes of the rate of rediscounting the commercial paper or discounting the promissory notes of the member banks of the Federal Reserve system.[91] It is by rediscounting or discounting that the member banks can borrow additional reserves from Federal Reserve banks.

When, by action of the Federal Reserve, interest rates are increased, costs of production will indeed be increased to the extent that higher interest rates now have to be paid for the use of money in production. Thus, theoretically at least, there *is* a cost push. But those few who, like Congressman Patman, tried to make an issue out of the policy of tighter money as a case of cost push, missed the very purpose of monetary policy.[92] The theoretical cost push via higher interest rates serves as a means of combating an aggregate demand inflation by restraining its financial base. However, where the inflation itself is of the *cost-push* variety, Congressman Patman may have a valid point, although for a wrong reason, to the extent that wage push continues *in spite of* restrictive monetary policy, which then only adds to the unemployment effect of cost-push inflation.[93]

Profits would create cost push if profit *margins* per unit of sales were deliberately increased. Thus the question of profit push is part of the problem of administered prices, which has already been discussed.[94] A seemingly plausible argument pointing to the existence of profit push is the one advanced by J. K. Galbraith.[95] According to this explanation, firms that possess enough power to "administer" the prices of their products have tended to keep their prices trailing demand increases for their products. Thus, they have accumulated "unliquidated monopoly gains from unmade price increase."[96] Such unrealized potential gains are then periodically "cashed in" through subsequent price increases when wages or interest rates are increased.

Galbraith's argument amounts to saying that firms that are able to administer their prices increase them to the level permitted by the corresponding demand with *systematic delays*, and use the wage or other cost increases as a lever for demand-oriented price increases. According to Galbraith's argument, there is thus a deliberate but systematic profit-margin *restraint*. Then, when wages or other nonprofit incomes increase, prices are raised to the levels permitted by their *pre-existing* demands.

But Galbraith's argument stops short of a full explanation. What are the implications of his reasoning for the behavior of profit *margins?* Such delayed, cost-rise-prompted price increases would indeed result in "maximum" *total* profits as determined by the pre-existing demand and the by-now *higher* costs. But such prices may yield profit *margins* (profit per unit of sales) that are even smaller than before the price was raised. It all depends on the *size* of the cost increase that prompted the subsequent price increase. But whether the new profit margins were lower or higher or the same as before, their change, if any, would come about as a result of *pre*-increased production costs and would be permitted by the level of *pre*-existing demand. There is very little in this process that would characterize it as an independent or autonomous *profit* push.

A genuine profit push would occur if profit *margins* were deliberately increased above their levels as determined by *existing* demands. A possible reason for firms so to increase their profit margins would be if they expected corresponding demand shifts in their favor from a growing aggregate demand inflation. Such pricing behavior could be classified as resulting from an autonomous profit push to the extent that it would not be based on *pre*-existing demands, but would be *forcing* its own demand "validation" by way of subsequently inflated aggregate demand through public policy undertaken for the sake of maintaining full employment and fostering economic growth. Available statistics on the actual behavior of profit margins do not seem to support the thesis that there has been a profit-margin push of proportions similar to the systematic wage push. In fact, there has been a decline in profit margins since 1948.[97] The American steel industry appears to have been a conspicuous exception. But it was prevented from reaping full benefit from its systematic inflationary price policies because, during 1958–62, it operated at exceptionally low levels of capacity.[98]

The ultimate reason for the different behavior of wage rates, on the one hand, and profit margins, on the other, is to be found in the following fundamental distinction. Wage push is explainable within the framework of labor-union attitudes ("more, more, and more") that are shaped largely *outside* the demand-and-supply framework of the market.[99] Firms, on the other hand, must operate *within* this framework if they are to survive. W. Baumol has recently even attempted to show that firms that have the power to administer their prices do so with an aim different from the traditional objective of maximizing total *profits*. According to this theory, corporate firms, by virtue of corporate sociology and management psychology, tend to maximize their *sales* revenue instead, with such profits as are deemed necessary to provide funds for short-term self-financing and to maintain incentives for competitive long-term equity-financing.[100] But according to Baumol, such profits are, as a rule, below the level of what they would be if firms were to maximize them in accordance with the traditional principle of purely competitive business behavior.[101]

Although it remains to be fully confirmed against the facts, Baumol's new theory gives a deeper insight into Galbraith's observation that profit margins tend systematically to trail demand increases. It now seems that the old principle of straight profit "maximization" is a theoretical leftover from the original model of perfect or pure competition. According to that mental construct, price changes were spontaneous—that is, prices changed automatically in response to the uncontrolled behavior of market demand and supply, and firms could only adjust their output and related production costs to the expected market price. In so doing, they would naturally see to it that they were left with as much profit as their internal productive efficiency and the demand for their products at the existing or expected market prices permitted. It was such total profit from the firm's sales that was called "maximum." But it was a "maximum" of sorts. Only one of the several codeterminants of this maximum—namely, the firm's internal productive efficiency—was controlled by the individual firm, and even this only in part, since the firm had to pay the going prices of productive services, whatever they were.

The prevailing corporate firms of today do not operate in such a simple competitive environment. For reasons of contemporary technology and organization, they tend to be large, producing a large share of the total output for any given market. Furthermore, neither the total market supply nor the total market demand are uniform. Product preferences of potential customers vary. Products and attending services of each firm are therefore differentiated and are being varied at more or less frequent intervals. Such firms must of necessity fight for their market shares, which therefore cannot easily be predetermined. And since, in the absence of homogenous market supply and demand, each firm's prices must be administered by the firm, and since this can be done conveniently only at relatively long intervals of time, there is no way of "maximizing" the firm's profits in any deterministic sense. Such firms can only aim at specific profit levels in conjunction with the "maximum" sales they are capable of by means of competitive products and services, at competitive prices, and with the help of competitive advertising and other sales efforts.

X

One remaining question about the inflation generated on the production side concerns its propagation. Little new need be said about it. A production-generated inflation spreads throughout the price system in the same manner as a demand-caused inflation. But inflation-initiating increases in wage costs (or in other income rates, if they can be pushed up) have a particularly strong tendency to be emulated in addition to their direct cost effects on product prices.[102] In the case of wage push, such emulation occurs primarily through induced union pressures elsewhere in the economy, regardless of whether or not productivity improvements warrant such wage increases. Some take the view that this kind of wage emulation may be reinforced by competitive emulation of wage increases by employers themselves with a view to establishing or maintaining the reputation of a permanently high-wage (and fringe-benefit) firm in order to keep or attract good workers, especially when they are in short supply and tend to accumulate vested interests (in funded fringe benefits) in particular firms.

8. *REMEDIES FOR INFLATION: REAL ECONOMIC GROWTH*

Selection of adequate remedies for inflation presupposes a correct diagnosis of the causes that can trigger it. Each initiating cause indicates its own remedies. Since it is likely, however, that any contemporary inflation involves several triggers, simultaneously or consecutively, an effective policy against inflation will usually require several kinds of remedies.

To the extent that inflation may be triggered by a *demand shift*, two kinds of remedies are possible, one that deals with the demand shift itself and the other that copes with the underlying downward inflexibility of prices. If the demand shift is deemed undesirable in itself, selective credit controls may be used to eliminate it or to diminish its size.[1] Thus particular varieties of consumer credit may be restricted if demand shift involves consumer goods.

But in a society that prides itself on permitting its people and institutions to pursue their own buying inclinations, in accordance with their autonomous aspirations, demand shifts are most natural and regular occurrences. They cannot possibly be all suppressed except in a national emergency. Furthermore, it is really the downward inflexibility of prices that turns demand shifts into inflation triggers. Thus, remedies should primarily be sought to make prices more sensitive to demand decreases.

There is one possible policy to increase the downward flexibility of prices that deserves more consideration than it has received. A systematic information program on the true availability characteristics of various products may appreciably increase general sensitivity of demand to prices.[2] Such an increase in sensitivity on the part of buyers to the prices of various goods would act as a stimulus to producers to make their product prices more pliable to demand reductions. Where rigidity of contractual money incomes is responsible for the downward inflexibility of prices, increased sensitivity of demand to product prices might elicit a more flexible attitude on the part of the income recipients involved; for a generally increased sensitivity of demand to product prices could greatly aggravate the unemployment effects of rigid production costs (as the cause of inflexible product prices), should demand weaken.

The only comprehensive alternative to exploring and developing all the anti-inflationary potentialities of this simple remedy is to have bureaucratic price controls that would enforce price decreases whenever particular demands fell appreciably below the capacity level of production.[3] But short of a major national emergency, such direct price controls are neither desirable nor feasible.

II

If inflation that is triggered or aggravated by an excessive *aggregate demand* is to be avoided, aggregate demand must be geared to a realistic level of full employment, discounting the kinds of unemployment that develop independently of aggregate demand or require specific remedies.

In all advanced Western economies, the task of *guiding* aggregate demand toward full employment rests, in the final analysis, on the government, which alone possesses the means to this end. When the multitude of decentralized components of the aggregate demand tend to add up to an excess or a deficiency in its total size, only deliberate *monetary* and *fiscal* policy measures can maintain or right the balance.[4] There is no other single agent within the aggregate demand that would have the motivation, or command the power, needed for such flexible rectifications of the total national expenditures on goods and services. Thus, the remaining opposition to the *principle* of governmental guidance of the total size of the aggregate demand is purely academic, with no practical alternative.[5]

Monetary policy does not directly affect the demand for goods and services that originates in wants, prices, and incomes; nor does it control incomes that originate in production. Monetary policy can only control the supply (stock) of money by virtue of legal reserve requirements against commercial banks' credit.[6] Ideally, the task of the central bank would be so to regulate the supply of money in the economy that its multiple use for the consecutive purchases of goods and services would just add up to the necessary and sufficient size of effective aggregate demand at the full-employment level. But in a flexible monetary and financial system, as was described earlier,[7] such an ideal monetary policy is impossible. Since a given amount of money in circulation may be turned over for consecutive purchases of goods and services with varying frequency, the influence of monetary policy on the aggregate demand is not only indirect but also uncertain.[8] What particularly complicates the financial system today are the close substitutes for money itself for purposes of liquidity (a variety of very liquid securities), but over which the Federal Reserve now has no direct authority.[9] It is therefore possible that a restrictive, anti-inflationary monetary policy may be circumvented by a more extensive or intensive use of money substitutes for liquidity purposes. The opposite may happen in the event of an expansive, anti-recessionary monetary policy.

Given the flexibility of the financial system and its resulting evasiveness in regard to general monetary policies, and in view of the extensive use of credit in our economy, it is easy to see why specific credit controls may be a useful supplement to the monetary control of aggregate demand. Specific credit controls can directly restrict the use of credit for precisely the kinds of purchases that may have triggered the expansion of aggregate demand. There is no doubt that a restrictive monetary policy would be a more effective weapon against inflationary pressures from the demand side, if it were supplemented by selective credit controls.[10] Objections against the use of such specific credit controls, save during a national emergency, are based on similar, if less convincing, considerations than those against controlling mere demand shifts.[11]

An additional problem affecting monetary policy as a tool for regulating the size of the aggregate demand is linked with the relationship between the central bank and the general government. When a central bank, like the Federal Reserve in the United States, is administratively independent of the general government, particularly of its executive branch, the problem arises as to how to coordinate monetary policy with the fiscal and other policies of the general government that influence aggregate demand. As they are administratively separated, the two may work at cross purposes. On the other hand, if a central bank is dominated by the general government, there is a danger that monetary policy will be subordinated to the specific objectives of government finances or that it will be pressured into "validating" pluralistic cost-push tendencies, instead of serving as a tool for guiding the total size of the aggregate demand so as to avoid inflation and minimize recessions.[12]

When the two sides of the problem are carefully examined, the conclusion points toward sensible coordination of monetary policies of the central bank with the fiscal and other economic policies of the general government. The criterion for such coordination must be a firmly established objective of *noninflationary economic growth,* with full employment to be achieved *without unnecessary interference with the composition of aggregate demand.* Thus, for example, when overriding considerations of national interest require sudden or sizable increases of government purchases of goods and services, monetary policy and the revenue side of fiscal policy must cooperate closely to contain the incipient inflationary pressures by holding back other segments of aggregate demand. Presently we shall see how the two must cooperate when expansion rather than containment of aggregate demand is sought.

III

This conclusion brings us to consider *fiscal policy* as the other major tool to help direct aggregate demand toward a realistic full-employment level. The term indicates the use of public finances, on both their revenue and expenditure sides, for purposes of influencing aggregate demand so that it will be sufficient to maintain all the economic growth that can be had short of inflation. Through the use of fiscal policy, aggregate demand can be enlarged by an increase in government expenditures on goods and services or by a tax reduction used as a stimulus for increasing nongovernmental purchases of goods and services. By changing taxation and government expenditures in the opposite directions, aggregate demand can be checked when deemed excessive.

When compared with monetary policy, fiscal policy, by its very nature, has one advantage and two disadvantages. The obvious advantage of fiscal policy is that a change in government expenditures for goods and services *directly* affects the size of the aggregate demand and also subsequently *indirectly* affects spending by the recipients of government expenditures. Changes in taxes do not, of course, change spending directly, but they do change disposable income out of which spending is made.

Of the two disadvantages of fiscal policy, one is that taxes and government appropriations in democratically governed countries are prerogatives of legislative bodies. This makes fiscal policy slow in its development and subject to capricious political pressures as to content and size. A partial remedy for this relative disadvantage would be to authorize the executive branch of government to effect revenue and expenditure changes in accordance with the requirements of fiscal policy within such predetermined limits as would safeguard the ultimate democratic control over public finances. In the United States, where the chief executive is directly elected by the people, such a modification of fiscal policy should not prove politically impossible.[13]

The other disadvantage of fiscal policy is that changes in government expenditures, particularly decreases, must be determined *primarily* in relation to the nation's needs for collective services,[14] rather than for purposes of guiding the total size of aggregate demand. This reveals the *inescapable conflict between* the *primary purpose of public finance, which is the procurement of public goods,* and *its secondary purpose,* which is to act *as fiscal policy for upholding sufficient aggregate demand.*

The second disadvantage of fiscal policy tends to obscure the true meaning of what is often presented as a technical issue. This concerns the use of tax reductions as a stimulus to increasing nongovernmental purchases when aggregate demand appears insufficient, rather than the expansion of government expenditures. The first method is usually claimed to be safer from surprising inflationary pressures, the assumption being that some of the tax savings will not be spent, whereas an increase in government expenditures always increases aggregate demand by its full amount.

This argument is not fully convincing. First, selective tax reductions, particularly of business taxes, are usually hailed as unleashing incentives in their beneficiaries to spend *beyond* the size of the immediate tax savings themselves. Second, if aggregate demand is indeed insufficient for full employment, it can in principle be increased by enlarging *any* component of aggregate demand. The only *technical* preference (in relation to the goal of noninflationary full employment) for selecting for increase one segment of aggregate demand rather than another would be in consideration of specific bottlenecks that may arise from increased purchases of particular goods in short supply. In the case of an increase in government expenditures, the corresponding purchases should, of course, be known in advance. When, however, taxes are reduced to elicit more nongovernmental spending, it is more difficult to foresee where the ensuing purchases will converge.

Thus, technical reasons for favoring one method of increasing aggregate demand over another are not entirely conclusive. It is more likely that the method of tax reduction for increasing aggregate demand is favored by those who like to view government expenditures as unnecessary waste or at best a necessary evil. Those, on the other hand, who share the conviction that our "affluent society" has systematically neglected much needed public goods and services, will just as eagerly seize an occasion of insufficient aggregate demand to step up government expenditures on goods and services. Here is a recent example. Professor Arthur F. Burns, former Chairman of the Council of Economic Advisers to the President, was critical of the Kennedy Administration for its resistance, in 1961, to reducing nonmilitary public expenditures to offset increasing defense expenditures. He would have preferred to supplement with tax cuts whatever further deficiency there may still have been in the total size of the aggregate demand.[15]

Analogous preferences underlie opposing suggestions for checking the inflationary impact of an excessive aggregate demand. Technically, the problem can be met either by increased taxes or by decreased government expenditures. The devotees of the sanctity of "private" goods, no matter what these goods may be, are likely to favor decreases in government expenditures, and the worshipers of "public" goods, whatever specific purposes these goods may serve, will usually prefer tax increases, especially for business.[16]

Clearly, what is primarily involved in this kind of controversy is not some technical aspect of the two alternative approaches to fiscal policy, but the underlying *judgment* about the relative desirability of more private or more public goods.

IV

Since the Burns-Council controversy in 1961, a remarkable convergence of attitudes on the subject has taken place. In the course of 1962–63, most business and labor groups turned in favor of a sizable reduction of personal and corporate income tax rates, from top to bottom. This consensus in favor of a general tax reduction as a stimulus to economic growth[17] was made easier by explicit international suggestions for reduced taxes, coupled with transitional budget deficits, as essential instruments for increasing the sluggish rate of American economic growth. These international suggestions[18] implied that the resulting increases in the aggregate demand would not be inflationary and therefore would not aggravate the deficit in American international payments. The goal was to increase the over-all rate of American economic growth to 4½ per cent, which was expected to reduce the rate of unemployment to 4 per cent.[19]

To implement this goal, President Kennedy submitted to Congress, on January 24, 1963, a comprehensive income tax reduction and reform proposal, lowering personal income tax rates from 20–91 per cent to a new range of 14–65 per cent, to be effected over a period of three years. Corporate income tax rates would be reduced from 52 to 47 per cent, and from 30 to 22 per cent on the first $25,000 of corporate income. The total revenue loss from the proposed reduction was officially calculated at $13.6 billion, which, however, would be reduced to $10.2 billion in consequence of the proposed tax-base-broadening reforms. Subsequently, in the course of prolonged congressional hearings throughout 1963, the tax reduction proposal was trimmed to about $11 billion and to fewer tax reform measures, but was to be implemented in two rather than three years.[20]

The new American fiscal policy represents a package composed of lower taxes, increased private demand, and a transitional Federal budget deficit[21] of some $10 billion in 1964 and $5 billion in 1965. Thereafter, if things go right, the resulting expansion of GNP should balance the budget at a level of about 4 per cent unemployment. Although budget deficit was expected to increase directly the effective aggregate demand for goods and services, the proposed tax reduction was predicated on similar demand effects, through larger disposable incomes, in addition to improved investment incentives. This twofold fiscal policy appears to be a reconciliation of the 1961 Burns-Council controversy, combining the elements of both sides.

As taxes are seldom reduced, one would expect jubilation when such cuts are seriously considered. The fact that President Kennedy's tax reduction proposal encountered a mixed reception was due primarily to continued budget deficits which would accompany reduced taxes. There were also disagreements concerning the reform provisions of the tax proposal. But the center of the controversy was the deficit.[22] Let us examine this problem.

The main purpose of taxes is to raise the revenue to pay for nonmarketable government services. Our Federal tax structure was shaped with a view to pay for World War II and the Korean War. Thus, in spite of the continued Cold War, there should be some scope for both a general tax reduction and a selective tax reform. This much is clear enough. But our increasing knowledge about the working of the nation's economy has revealed that there is a more complicated relationship between the nation's production and government finances than meets the eye.

It remains, of course, intrinsically true that government revenue and government expenditures must somehow balance. Yet, attempts to balance them when the nation's economy experiences substantial and protracted unemployment, such as has consistently been the case since 1957 (with unemployment ranging between 5 and 7 per cent of our growing working population), do not help the economy to make a fuller use of available labor and capital. In an underemployed economy, lower taxes and/or higher government expenditures, with transitional deficits, would generate demand for additional production and give rise to incentives for more investment in productive capacity. At the resulting higher levels of production the lowered and partly restructured tax rates would yield higher tax revenues, which would eventually balance government expenditures.

If government finances are not to act as a drag on the nation's economy, government revenue and expenditures must be precalculated so that they will balance at a level of the nation's total production, which will be closer to full employment than was the 1962–63 level. If government revenue and expenditures are planned to balance when the nation's production and employment are substantially below what they could and should be, then there is no known way to take up the slack in the nation's production and employment.

The slack can be absorbed either directly, by increased government expenditures in excess of expected tax revenue at existing tax rates, or by reducing taxes below the existing level of government expenditures, thereby permitting consumers and producers to activate idle resources through increased private purchases. The new American fiscal policy combines the two known possibilities.

To really understand the current controversy concerning government finances, one must keep in mind the underlying aim, which is to re-establish full employment. A growing, fully employed economy is needed not only for the obvious sake of employing all Americans who are able and willing to work and whose employment depends on the strength of the total demand for goods and services. (This would still leave between 3 and 4 per cent unemployed for a variety of specific reasons, which are not due primarily to the level of total demand.) We also need a fully employed economy in order to meet our increasing needs for more private and public goods and services, and for the sake of our competitive economic position in the world.

Neither the danger of renewed inflation, nor the difficulties of balancing our international accounts, can be validly invoked against reasonable full employment as our basic economic goal. The attainment and maintenance of the desired level of the nation's production requires, first, that our public finances be balanced at a level of total production nearer to full employment; second, that wage increases be within the economic limits of the nation's productivity increases (increases in output per unit of labor and capital); and, third, that price changes reflect corresponding demand-and-cost changes. These combined requirements of a fully employed economy have the additional power of preserving the stability of the general level of prices, thus checking inflation and strengthening our competitive economic position in the world. The wage-price behavior requirements for noninflationary full employment will be further discussed below.

If, on the contrary, government finances are planned to balance, *regardless* of the level of the nation's production, they may actually not balance at all, and the economy may forever linger below its full employment level of production. A balanced budget generates no *net* addition to the total demand for production, and such addition has clearly been needed. The resulting national income may not even yield sufficient tax revenue to balance the "balanced" budget. We have had such a doubly self-defeating fiscal policy since 1957.

When such technical requirements of an orderly economy as a balanced budget, balanced international accounts, and general price stability are elevated to the artificial status of *independent* objectives, they displace such basic human goals as full employment and maximum production. Then such technical requirements become idols that are bound to crumble. Integrity of technical requirements can be upheld only when they are put in the *service* of human welfare. If arch "liberals" tend to forget that welfare objectives can be effectively served only by disciplined technical means, the tragedy of their arch "conservative" opponents is that they are prone to confuse the discipline of means with the basic human ends themselves.

This is the essence of the "new" insight concerning the basic relationship between government finances and the nation's economy. Because the insight is relatively recent, there are still some disagreements about it among professional economists themselves.[23] Uncertainties continue to persist on secondary aspects of the public finances–national economy relationship. No one knows, for example, precisely how much of the proposed tax savings would actually be spent on increased consumption; how much investment-incentive value such increased consumption spending would have; and by how much reduced tax rates and reformed tax structure would directly increase investment incentives.[24]

Since precise quantitative effects of the proposed tax revision cannot be known in advance, disagreements are unavoidable. But this is necessarily so with all quantitative forecasts of human effects. And yet we must make decisions in advance of their quantitative results. In view of the incontrovertible logic concerning the basic public finance–national economy relationship, the proposed tax changes with contrived transitional budget deficits were bound to prevail. There is no other known way to our undisputed goal of a full-employment economy.

How does the current emphasis on expansionary fiscal policy affect monetary policy, the traditionally favored public policy for stimulating economic growth toward, and stability at, full employment? This is the policy of increasing the supply of money in the economy through larger purchases by the Federal Reserve of publicly held Federal securities, or through lower interest rates at which commercial banks can borrow additional reserves at Federal Reserve banks, or through lowering the legal reserve requirements of commercial banks (now between 12 and 16½ per cent) against their demand deposits (checking accounts).

As already indicated above,[25] there are two drawbacks to monetary policy as a means of economic expansion. First, as instruments of an expansionary policy, the various measures of monetary policy promise less directness and are therefore of more doubtful effectiveness than either the lowering of taxes or increasing government expenditures. Increased government expenditures directly add to the total *demand* for goods and services, and lower taxes leave more of the earned *income* in the hands of individuals and businesses. Monetary policy, on the other hand, does not add directly either to total income or to total spending. It only makes it possible for individuals and businesses to dispose of their government securities for *cash* at somewhat higher prices and to *borrow* more at perhaps somewhat lower interest rates. Second, such expanded possibilities for cashing government bonds or for borrowing new money may be seized upon, if at all, only at interest rates which, by international comparison, could appear so low that they would drive out of the country large amounts of foreign and domestic dollar holdings in search of higher interest rates abroad. Such a domestically effective monetary policy could therefore turn out to be entirely incompatible with the precarious state of our already severely reduced monetary gold stock and with our chronically passive balance of international payments. Thus, for all practical purposes, fiscal policy is now our chief instrument for economic growth toward higher levels of employment.

It would still be incorrect, however, to conclude that there is no further scope now for monetary policy as an instrument for economic expansion. Monetary policy may be called upon to *support* the effectiveness of an expansionary fiscal policy, primarily by helping to finance transitional Federal deficits through enlarged purchases of the publicly held Federal securities in the open market, thus enabling the public to buy more of the new Federal bonds. How far this help should go must be determined by the amount of idle funds already in the economy that can be activated for increased purchases of goods and services or of new Federal bonds. It is for monetary policy so to limit its financial support to an expansionary fiscal policy that the resulting total demand, both private and public, for goods and services will not be in *excess* of the supply of goods at the full-employment level of production, for this would clearly be inflationary. Essentially, this appears to be the position of the Board of Governors of our Federal Reserve system, as voiced by Chairman Martin when he testified on the subject before the Joint Economic Committee of Congress, on February 1, 1963.[26]

In conclusion, monetary policy's role in relation to economic expansion out of large-scale unemployment toward a closer-to-full-employment rate of economic growth is of a *permissive* and subsidiary kind. Monetary policy should be so conducted that the *amount* of monetary reserves and the resulting *conditions* of borrowing will be sufficient for the consumers, the businesses, and the various levels of government together to finance such aggregate purchases of economic goods and resources as will sustain the rate of economic growth along the rising path of full employment. Not much more can be expected of monetary policy alone. It is up to fiscal policy to participate actively with the consumers and businesses in mobilizing the available but idle resources for production to satisfy our growing private wants and public needs.

V

The cost-pushing pressures on prices implied in the remaining fear of inflation from an increase in aggregate demand during high unemployment bring us to consider remedies for inflation generated from the production side.

Since 1955, the United States has experienced so-called creeping inflation.[27] As this inflation has been accompanied by a relatively high rate of unemployment and by a low rate of economic growth, it was generally ascribed to cost-push causes. Since 1958, there has actually been a remarkable stability in wholesale prices and a slower creeping-up of consumer prices. On the other hand, this same period has been characterized by a persistently higher rate of unemployment and a lower rate of economic growth.[28]

Since cost push means an autonomous increase in some cost component per unit of output,[29] it tends to lead to price increases or to profit squeeze or both. It has been argued, however, that since such autonomously increased costs also constitute increased money incomes, these will translate themselves into a commensurate increase in aggregate demand, thus providing sufficient "purchasing power" to buy the entire output at higher prices.[30]

This is a double fallacy. First, the argument accepts cost-push inflation as if it had no undesirable effects other than its special unemployment effect, which the argument is designed to deny. Second, the argument is deficient even in its limited scope. For the argument fails to consider that whatever the expected or pretended aggregate demand effect of inflationary income increases may be, it may *lag* considerably behind their *immediate* cost effects.[31] This lag may cause reductions in sales, output, and employment at increased prices before the unknown aggregate demand effect of money-income increases is implemented. Furthermore, there is no guarantee that the increased aggregate demand will sufficiently increase the particular demands for precisely those products whose increased costs have pushed up their prices.[32]

The cumulative unemployment effect of a creeping cost-push inflation can be cushioned if aggregate demand is kept in line with the rising money costs and prices without significant lags, through deliberate monetary and fiscal policies designed to maintain full employment regardless and in spite of the cost push. But such a deliberate increase in aggregate demand, with a view to preventing or eliminating the unemployment effect of cost-push inflation, will not be fully successful either. It will eliminate only a part of the unemployment effect of cost-push inflation. This will happen because some of the deliberately increased aggregate demand will increase the expenditures on some goods beyond the amount required to "validate" the preceding cost push, while the demand for other products will remain short of what it would have to be if the unemployment effect of cost push were to be fully eliminated. Thus, attempts at deliberate "validation" of cost-push inflation by means of monetary and fiscal policies will increase inflationary pressures in the economy[33] while failing to eliminate the entire unemployment effect of cost push. Monetary and fiscal policies can change the aggregate demand as a whole, but cannot readily control changes in its composition. Only direct controls can do that.

As an aid to avoiding inflationary pressures and unemployment effects from disorderly wage increases and related price changes, the Council of Economic Advisers to the President has published "Guideposts for Noninflationary Wage and Price Behavior." The set of interrelated criteria, contained in the President's Economic Report of January, 1962,[34] may be reduced to the following essential propositions.

Since, in real terms, money can buy only what has been produced, average increases in *real* income can come only from output increases per unit of resources used. If average *money*-income increases in the economy exceed output increases per unit of resources used, inflationary pressures are generated, and, as the Report should have added, unemployment will tend to increase, since various demands will lag behind increased supplies at unchanged or higher prices. In addition, overpriced labor will increasingly be displaced by more intensive mechanization, which otherwise would not be economically justified.

To prevent the economy-wide average of money-income increases from exceeding the limits of real output increases, a set of inferred criteria or decision-making rules must be observed in the processes of organized wage-and-price administration.

The basic rule for increases in the rate of labor income per hour (including overtime and all fringes) is that they should conform to the rate of economy-wide output increases per unit of *resources* (and not just per unit of *labor* used, as the Report seems to imply). But there are two modifiers of this basic rule intended to serve as monetary incentives for labor to move into and out of particular industries, depending on changes in demand for various products and in technology. Actual hourly labor-income increases in particular industries, firms, or skills should therefore exceed or fall short of the basic rule, depending on whether the labor supply in particular cases is short, or in excess, of the actual labor requirements. Similar modifiers may be used in order to redress significant inequities in labor income as between various industries, firms, or skills.

The basic rule for administered price changes related to negotiated labor-income changes is that particular prices should remain unchanged, be decreased, or increased, depending on whether the actual rates of output increase per unit of resources used in particular industries or firms coincide with, exceed, or fall short of, the rates of actual hourly labor-income increases in the respective industries or firms.

This basic rule for administered price changes in relation to negotiated labor-income changes should be modified in accordance with whether the existing profit rates in particular cases fall short or are in excess of what is required to maintain or attract sufficient capital. It should be mentioned, however, that this modifying consideration would be less important if productivity improvements were consistently measured in relation to the combined use of labor and capital rather than in terms of labor input alone. This point has been stressed above.[35]

The official "guideposts" in the President's Economic Report, however, leave entirely unanswered the question as to how the criteria for a full-employment and noninflationary wage-price administration may be implemented. Caution in this regard is understandable, since the criteria themselves are in need of further elaboration and clarification.

But there is a fundamental aspect of these criteria that clearly indicates the direction in which their implementation will have to be sought. The Report itself states that "the guideposts suggested here . . . are not concerned primarily with the relation of employers and employees to each other, but rather with their joint relation to the rest of the economy." And the Report emphasizes that *labor* and *management* "should [not] bargain implicitly about the general price level" and also, as the Report should have added, not about the level of employment. Full employment and general price stability are our recognized, and much needed, *national* goals.

To put it plainly, collective-bargaining decisions and related price administration have systematically contributed to inflationary pressures and to unemployment. It is the very purpose of the inferred wage-price criteria to prevent such systematic injuries to the common good of *all*, including labor and management themselves, and not just "to the rest of the economy," as the Report puts it.

It is obvious, therefore, that if the wage-price criteria are to be observed in order that the common good be preserved, collective bargaining and related price decisions will have to be adjusted to these criteria. And this requires first of all that collective-bargaining negotiations take place within a more orderly procedural framework to permit the criteria to be fully considered and applied. We shall discuss this question after a more detailed examination of the wage-price criteria themselves.

Thus, if creeping inflation and/or profit squeeze with unemployment effects are to be avoided, the average rate of periodic increases of all monetary earnings from production must not exceed the average rate of national productivity improvements calculated at existing prices.[36] This requires some further clarification. The average rate of total periodical income increases must be based on the average rate of productivity increases over the current period. The average rate of productivity increases over the next period (following a given periodical income increase) is not yet known. Furthermore, it remains to be seen whether the expected productivity-caused increase in future output can be sold at existing prices. The use of the expected *future* productivity as the criterion for current income increases would therefore increase tensions and disagreements concerning income distribution and could be the harbinger of future inflation.

There is, however, a cyclical problem concerning productivity. Although productivity improvements result primarily from technological and organizational rearrangements, productivity changes to a certain extent also depend on output changes within a given technological and organizational structure of an existing industrial capacity. An overstrained full-employment capacity may result in lower output per unit of resources used, because additional labor now works with relatively less capital. A substantially underutilized capacity in a recession, on the other hand, may also cause a lower output per unit of resources because of the higher overhead cost per unit of output.[37]

Since a "current" collective wage increase is to last for at least a year or two, the question arises whether cyclical changes in productivity should not be simply ignored as far as the use of the productivity criterion for periodical income increases is concerned.[38] If and when the rate of productivity is impaired under the impact of a recession, a productivity criterion ignoring the changing impact of the business cycle on productivity may be feasible, so long as productivity is likely to improve cyclically within the contractual period in question. On this assumption, the policy would have an antirecessionary, but not inflationary, side effect on demand, leading to increased production. If and when, however, productivity is impaired by cyclical overultilization of capacity, the policy of ignoring cyclical influences on productivity would escape inflation only if it spurred technological and organizational improvements without cost-induced price increases.

VI

The preceding two propositions concerning the two productivity limits ("average" and "current") on periodical income increases are as true as the simple fact of common experience that it is impossible to distribute more than there is. The difficulty with the productivity criterion for income increases is not in its logic but in its application: How should nationally available productivity increases be *distributed* among the various participants in production?

Following the great American economist J. B. Clark, one may feel that available productivity increases can and should be distributed among the various categories of participants in the productive processes in accordance with their respective marginal (additional) contributions to production.[39] But this theoretical criterion for the apportionment of periodical income increases has two practical shortcomings. First, the structure of productive cooperation of various categories of participants in a highly developed industrial economy is so complex that it cannot be readily unscrambled into specific contributing elements according to the degrees of their respective productive contributions. Even when, at the points of their direct productive impact, specific improvements in productive efficiency seem to result from a particular observable change (technological, managerial, political), it will still be found that a scattered but interlocked variety of more remote changes preceded the directly observable impact-change itself. In addition, the latter's productivity-improving effectiveness requires accompanying or subsequent adjustments on the part of other cooperating factors. Take a new machine, for example. When the machine has been installed, labor and all the other productive inputs, often of great number and variety, must be adjusted to the machine's best use in production.

Productivity improvements in highly developed industrial economies most often result from complex and multiple causes and lead to manifold social effects, which can seldom be measurably imputed to specific participating factors.[40] But even if precise mathematical measurements of productivity contributions were somehow possible, it might still not be the most desirable or even acceptable method of distributing the fruits of productivity improvements. There are many forms of psychological and institutional immobility of labor and of other resources in the advanced industrial economies of today. In consequence, marginal contributions to production by various participating factors in various industries and areas will differ greatly. A mechanistic method of distributing income increases in conformity with widely differing marginal productivities (still assuming that they can be correctly calculated) would lead to all kinds of growing income inequalities. These would be ethically questioned and psychologically resented because of the remaining doubts about the correctness of mathematical imputations and because of unavoidable differences of opinion about the fortuity of widely differing backgrounds of opportunities enjoyed by the various participants in the productive process. This is the unavoidable consequence of the basic fact that we live in a very "imperfect" world with all kinds of "immobilities," spacial and otherwise, which haphazardly interfere with the distribution of opportunities and resulting marginal productivities.

One must conclude that there is no ready-made automatic formula for a fair and noninflationary distribution of the fruits of aggregate productivity improvements. Such distribution can only be "talked over" and worked out on the basis of some social consensus (sensible compromise) necessitated by the complex social character of the causes and effects of productivity increases. In the United States, it has hitherto been conveniently assumed that such a consensus was exclusively a matter for specific unions and management to work out. This traditional assumption implied that business management, representing entrepreneurship and capital, and union labor were the only sources of productivity improvements and therefore the only rightful claimants of the fruits of such improvements. As already indicated above, this implication is clearly untenable.

Productive efficiency depends on many factors, including, very prominently, a variety of public institutions and policies, which belong to the general public as the sum total of individual, associated, and collective consumers.[41] Furthermore, the record of union-management consensus on the distribution of productivity-generated income increases is anything but enviable. Who will ever know the amount of economic loss that has been caused by strikes and related production stoppages and by inflationary settlements of union-management disputes, which led to miscalculated wage and price increases, reduced output and employment, and were thus damaging to everyone, including labor and management themselves? The establishment in the United States in February, 1961, of the President's Advisory Committee on Labor-Management Policy, with members drawn from labor, management, *and the public,* implies official recognition that social consensus on the distribution of the fruits of productivity improvements transcends the specific interests of particular unions and management alone.[42]

The reason why collective wage contracts between management and labor unions are nevertheless the crucial element in the process of periodical distribution of the fruits of productivity improvements is in the quantitative preponderance of wages in production costs, in the pattern-setting influence of collective wage contracts in key industries on wages and wagelike incomes elsewhere, and in the fact that other income claimants are in effect paid out of what wage contracts "leave" in the hands of management.[43] If, after a collective wage increase, management feels that expected sales at existing prices will not yield enough revenue to recover new labor costs and to compensate other income claimants proportionately, prices will be increased, demand permitting. To the extent that demand is sensitive to price increases, unemployment will follow with or without a price increase. Collective wage settlements and price-setting are directly related because all productive incomes and profits depend jointly on product prices as one determinant of sales revenue.[44]

Because productivity improvements result from multiple causes and because the precise structure of this complex causation cannot be quantitatively determined, it follows that, as a first approximation, the basic pattern for the distribution of the fruits of productivity improvements between labor and other income claimants should follow the existing pattern of functional income distribution. This would require that collective wage increases conform to the *average rate of national productivity improvements* over the period *preceding* the union-management contractual settlement. The basic distributional pattern would thus also conform to the existing national wage structure.[45]

If the basic distribution pattern followed differential productivity improvements by individual firms or industries, it would gradually result in violent wage differentials that could neither be justified ethically nor maintained economically.[46] We have discussed this already.[47] The underlying technological and commercial differences among industries, and even firms, in an era of uneven automation and systematic advertising, clearly cannot be basically imputed to differences in productive contributions of labor, which very often is of similar ability and performance in different industries with widely differing productivity improvements. Furthermore, such a basic distributional pattern would tend to freeze the existing national structure of product prices to the extent that they are cost-oriented. And this would distort the basic allocative function of the price mechanism.

If a frozen price structure is not workable in a market economy, neither is a frozen wage structure, which would result from unmodified application of the average productivity criterion *alone*. There are good reasons of justice and of necessary economic incentives why wage increases should not simply conform to the existing general wage structure.[48] Furthermore, if the basic distributional pattern followed solely the national average rate of productivity increases, it would result in systematic price increases in those branches of production where productivity improvements, if any, *trailed* the national average. Thus, unless prices declined proportionately in industries where productive improvements exceed the national average, creeping inflation would continue systematically. Supplementary criteria for modifications of the basic distributional pattern for income increases are therefore needed.

The first supplementary criterion to be taken into account in collective wage contracts is the criterion of *relative labor scarcity*. For industries and skills where labor is short (and the shortage has not been deliberately contrived), wage increases should exceed the rate of national productivity improvements to the extent necessary to act as an incentive to attract more labor into the respective skills and industries. On the other hand, in fields where there is a labor surplus, wage increases should be below the national productivity average to the extent necessary to establish a disincentive in the respective skills and industries. Needless to say, however, in areas of *chronic* labor surplus, special measures would still be necessary to help expedite the solution of the problems of depressed areas and obsolete skills or lack of skill. These problems cannot be solved by the strength of the incentives and disincentives that stem from the operation of the price system alone, or even from general monetary and fiscal measures. Deeper sociological, psychological, technological, organizational, and geographical factors are involved here, which call for special remedies involving planned cooperation of private and public efforts for reorientation of available resources, as well as retraining and resettlement of human skills.

To reach a reasonable quantitative consensus on wage-increase differentials, based on considerations of relative labor scarcity as a modifier of the basic average productivity criterion, may be one of the most difficult tasks of future collective bargaining.[49] The required application of the labor-scarcity criterion to union-management contract settlements thus clearly indicates the need for collective-bargaining negotiations to take place within a more systematic framework of negotiation procedures than has generally been the case so far. This aspect of the problem will be discussed further.[50]

VII

Wage policy is directly related to the problems of *price policy*. The one needs correct economic and welfare criteria as much as the other. It is *cost-induced price changes* that are pertinent for public policy to cope with cost-push inflation. This calls for a second supplementary criterion for a workable, fair, and noninflationary wage-price policy. In industries where the basic distributional criterion for periodic income increases (the national average of productivity increases), as modified by the first supplementary criterion (relative labor scarcity), would lead to wage increases short of the rates of actual productivity increments in the respective industries or firms themselves, product prices should be reduced as much as a particular industry's cost behavior would permit. Such price reductions would offset the difference between the actual rate of wage increase and the industry's higher productivity rate. In industries, however, where the same two wage-increase criteria would result in wage increases in excess of the respective rates of productivity increments in those industries, prices usually would have to increase in order to recover additional labor costs and to protect the income position of nonlabor participants in production. The inflationary impact of such necessary price increases would be offset by price decreases in other industries, as explained above.

A price-change policy in conformity with this second supplementary criterion would not only secure the stability of the general level of prices, but would also act as a powerful incentive to economic efficiency and growth. Such a price policy would encourage expansion of the most productive industries by attracting to them additional domestic and foreign demand through systematic price decreases. These two salutary effects—general price stability and expansion of industries, which are both most productive and demand-attracting—would also strengthen the country's position in international trade, which is badly needed, particularly in the

United States because of its world leadership obligations, in face of the growing competition from Western Europe and Japan.

VIII

This important question now arises: How is this second supplementary criterion (pertaining to price policy) to be implemented, short of direct price controls? The answer is to be sought in the following, rather obvious, consideration. If labor is to agree to the basic distributional criterion (national average of productivity increases) and to the first supplementary criterion (relative labor scarcity) of a fair and noninflationary wage policy, it can be expected to do so only if management, in its turn, is willing to follow the logically related second supplementary criterion concerning cost-induced price changes. The three criteria form a *unity*, in that only all of them taken *together* can determine a workable, fair, and noninflationary distributional pattern for income increases in conformity with the true (noninflated) dimension of periodical productivity increments in the economy.

Once this interrelation of wage and price criteria is fully recognized, the simple logic of the indicated wage-price policy should assert itself with convincing clarity. When the three interrelated criteria of a constructive wage-price policy are so understood, accepted, and adopted,[51] we can expect that within this new framework of reason and fairness the interplay of normal interests[52] on the part of labor and management will serve as an effective agency for the *self-implementation* of these criteria. Herein is the greatest promise of the indicated wage-price policy. It can operationally rely on self-implementation, once its "rules of the game" (the three interlocked criteria) are understood and accepted. There is no need for any extraneous political and bureaucratic system of price controls.

It may be objected at this point, however, that the proposed wage-price policy in accordance with the three wage-price criteria, while satisfying the conditions for the over-all price stability, would still fall short of full justice in income distribution. Is the objection valid? The suggested policy would modify the existing wage-price structure in the economy through its two supplementary criteria. The existing wage structure would be modified by changes in labor scarcity differentials between various labor groups, and price changes would conform to such wage changes *in relation to* differential productivity improvements. Productivity increments would thus be distributed as broadly and evenly as is economically feasible without pushing the economy into social strife, waste, and the injustices of inflation. Whoever felt strongly that his wages should be still higher than the combined criteria would permit, would have to seek the opportunity to shift into some higher paid labor group or location. No more can be asked in strict justice. Reasonable mobility of resources, including labor, is indispensable for economic and social progress.

Only when whole groups or areas are adversely affected by major demand shifts away from their products, or by major technological changes away from their skills or locations, would valid cases exist for specific public policy measures to increase and expedite their mobility toward new skills or locations. But such measures belong to the field of social policy to be financed through political redistribution (through taxation) of the functionally distributed income (wages, interest rates, profits, rents). Functional distribution of income can only be made to conform to the existing noninflationary demand-and-supply conditions in related markets for final products and for productive factors; it cannot fundamentally rearrange the underlying opportunities themselves. These are matters for social policy operating outside the structure of functional income distribution.

IX

To enable labor and management to assert their true interests within the scope of the three wage-price criteria, union-management relations need certain institutional improvements. One urgently needed correction is to improve the machinery of collective bargaining by giving it a procedural framework conducive to orderly negotiations. The union-management negotiations that preceded and accompanied the steel strike in 1959, for example, or those concerning the New York newpapers in 1961–62 and again in 1962–63, dramatized the basic deficiency of the existing procedural *laissez faire* in collective bargaining.[53]

As a result of this manifest deficiency in the institution of collective bargaining, there is a growing feeling that collective bargaining simply cannot measure up to the logical requirements of a constructive wage-price policy[54] and should therefore be replaced by compulsory arbitration, or by some even more direct form of wage control. This pessimistic attitude, while understandable, misses the essential point. Social problems that lack self-evident quantitative solutions equally acceptable to all cannot be mechanically resolved by authoritarian dictation any better than by the conflicts of unrestrained group interests. Wage-price problems are clearly in this category, and so are problems pertaining to automation and its employment effects. They can be resolved only by rational *consensus*. But to accomplish this, collective bargaining must be kept within the bounds of an *orderly* dialogue.[55]

In civilized society, an assembly that is to reach meaningful conclusions, whether this be a high-level legislative body or the board of some small voluntary association, always has a chairman to act as a *procedural moderator*. The institution of collective bargaining makes decisions on questions of basic importance to the participating parties and to the general public. Hence, it should be self-evident that at least all *major* cases of collective bargaining should be presided over by an expert procedural moderator. His function would be to expedite collective bargaining negotiations; to keep bargaining sessions orderly within the framework of the established wage-price criteria and within the bounds of the agreed agenda sequence; to insist on factual description and logical explanation of claims, assertions, and evidence used by each negotiating party; to summarize the main points discussed, the consensus reached, and the remaining disagreements of each preceding bargaining session.

It is quite clear from this that the procedural function of the proposed moderator would not involve the power of arbitration, or even mediation in its technical sense, as far as the *content* of the collective-bargaining agreement is concerned. This is for the two parties to work out, as the word consensus implies, within the established logical criteria for a noninflationary, full employment-oriented wage-price policy.[56]

The priority which the public policy agenda in the West has to give to the basic problems of wage-price relationship and collective bargaining stems from the understanding of the intrinsic nature of the pluralistic market economy operating within a democratic political framework.[57] In such an economy, neither "labor" nor "capital" can substantially and permanently improve its relative income share from joint production by unilateral action at the expense of the other.[58] Within such an institutional framework, either side can fight back in order to protect its relative income position. But in the battle of how to divide the product of individual firms and industries, the total productive performance of the economy is impaired, and individuals and weaker groups suffer arbitrary injustices in consequence of the inflation, the unemployment, and the slowing down of growth that such battles generate.[59]

This is one aspect of economic arrangements in a free society where cooperation instead of competition is indicated. Competition is a unique source of efficiency in production and in functional income distribution within each aggregate distributive share.[60] Economy-wide distributive shares, however, are subject to the limit determined by the joint productivity of all the participants. Collective bargaining must be made orderly, precisely with a view to leading to a consensus *within* this limit. "Competition" in this framework leads to a systematic inflationary transgression of the general limit, if not necessarily on the microlevel of highly productive firms and industries, certainly on the macrolevel of the economy as a whole.

The need for wage-price criteria, consistent with the national objective of noninflationary full employment, and their implementation through social cooperation is now generally recognized. The President's Economic Report of January, 1962, contained a section on "Guideposts for Noninflationary Wage and Price Behavior,"[61] discussed above.[62] In November, 1962, the Organization for Economic Cooperation and Development (OECD) published a report, *Policies for Price Stability*, stressing wage-price criteria consistent with noninflationary growth with full employment, and reporting that all Western countries were in the process of developing public policies to that effect.[63] Conceptual novelty and early stages of these policies would seem to explain why the results so far have been meager. However, there has already been an impact of the new approach, particularly in the United States and West Germany. Free trade within the European Common Market area and progressive reduction of mutual tariffs between the Common Market, the United States, and other parts of the free world should act as an influential reminder to labor and management everywhere that noninflationary behavior of wages and prices is as important in relation to the balance of international payments as it is for full employment.[64]

X

The implementation of the three wage-price criteria by social consensus and through improved union-management relations would establish the necessary conditions for a fair and noninflationary income distribution with corresponding price changes that together would maintain general price stability without sacrificing full employment. These effects would, in turn, maintain conditions favorable to improving productive efficiency and to achieving the highest sustainable rate of economic growth.

But several problems still remain untouched, either because they cannot be adequately dealt with within the limited scope of this study or because they fall outside the operational reach of the suggested measures. These remaining problems may conveniently be grouped into three categories. The suggestions discussed in this chapter do not deal with *technical* questions concerning the implementation of the proposed modifications. One major technical difficulty is that statistical information needed for making the wage-price criteria fully operational is not yet sufficiently developed, especially at the industry level. Modern accounting techniques should, of course, provide such data at the management level.

Secondly, even if the suggested modifications of the wage-price policy are adopted and the necessary technical details are worked out, there will still be a need for some *specific adjustments* in the behavior of certain parts of the economy that the three general criteria and improved union-management relations cannot sufficiently influence in a direct way. Examples of this kind are the already mentioned declining skills and depressed-areas problem and the complex farm problem.

Finally, there is a broad remaining problem that is or should be entirely outside the scope of the three wage-price criteria. This is the whole category of politically shaped *welfare measures* (social security, unemployment compensation, medical care for the aged, etc.) aiming at various degrees and forms of social redistribution of income after it has been functionally distributed in accordance with the suggested criteria. Pioneering welfare innovations have more recently developed within the framework of collective bargaining, using the vehicle of "fringe benefits." In view of the already overstrained cost structure of production, it would be wise if this pattern of our expanding welfare provisions were reconsidered. In principle, only welfare measures directly connected with the improvement of working conditions should be subject to collective bargaining. Broader aspects of social welfare belong to the areas of cooperative self-help and social legislation. In addition to alleviating rising but widely differentiated pressures on the costs of production, such a shift in financing welfare measures is the only promise we have that *everyone* will come to share an increase in social welfare. And this is another reason why wasteful and discriminatory cost pressures on production should be eliminated and avoided.

These remaining problems are mentioned here only because their solution must be geared to the working of the economic system within the scope of the three wage-price criteria and their implementation. These latter are the foundation. The other group of solutions must be built *upon* this foundation. Otherwise, they arbitrarily hinder what is more important to the general welfare, an orderly and efficient economy.

Once the wage-price behavior conforms to the three interrelated criteria for the fair and noninflationary wage-price policy, the problem of cost-generated creeping inflation is checked at its roots. Monetary and fiscal policies can then be directed toward the maintenance of sufficient aggregate demand for a sustainable full-employment growth of the national product and income. Except for the special output-income problems in agriculture and localized or specialized chronic unemployment, all of which require specific remedies, a maximum rate of economic growth with full employment will then become the manageable responsibility of monetary and fiscal policies.

The share of monetary policy in this responsibility will have to be determined by carefully considering its bearing on the problem of the balance of international payments. Fiscal policy, on the other hand, should be conducted within a system of taxation which will not stifle the incentives necessary for efficiency in production and for sufficient growth.[65] In addition, the public expenditures framework of fiscal policy must be geared to providing the most useful public goods and services, as preferred by a well-informed electorate.[66]

9. *INFLATION OUTSIDE THE WEST: RAMPANT OR HIDDEN*

So far we have examined the root problems of economic growth in each of the world's three great economic subdivisions. Inflation was shown to be the crucial limit and obstacle to economic growth in the advanced economies of the West. But the phenomenon of inflation is clearly not limited to the West. Although in the economies of the newly developing countries and the Soviet orbit there are growth problems that are both more basic and more important to them than inflation, inflation is, at least partly, a common characteristic of all contemporary economies. Moreover, it can be shown that the key problems of economic growth in the new nations (cultural lag and entrepreneurial gap) and in the Soviet orbit (obstacles keeping democratic socialism from asserting itself as the demand-and-supply shaping force) are closely associated with the inflation in their economies. Inflation thus assumes a broader significance in the framework of the global problem of economic growth. In this sense, inflationary pressures are comprehensive indicators of the existing limitations and of specific obstacles to economic growth in all contemporary economies.

Since there are great developmental, organizational, and operational differences between the economies of the West, of the newly developing countries, and of the Soviet orbit, inflation, although a phenomenon common to all, is in each of the three economic areas caused in different ways. And yet, underlying these various inflation-generating forces, there must be still more basic factors common to all societies. Inflationary pressures are generated by excesses in effective demand over the effective supply of productive resources and services, functional incomes, and output of finished goods. Such demand pressures result in open inflation (rising prices) whenever there is a price system which is responsive to changes in demand and supply.

The purpose of this chapter is to single out the specific factors that generate inflationary pressures, and the ways in which they do so, in the developing countries and in the Soviet orbit; to compare these factors and their *modus operandi* with those in the West; and then to extract from all their common source.

II

Inflationary pressures in the newly developing economies outside the Soviet orbit are both similar to and different from those in the industrially advanced countries of the West. If the effective aggregate demand at existing prices increases at a faster average rate than the rate of output can increase, inflationary pressures will be generated regardless of the stage of economic development. Similarly, inflationary conditions will develop in any kind of market economy if the rate of combined money-income increases exceeds the rate at which output expands relative to the amount of resources used. If political and other institutional factors in the newly developing countries permit or even foster such excessive demands for output or for incomes or both, inflationary pressures will result.

In the newly developing countries, politically motivated demand for capital goods, and for expanding government bureaucracy, tends to be excessive in relation to voluntary savings and tax revenue, because of the eagerness of their more or less authoritarian governments to foster rapid economic development and to build their political power under the impetus of prevailing nationalism. The existence of wage push in these countries, on the other hand, is less self-evident.

When Western nations were in comparable stages of political and economic development, labor was not effectively organized. In the newly developing countries of today, even in Africa, labor is more self-assertive and, in some of these nations, quite well organized. This makes them potentially vulnerable to a wage push similar to that in the advanced industrial countries of the West.

But there is one particular aspect of inflation in the new nations that clearly distinguishes it from the inflationary problem in the West. In the developing countries, inflationary pressures are closely associated with their chronic shortages of entrepreneurial aptitudes and technical skills relative to other resources and to aggregate demand. Under the pressure for rapid economic development, the newly developing countries tend to emulate the developed economies by introducing advanced industrial technology through excessively labor-saving capital investment *ahead of* corresponding changes in their inherited attitudes and aptitudes and *ahead of* slowly developing technical skills. This double disparity tends to generate multiple-bottleneck-types of inflationary pressures along with persistent unemployment. The resulting inflation is caused *jointly* by an excessive as well as ill-composed aggregate demand

and by rising costs, well before the full use of the existing capacity to produce, because of chronic shortages of entrepreneurial aptitudes and technical skills.

Thus, the two universal types of inflationary pressures, from the demand and cost sides, in newly developing economies hinge primarily on the rate at which entrepreneurial aptitudes and technical skills increase relative to the rate of investment in advanced capital tools and in relation to the prevailing native resources. It is the scarcest productive factor that is the crucial determinant of a country's growth in real output and in productive efficiency. In the newly developing countries, the scarcest productive factors are entrepreneurial aptitudes and technical skills. The slow rate of real economic growth and the concomitant inflation in these countries[1] are therefore reducible to the still prevailing basic error in failing to consider human attitudes, aptitudes, and skills as their shortest resource, along with capital equipment.[2] Inflationary pressures in the new nations are thus directly related to their particular root problem of economic growth.

III

In the Soviet system, inflation not only has causes different from those in both the West and the newly developing countries, but also has different manifestations. In fact, if one were to insist that the rising level of prices constitutes the phenomenon of inflation, one would come to the conclusion that, according to the official Soviet price statistics at least, there has been little or no inflation at all in the Soviet economy since 1949.[3] When, however, one recalls that in spite of active inflationary pressures the price-level-increasing symptoms of inflation may be "repressed" when prices are effectively controlled, the absence of a rising level of official Soviet prices may not constitute even a prima facie evidence for the absence of inflationary pressures in the Soviet economy.

Both historically and analytically, prices have been primarily associated with the market-type economies. In such economies, demand for and supply of specific economic goods are basically independent of each other and more or less decentralized in their composition. It is through interactions of independent and decentralized components of demand and supply in corresponding markets that individual prices (as well as the composition and distribution of total output and income) are ultimately determined in a market economy; such prices therefore reflect the various degrees of scarcity of specific economic resources and products in relation to the effective demand for them.

In a market economy, prices perform three major functions. First, they serve as a convenient measure of exchange values of economic goods for transactions, and therefore they also make possible meaningful accounting and statistical aggregation of economic quantities. In addition to this immediate service, prices perform two further functions in a market economy. When viewed within short periods of time, individual prices serve as a *rationing* device whenever, at a given price, the available supply of a good falls short of the existing demand for it, and vice versa. In such situations, the price will tend to rise in order to eliminate the excess demand, or to fall (when supply becomes excessive) in order to attract additional demand or to reduce excessive supply. From the point of view of longer time spans, on the other hand, prices in a market economy perform also an *allocative* function; a strong demand for an economic good, by firming the price of that good, tends to expand its production, and vice versa.

The *extent* to which, in a market economy, prices perform the rationing and allocative functions depends on the various degrees of social decentralization of economic decision-making on the supply and demand sides as well as on the varying degrees to which different prices respond to the underlying changes in supply and demand of particular goods. We have seen that in contemporary Western economies such responses may be sluggish when wages are determined through collective bargaining and prices are management-administered.[4] Such inflexibility of prices constitutes the main justification for the need of short-run adjustments of aggregate demand by means of monetary and fiscal policies,[5] as well as for appropriate "guideposts" for noninflationary wage-price behavior.

IV

The Soviet economic system is managed and controlled from one dictatorial political center by means of a comprehensive economic (supply-and-demand) plan. This is the political and economic consequence of the basic legal prohibition of private ownership of productive assets. Because of the total political integration and centralization of the Soviet economy, even after the recent attempts at "decentralization," the price system can in principle play only a subsidiary role, if any.

Soviet prices are politically administered on the basis of preplanned physical demand-and-supply relationships, which reflect the economic and other objectives of the Soviet political center. *Industrial prices* of specific products are set in accordance with the estimated average labor costs (preplanned money wages) of production in the respective industry, plus a planned profit markup intended to compensate for the use of nonlabor resources. The resulting profit-and-loss differentials among individual enterprises within each industrial group are then leveled out by means of differentiated profit taxes to, and subsidies from, the government. *Retail prices* of consumer goods, on the other hand, are administered with a view to forcing spontaneously changing demands for individual consumer goods into line with the preplanned or actually available supplies of corresponding products by means of variable sales (turnover) taxes.

From the fact that the Soviet economic system makes broad use of prices for a majority of economic goods at all stages of planning, production, and distribution, it can be concluded that Soviet prices perform at least the function of a convenient device to facilitate transactions, as well as to permit accounting and statistical aggregation of predetermined economic quantities. But the Soviet system makes little or no use of the *allocative* function of prices. Soviet prices are clearly not a significant supply-determining factor. This decisive function, which in a market economy is basically performed by the price system, is, in the Soviet economy, politically preempted by centralized planning, administration, and control of the Soviet economy. There is no indication that the dictatorial Communist governments intend to relinquish their absolute political power over production and distribution of economic goods to a genuine market mechanism that would reflect the actual needs and aspirations of the people, on the one hand, and real scarcities of resources on the other.

In regard to the *rationing* function of prices, a distinction must be made between Soviet prices of consumer goods and those of nonconsumer goods, from basic resources to the finished capital goods. Distribution of consumer goods in the Soviet system works as follows. Participants in the production of goods and services receive money incomes, from which a relatively small income tax and some compulsory savings are deducted.[6] The rest may be freely spent on the available consumer goods. People's disposable income, the composition of their wants, and politically administered consumer goods' prices then together determine the demands for particular consumer goods. Soviet consumer goods prices are so administered as to keep such particular demands in line with the preplanned (or actually available) supply of them. This kind of consumer goods rationing requires that consumer goods prices be flexible in relation to the intervening changes in particular demands. Without such price flexibility, the consumer goods whose demands increased beyond their preplanned quantities would have to be physically rationed.

Flexibility of Soviet consumer prices within the centralized framework of political price administration is made possible by means of manipulating the structure of turnover (sales) taxes, which are levied on all marketable consumer goods at variable rates averaging about 50 per cent of consumer prices.[7] But since the rates of these taxes obviously cannot be changed on a day-to-day basis within each individual retail establishment, the proverbial waiting-line and elbowing type of Soviet rationing act as supplementary means for bridging the gaps between preplanned supplies and free demands, whenever sudden shortages occur.[8]

If Soviet consumer prices are deprived of the allocative function, Soviet nonconsumer goods prices are virtually denied even the rationing function. It is only within very narrow limits of closely related alternative materials that Soviet plant managers have a measure of official discretion in input selection. But even this narrow selectivity depends only partly on official price differentials intended to minimize the use of scarcer alternatives. Except for this narrow managerial discretion, the function of Soviet prices other than those of consumer goods is limited to that of accounting aid only to support the preplanned physical allocation and direct control over it. If faulty planning or its deficient implementation results in inconsistent allocation of productive resources, corrections must be worked out outside the official price system, either through official physical reallocation or by means of "informal activities" of Soviet plant managers themselves. The latter resort to all kinds of black markets, barters, hoarding of materials and labor, and, of course, influencing and bribing of suppliers and higher-ups.[9]

V

Within the centrally preplanned, bureaucratically administered, and Party-controlled Soviet economy, with its politically superimposed price system, inflationary pressures, whether they manifest themselves in rising prices or not, tend to develop under three interrelated conditions: (1) if the plan is generally overextended in relation to the available resources; (2) if the plan is internally inconsistent in relation to the existing input-output structure of the economy;

and (3) if the administration of, and control over, the execution of the plan fail to implement its provisions. If any of these potential allocational shortcomings of the Soviet economic system develop, and the plan is not duly and promptly corrected, unplanned shortages will appear and spread their effects throughout the economic system according to its existing input-output-input sequences. As a rule, Soviet economic plans and the administrative commands flowing from it "fully commit, and even overcommit, the resources of the whole economy and of each enterprise."[10] Clearly, then, there are bound to be many internal planning inconsistencies and further shortcomings in the implementation of such a generally overstrained national economic plan. Thus, the Soviet economy labors under chronic inflationary pressures from these three basic sources.

The political nature of Soviet price administration now shelters the official Soviet price system from the impact of these pressures. Inflation of Soviet *consumer* prices, which are responsive to demand changes, is being prevented by keeping the total of personal income increases behind productivity improvements.[11] However, as a result of post-Stalinist increases in minimum wages and pensions, of selective wage increases, and of discontinuation of compulsory personal saving in government bonds, the monetary equilibrium in the Soviet consumer goods markets has recently been disturbed. In 1962, the Soviet regime counteracted by increasing the prices of butter and meat by 22 per cent and by postponing indefinitely the scheduled reduction of personal income taxes. This is the clearest, but by no means the only, symptom of a recent direct inflation within the Soviet price system.

In the area of *interindustry* products, there are black as well as gray markets to which Soviet plant managers resort when they are desperately short of irreplaceable inputs.[12] Presumably, in these illegal markets, demand pressures do result in rising prices. But no statistical information on such price increases is available. However, in recent years the post-Stalinist thaw has been reflected in this central area of the Soviet economy also. The Soviet press has been reporting extensively about widespread black marketeering and other illegal dealings by Soviet plant managers with the connivance of government and party officials. To counteract such massive "informal" modifications of, and adjustments to, the centrally planned requirements, the death penalty was reintroduced in 1962 for a variety of "economic crimes."

In summary, inflationary pressures in the Soviet economy manifest themselves primarily in planned and unplanned shortages of resources and products, in qualitative deficiencies, in below-productivity wages, and in all kinds of "informal" and illegal dealings on the part of Soviet managers. These chronic inflationary symptoms in the Soviet economy are reducible to the same two basic causes that lie at the bottom of all inflation. The central fact that the political management of the Soviet economy tends systematically to overcommit the available resources is analogous to excessive aggregate demand as the source of inflation in a monetary market economy. Black market operations and related dealings in the Soviet economy also bespeak demand as the cause of inflation.

The manifold wasteful practices in the implementation of the plan, on the other hand, must be characterized as indicative of a systematic, built-in cost-pushing aspect of the Soviet economy. This cost-pushing aspect is particularly characteristic of Soviet enterprises where managers feel compelled to hoard materials and labor and to detract from the planned quality of products in order to protect themselves against the danger of falling behind the quantitative output requirements of the plan.[13] Such a cost-increasing tendency is inherent in an economic system that is based on detailed political enforcement of what are essentially arbitrary and centralized economic dispositions. Such an economic system lacks both workable incentives and reliable methods for efficient use of its resources.

In the Soviet economy, too, inflationary pressures are directly related to the root problem of Soviet economic growth, that is, to the gap that separates the totalitarian dictatorship of the Soviet Government from the supposed socialist character of the Soviet economy. If the Soviet economy were guided by a spontaneous system of democratic socialism, the aggregate demand on Soviet production would be eased by the reduction of the existing Soviet power objectives at home and abroad, which now absorb almost one-half of Soviet resources. Similarly, because of more effective incentives and greater use of the price system in allocating available resources, democratic socialism would reduce some of the wasteful use of resources that now characterizes the Soviet economy.

This is not to say that inflation would cease to be a problem if genuine socialism prevailed in the Soviet economy. Undoubtedly, new inflationary tendencies would develop, both on the demand and on the cost sides. Demands for consumer goods and certain public services would rise greatly, and organized pressures for wage increases would emerge. But such inflationary pressures would then operate within a political and economic system that would register them more directly and would therefore permit a more rational control over them.

VI

It is now possible to answer the question as to what are the underlying common causes of inflation, regardless of the differences in economic systems and in stages of economic development. The root causes of all inflation are *excessive claims for output and income from production* and *inefficient use of available resources.* Excessive demands on production and wasteful use of resources both stem from *imperfections of economic knowledge* and *inadequacy of economic institutions.* Such imperfections and inadequacies are universal because they are human. But there are significant differences in time and place.

In the Soviet economic system, imperfections of economic knowledge and inadequacy of institutions are *fundamental.* By its political conception, its institutions, and its operating methods, the Soviet system precludes the possibility of establishing and maintaining a balanced relationship between the needs and aspirations of the people, on the one hand, and production, on the other. First, people's needs are arbitrarily determined by the self-appointed Communist dictatorship. Second, the absence of meaningful decentralization and competition in Soviet production prevents the possibility of reliably calculating the degree of its efficiency even in relation to its arbitrary objectives, let alone in relation to people's real wants.

In a decentralized economic system in which independent components of demand and supply influence prices, and price changes have influence on demand and supply, inflationary pressures can not only be detected but can also be eliminated or controlled, provided there is the *will* to do so. In the existing Soviet system, there might be the will to eliminate inflationary pressures, but there is no *effective way* of doing it, because such pressures pervade the entire system, so that most of them even elude detection. The first decisive step toward controlling inflationary pressures in the Soviet economy will be made when its formal but still suppressed socialist character asserts itself as an effective demand-and-supply shaping force.

10. *ECONOMIC GROWTH FOR WHAT?*

The broad framework of this study requires that its conclusions now be pulled together so that their contribution toward the understanding of the root problems of economic growth, in the context of Soviet global designs, may be clearly perceived.

This is Moscow's story. In the next ten years, the Soviet economy will grow at such a rate as to overtake the per capita output of the United States.[1] In the ten years after the decade 1964–74, Soviet economic growth will overcome the scarcity of a number of consumer goods and services and make them freely available to the Soviet people. Thus, an effective start will have been made toward the ultimate communist society of universal abundance; such as society of abundance will eliminate all class differences, thereby putting an end also to the institution of government, which, according to Marxist tenets, is the agent of social compulsion in the interest of the dominating class.

Following Stalin's theory of "capitalist encirclement" as the last obstacle to the "withering away" of the state, Khrushchev has developed his theory of "peaceful" coexistence between the Soviet bloc and the West. No new war is needed to remove the capitalist encirclement of the Soviet orbit, because in the peaceful competition between Western capitalism and Soviet socialism the latter will win hands down. Capitalism is doomed, not only in the underdeveloped countries, which are turning to Communist methods for quicker economic development, but even in the West itself, because its capitalist growth is waning.

II

Such is the surface version of Khrushchev's blueprint for world expansion. But the new Communist program for the next "twenty years" also has some finer print, which reveals that if continued "peaceful" coexistence and competition should not yield the predicted results, "the possibility of nonpeaceful transition to socialism should be borne in mind."[2] This means that organized Communism intends to step up internal troubles in Asia, Africa, and Latin

America whatever the outcome of the recurring crises in Berlin may be.

Discounting its purely propagandistic and oratorical trimmings, the new Communist Party Program amounts to a declaration of the following Soviet intentions.

First, there will be no official, gradual liberalization of the Soviet regime. The reasserted Marxist dialectical goal (the goal of the utopian communist society) continues to be involved as a pretext for an indefinite continuation of the totalitarian Soviet rule; it remains in full force as the basic dogma of Communism.

Second, the newly developing countries outside the Soviet orbit are the current target for Communist expansion.

Third, the West will be subdued, one way or another, as soon as the Soviet Union, as Khrushchev boasts, goes ahead in the production of things needed for the control of the world and of outer space.

How should we counter this universal Soviet "economic" offensive?

For one thing, the new Soviet Program must not be cynically brushed aside as was Hitler's *Mein Kampf*. It must be taken for what it truly means. Then, in addition to keeping up with the Soviets in military and space technology, we must concentrate on the specific key problems of economic development in the developing countries, the Soviet orbit, and in the West itself.

III

With respect to the underdeveloped countries, we must aid their efforts for genuine economic development so that they will not be pushed or misled into the Soviet trap. If their economic growth is to proceed toward ever increasing well-being, the *broad human foundations* for economic development must be laid and strengthened from the start. The underdeveloped countries must be made to see that the Communists are trying to lure them away from this firm ground so that Communist deceit and power may be able to move in with little resistance.

The issue in the underdeveloped countries is not, as Soviet propaganda would have it, *capitalism* vs. *socialism*. This erroneous impression, which we ourselves have shared, must be dispelled. The humanistic capitalism that the West has so patiently and painfully developed is a very complex social and economic system, which, in addition to its articulated human basis and pluralistic structure, presupposes technological maturity in the Rostowian sense. Thus, contemporary capitalism as a social and economic system is not yet applicable to the existing conditions in most of the underdeveloped countries.

The real issue for these countries is not the organization of production itself. When there are few, if any, experienced private entrepreneurs, there is little choice other than to organize the early stages of economic development within the framework of cooperative and political management. The real issue is *what* is being developed, in what sequence, and in whose interests. A balanced system of dispositions for the allocation of resources and distribution of products must be developed that will reflect both the true needs and aspirations of the people and the most efficient use of available resources and skills. If this is done under the slogan, or even within the programatic tenets, of socialism, it is quite all right, so long as it is a democratic socialism "of the people and for the people," and not just a semantic pretext for a Communist or similar autocratic rule. When the people have the power to dispose, there can be no doubt that a pluralistic society will emerge in due time.

Instead of fighting labels, we should pursue substances. Instead of seeing the touchstone of the ultimate intentions of the government of a developing country in the managerial organization of production, we should make that country's system of economic dispositions the true measure of its humanistic orientation.

If the new nations will shift emphasis toward systematic strengthening of their human foundations, their economic development will be speedier and more rewarding, their specific inflationary pressures will be reduced, and Communist inroads will be minimized. If we so extend our economic aid to the newly developing countries that their human skills are strengthened, we will bring about their best possible economic growth and at the same time halt Communist expansion.

IV

The crucial problem of the future of the Soviet world is not whether or when it will enter the ultimate communist stage of its development. That stage will never come. It is a fantasy if not a cynical pretext. The real problem is whether there is a chance that the Soviet system may turn away from its misuse of the Communist economy for purposes of power politics at home and abroad and embark on the course toward high mass consumption and social welfare, and through it, to world peace and broader freedom. When this opportunity is carefully examined, only one possibility remains.

In the legal framework of the Soviet constitution and in Soviet political psychology, the Soviet system is referred to as "socialistic," meaning the common ownership and social management of all the country's resources. In reality, the country is managed as if everything in it, including its people, were owned by the exclusive group that rules it—the Communist new class. But this all-possessing and all-dominating class does not dare to admit its exclusive domination over all things and all the people. The new class acts as a collective slave master, but it talks "people's socialism," not just as a nominal label or advertising slogan, but in operational terms, in order to create the impression that socialism really exists in the Soviet Union and its foreign dependencies.

Djilas, who himself shared the reality of the new class in its top echelon, fixed this blatant contradiction within the Communist system as the source of its eventual disintegration and transformation. From the central insight that this courageous rebel has given us, one can deduce important implications for a new strategy for world peace and human freedom.

We must add another dimension to our foreign policy and public relations abroad. We must adopt the objective of a genuine socialist transformation of the Soviet system. We must be able to present to the people of the Soviet Union with clarity and compelling conviction the following dilemma. The promised transformation of Soviet society and economy into a utopian classless and stateless society of limitless abundance is obviously nonsense. To cling to such a vain hope is to continue indefinitely the autocratic rule of the new class. The only possible hope for the Soviet people is to press courageously and with untiring perseverance for the transition from the existing autocratic system to the democratic socialism which, according to the Soviet constitution and the Communist oratory, is already *supposed to exist.*

There are many opportunities to single out and dwell on the daily manifestations of the basic contradiction between the vociferously protested formal socialism, on the one hand, and its persistent perversion by the autocratic Communist leadership, on the other.

We must overcome our traditional reluctance to "interfere" in the internal affairs of others. This rule clearly does not apply in the case of the Communist governments. In their major pronouncements as well as in their daily propaganda at home and in the world, the Communist governments concentrate their watchful criticism on our economic system, on its real and its alleged shortcomings. Khrushchev himself never tires of asserting that our system is doomed.

By contrast, we are still wearing the strait jacket of the outdated diplomatic approach whereby it is improper to comment on, let alone systematically to criticize, the domestic affairs of another country. But the contemporary world, particularly the newly developing countries, is eagerly attuned to the punchy Soviet "economic approach." We must learn to speak the economic language of the people of the Soviet Union, and must redirect the desperate hopes of the masses on three continents by stressing the fundamental contradiction within the Soviet system.

The longer we delay, the slower will be the hoped-for changes in the Soviet Union and the more difficult it will be to repair the immeasurable psychological and political damage that the Soviet economic offensive has already inflicted on the attitudes and convictions of the newly developing peoples.

If the deep internal contradiction within the Communist system is forced into the open, the totalitarian grip of the Communist new class on the peoples of the Communist-dominated countries will gradually weaken, its global expansionism will be checked, and democratic socialism will begin to assert itself as a demand-and-supply shaping force. Then their economic growth will be redirected toward human welfare, and world peace will be maintained.

V

The West itself must put its economic house in order. Western Europe has improved greatly since the war. Its rate of economic growth compares well with that of the Soviet Union.[3] But its contribution to the common defense against Soviet global expansionism is behind its economic potentialities, while its participation in the aid to the newly developing countries is only beginning.[4] A larger measure of political union of Western Europe would further increase Europe's economic growth, which its increasing obligations require. Furthermore, a speedier political federalization of Western Europe is also called for in order to give impetus to Europe's traditional cultural leadership. And this is vital, if the growing Western affluence is to maintain its *humanistic* justification.

The industrially advanced Western societies, the United States no less than Western Europe, are caught in a protracted crisis of their pluralistic social and economic structure, which requires a clarification of its purpose and a better coordination of its functioning.

This is the situation of the United States. To achieve full employment and to meet our world obligations, we must have a more rapid economic growth. This presupposes an expanded effective demand and lower production costs. But even so, we will still be caught in the dilemma between the increasingly automated mechanization of production and chronic unemployment.

Automation is the way to more abundant and cheaper production. But people still must earn their living from participating in production. If we are to move ahead with faster mechanization, we must do so by expanding our total production far enough to maintain full employment of a growing labor force. If this cannot be done, automation must move at a slower pace. But then there will be less economic growth.

Much of the impetus for automation has come from the experience that labor costs have been outrunning productivity under conditions of nonautomated technology. Once automation expands, its increased productive efficiency makes higher wages possible, but on two conditions. First, the labor to be employed must have the skills that automation requires. Second, there must be enough automated production, or an increasing expansion of accompanying nonautomated services, either public or private, to employ all the labor that is willing and able to work. For an economy such as ours, which is increasingly short in the comparative provision of many public and private services, the second alternative is worth serious examination.

Thus, even within the frame of reference where unemployment tends to be blamed on automation, the underlying cost-pushing attitudes remain our basic unresolved problem. There is no solution other than that of accepting the interrelated criteria for a fair and noninflationary wage-price policy. These criteria are: First, the national average of realized productivity improvements; second, relative labor scarcity; third, a corresponding price policy to offset positive or negative differences between wage increases in accordance with the first two criteria, on the one hand, and the particular industry's productivity improvement, on the other. When organized economic groups deviate from these wage-price criteria, their actions hurt the employment prospects of their own members, as well as the common good of society as a whole, through the slowdown of economic growth and other negative effects of inflation.

If our pluralistic system is to survive, its constituent organizations and groups must realize that their only *raison d'être* is to be *instrumental* in obtaining the personal and family good of their individual members as well as the common good of the entire society. If they degenerate into power-accumulating machines for their own organizational prestige or for the personal ambition of their leaders, as some of them already have done in the past, they become a source of increasing social tensions and difficulties.

A radical clarification of the confused attitudes by economic organizations and groups in our pluralistic society is essential. If it is not achieved, there can be but one outcome—progressive political centralization and control. The return to an imaginary *laissez faire* society of independent individuals would be impossible. Such a society never really existed, and it certainly cannot in the era of Communist global expansionism, the race for outer space, automation, and urban megalopolization. We had best reform our pluralistic society. But the basic problem of our pluralistic attitudes should not make us forget that in times of increasingly pressing public demands on production, aggregate demand, too, may again play inflationary havoc with our economy. Inflation-preventing monetary and fiscal policies for economic growth must still remain our firm resolve.

We must succeed in controlling the two-pronged inflationary pressures so as to secure all the economic growth that our human know-what and know-how, our natural resources, our technological possibilities, and improved working of our pluralistic institutions will permit.

VI

Economic development and growth dominate the thoughts and policies of the contemporary world. The Soviet Government has based its new plan for world conquest on its version of the expectations of economic development and growth in its own orbit, in the underdeveloped parts of the world, and in the West. To counter this offensive, we must first know what are the key problems of economic development in each of the three main segments of the contemporary world. This has been the subject and purpose of this study.

11. CONFLICT OR CONVERGENCE?

Having examined the root problems of economic development and growth in each of the world's three broad subdivisions, do we have a basis for some judgment concerning the future evolution of the tripartite economic structure of the world? More particularly, is it possible to discern in the diversity of the key problems and their underlying circumstances some dependable tendencies toward increasing similarities, or is it more plausible to expect the differences to widen?

Admittedly, these are highly speculative questions. But any judgment about the future of complex social relationships is speculative at best, because of the pre-empirical and indeterministic nature of the subject. The choice is between rational speculation and intuitive imagination. The first condition for justifiable speculation about the future is a sufficient knowledge of the facts of the past and of the resulting problems of the present. If our study has achieved this, it should permit us to say something meaningful about the future of the three economic subdivisions of our world.

II

As a starting point, let us *assume,* before we substantiate it as a probability, that each of the three areas will effectively resolve its own specific root problem of economic development. If we make this assumption, what results are we likely to get? Would the existing disparities between the three economic areas be reduced?

Given the specific root problems of economic growth in each of the three subdivisions of the world, our assumption would give rise to the following directional movements. The developing countries would consciously and systematically promote the strengthening of the human foundations of their economies, aiming specifically at the development of technical skills and entrepreneurial aptitudes and, generally, at elevating the broad levels of culture in its scientific and humanistic aspects. The Soviet Union, its satellites, and eventually China itself, would experience pressures for increasing socialist participation of the people in decisions, first on peripheral levels of their economies, and eventually in the center also. The West, finally, will solve its root problem of economic growth if it starts promoting a workable wage-price behavior that will breed neither inflation nor unemployment, and if, within such a consistent framework of wages and prices, it will keep expanding the aggregate demand by as much as the application of new knowledge to the available resources will permit.

If the assumption concerning the solution of the specific key problems of economic growth is justified by discernible tendencies in the facts of each case, certain important similarities between the three economic areas would begin to emerge.

A strengthening of the human basis of political and economic development, in the newly developing countries, and an effective socialist participation on the part of the people in the economic decisions within the Soviet orbit, would lead toward increasing assertion of genuine human aspirations as the chief objectives for economic growth. There would thus be at work a tendency toward convergence of all the three great economic subdivisions of the world in regard to the most important aspect of any economic system.

III

The principle of effective self-determination of human needs and aspirations as the guiding criterion for economic development has two important ramifications. The first one concerns the choice between goods for individual and family consumption and those for public use on the various levels of voluntary and compulsory (government-imposed) social cooperation.

When needs and aspirations are determined by the people, the selection among goods for "private" consumption and those for "public" use tends to be made on the basis of the relative merits of each case, the degrees of correctness of such assessment depending on the degrees of understanding and information. Relative merits of private versus public use depend on two complementary criteria. When a particular need or aspiration can be satisfied either way with similar *convenience*, the deciding consideration then obviously becomes cost. Which alternative is relatively cheaper? On the other hand, when the alternative ways to satisfaction, through private consumption or through public use, are of approximately the same *cost*, it is the greater convenience that will eventually decide which method of use shall prevail in particular instances. People who are informed about the relative conveniences and relative costs of the various ways in which particular needs and aspirations can be satisfied, and who are also free to choose accordingly, will clearly make their decisions in accordance with the two complementary criteria. To choose a method of satisfaction that is neither the most convenient one nor the cheapest one available can only mean that the choosers are either not properly informed or not free to choose, or both.[1]

The second ramification is implied in the first, as its institutional extension, but deserves to be made explicit. In a self-determining society, all socialization,[2] that is, the various forms of private and governmental institutions, will eventually be judged and dealt with as instruments for a balanced satisfaction of personal and family interests, on the one hand, and of the common good of the society as a whole, on the other.

These two ramifications reflect the realization that economic goods as well as social institutions are only the *means* and not the ends of human existence.

IV

It is now possible to ask what the gradual convergence toward the common principle of self-determined human needs would *specifically* entail for the newly developing countries, for the Soviet orbit, and for the West—first, in terms of relative *production* of private and public goods; second, with respect to the *organization* of production; and, third, concerning the degree and structure of *socialization*.

Because self-determination of needs is a relative novelty in the new nations, it must be expected that their aspirations will continue to be strongly influenced by their political leadership, which, in turn, must be expected to continue to stress the priority of public goods and services for education, transportation, public health, electric power, and basic industrialization over the private goods for personal and family consumption. But pressures for more consumer goods for private use are bound to mount as people become more conscious of their current personal needs vis-à-vis the projected well-being of future generations and the power of the state. An often neglected reason why political leadership in the underdeveloped countries (and even more so in the Soviet orbit) keeps pushing economic development for power purposes of the "state" and for the "future" rather than the "present" is that the members of the ruling elite do in fact enjoy many personal amenities of life that the masses are denied.[3] Therefore, it is only when nationalistic political leaders are exposed to pressures from the people that they are forced to adopt a more balanced approach to economic development for the sake of the people as well as that of the "state," and for the benefit of the present as well as that of the future.

The criteria of relative convenience and costs that emerge from the principle of self-determination of human needs in a world of scarcities must also be expected to be increasingly applied to the organization of production in the developing countries. This would lead to a progressive widening of the scope of *decentralized,* both public and private, enterprise as a more convenient and cheaper way to produce most of the particular products and many services. Related to this organizational development is a more general tendency for social institutions, private as well as public, to have their instrumental significance continuously *reappraised.* In the new nations, we may expect a relative decline in governmental bureaucratization of societal activities and a commensurate increase and articulation of voluntarily associated activities.

V

The assumption of the principle of self-determination of ends and wants *in the Soviet orbit* is also bound to have a far-reaching impact on the relative proportion of private and public goods, on the organization of production, and on the forms of socialization in general.

Once the Soviet people begin effectively to influence the formulation of demands on Soviet production, a pronounced increase in the proportion of goods for current consumption by persons and families is clearly to be expected. The only question is how rapid and how radical this expected change will be. The huge accumulated backlog of consumer needs and aspirations in the Soviet orbit and the proven ability of the Soviet economy to turn out a fast-growing output will act as particularly strong stimuli in favor of a substantial relative increase in the output of private consumer goods at the expense of power-oriented public goods, which have so far enjoyed an absolute priority. Other Communist-dominated countries, including rebellious Communist China, will have little choice but to trail Soviet developments. There is no reason why a prospective democratic socialism in the Soviet orbit should stop at just changing the proportion of private and public goods. Great institutional changes toward increasing decentralization in the administration of the Soviet society and economy must also be expected to evolve in accordance with the two criteria of relative convenience and cost.

Because integral socialism, even though it must be democratic and decentralized in order to be workable, does not envisage private ownership of land and capital, private enterprise in the Soviet orbit cannot be expected to start re-emerging rapidly. But this legalistic view, which is formally correct, is easily misleading. The decentralization of authority and institutions, without which socialism cannot be effective since society as a whole cannot democratically manage production in a direct way, leads not only to a spontaneous determination of demands from the grass roots up, but also to various degrees of effective self-administration of individual production units. Once an enterprise, or an associated group of enterprises, is entrusted with power of decision over the selection and combination of inputs and the specification of outputs, it behaves as if it had legal ownership and control over the material resources it uses. Furthermore, such a decentralized managerial autonomy is feasible only within an economic system in which planning and executive decisions are supported by a meaningful economy-wide price system, which alone can reflect true scarcities in relation to the determined needs and aspirations.

The two specific requirements of genuine and effective socialist economy (self-administration of enterprises and a meaningful price system) thus lead gradually to an outcome similar to a predominantly private enterprise system in many of its aspects—except for the legally formalized private ownership of land and capital. But even this is bound to emerge, once entrepreneurial autonomy asserts itself as an effective instrument of production serving the self-determined needs of the people.

VI

What may we expect from the solution of the two-pronged problem of inflation *in Western economies*? Two important developments can easily be discerned.

The existing inflationary bias, which is built into the very structure of the existing pluralistic societies and economies in the West, cannot possibly be eliminated unless organized economic groups, primarily labor unions and business corporations, accept and live up to clear-cut criteria for wage and price behavior that will neither generate inflation nor breed unemployment. Once suitable wage-price criteria are developed and accepted, and institutions are adapted to the procedural requirements of such criteria,[4] the West will have eliminated the inflationary bias from its social structure and economic organization. As a consequence of such adjustment, the pluralistic West will have used "socialization" to create balanced self-determination, and better satisfaction, of human wants and aspirations. In particular, the problem of inflationary pressures will then be limited to the demand side, where it can more readily be managed by flexible monetary and fiscal policies.

When, as has been the case since World War II, monetary and fiscal policies are burdened with the responsibility for *all* inflation, regardless of its origin, these policies tend to be either ineffective or overly restrictive. Liberated from inflationary pressures stemming from organized wage and price administration, monetary and fiscal policies can serve more boldly the interrelated objectives of maximum economic growth with full employment and general price stability. With more scope for economic growth, we may expect, particularly in the United States, that a larger proportion of increasing production will go into much needed public goods and services such as faster and more convenient urban transportation, improved health services, more abundant and diversified recreational facilities, and opportunities for education, defense, and space exploration.

Thus, the industrially advanced countries of the West will accomplish a fuller and more balanced satisfaction of their expanding human wants and social ends.

VII

This reasoning was based on the *assumption* that each of the three economic subdivisions would recognize its specific root problem of economic growth and would effectively begin to solve it. We must now face the deciding question as to how *realistic* this assumption is.

There is some evidence that the *underdeveloped countries* are becoming increasingly aware of the primary need for human development as the condition for their economic growth as well as for general national strength. These countries are all members of the United Nations. There they are in direct contact and contest with the cultural factors and influences from the rest of the world. Lacking sinews of national power, the representatives of these countries cannot but realize how fundamentally important it is to develop the qualities and abilities inherent in their people.

The new nations—in the framework of the United Nations and its special activities, through participation in other international arrangements of all kinds, through association with the European Common Market, as beneficiaries of Western foreign aid and technical assistance, and through educational arrangements for their students abroad—are promoting the development of the human foundations for their economic and political development.

Three recent events of special significance may serve to illustrate the beginning of a trend toward the solution of the key problem of economic growth in the newly developing countries. From October 16 to 20, 1961, a Policy Conference on Economic Growth and Investment in Education of the member nations of the Organization for Economic Cooperation and Development was held in Washington. Interesting papers and statistics on cultural and educational needs and on the accomplishments and potentialities of the new nations were presented and discussed at the conference. The root problem of the economic growth of these nations was fully exposed and explored. The contribution of such ordered efforts toward the solution of the problem is obvious.

In January, 1962, the heads of state or government of twenty African nations met at Lagos, Nigeria, for a six-day official conference to explore possibilities of closer cooperation. A sort of "confederation of independent African states" emerged, to "follow a concerted policy in the most varied fields." Among the specific agreements on associated efforts and projects were the establishment of an "Educational and Cultural Council of African and Malagasy States" and of "joint veterinary schools."[5] After the first conference of this kind was successful, much more can be expected from other conferences and activities of the evolving "African Confederation." In fact, a continent-wide conference of heads of African states was held at Addis Ababa in May, 1963, which adopted a charter for an Organization of African Unity with a permanent secretariat to "develop co-operative programs in the fields of diplomacy, politics, economics, education. . . ."[6]

VIII

The assumption that *in the Soviet orbit* socialist participation of the people will prevail appears less realistic. But, as shown in Chapter 4, a basic contradiction within the Soviet system unquestionably exists, feeds on itself, and presses into the open. "De-Stalinization" of the whole Soviet system, "decentralization" of production, widespread and growing "informal activities" of the Soviet managers, the protracted and deepening crisis of agriculture in all Communist-ruled countries, renewed "socialist" protestations and "communist" promises of the new Soviet Party Program—these are undeniably manifestations of profound difficulties and great permutations within the totalitarian Communist reality.

The crisis of the Soviet system is real, although its specific outcome cannot be foreseen.

A genuine and effective socialism in the Soviet orbit is unavoidable, not because of its own intrinsic merits, but because it is the only way by which the people in a totalitarian society can begin to exert pressure when the technical knowledge of enough of them becomes indispensable for the system to function. In the Soviet Union, that time is approaching. In Chapter 4, we pointed out how the West can encourage this hopeful development. Willy-nilly, other Communist-dominated countries, including Red China, will in due time be forced to move in the same direction.

IX

How realistic is the assumption that *the West* will solve its root problem of economic growth, which is the inflationary bias that is now built into its pluralistic structure?

Since 1957, there has been a growing awareness in the West of the chronic inflationary pressures on the cost side of production.[7] This awareness received abundant expression in official warnings to unions and management to use restraint in their wage-price behavior. Many books, articles, congressional hearings, and studies of inflation considered the problem.[8] Yet no public policy was developed.

In the United States, a basic change occurred in 1961, when growing pressures of international competition, particularly from the European Common Market, severely aggravated the United States balance of international payments, reducing the American monetary gold stock from more than $24 billion in 1949 to less than $16 billion in 1963. Under these pressures, President Kennedy announced on February 2, 1961, that he would appoint twenty-one representatives of organized labor, business, and the public to serve on the new Advisory Committee on Labor-Management Policy. Among the assignments with which the President charged the committee was to advise "with respect to actions that may be taken by labor, management, and the public which will promote free and responsible collective bargaining, industrial peace, sound wage policies, sound price policies and stability, a higher standard of living, increased productivity, and America's competitive position in world markets." The committee has had regular monthly meetings.

A still more important step toward the solution of the inflationary pressures inherent in the pluralistic structure of Western economies was made when President Kennedy's Council of Economic Advisers, in its first economic report, issued on January 22, 1962, published a set of "Guideposts for Noninflationary Wage and Price Behavior."[9] This represented a pioneering *official* attempt to formulate specific criteria to guide the determination of collective wage increases and related administered price changes.[10] Similar developments are under way in other Western countries.[11]

It appears that the European Common Market, in freeing trade, investment, and mobility of labor within its large economic area, has given new impetus to economic competition and efficiency everywhere in the West. As a consequence, Great Britain and other nonmember countries in Europe wish to join the Common Market, and the United States is attempting to work out wide mutual tariff reductions with the Common Market. It was the interrelated consequences of the European Common Market that persuaded President Kennedy and his Council of Economic Advisers to formulate and publish specific wage-price criteria in the official economic report where, in the past, there were only vague exhortations to labor and management to use "restraint."

We may therefore conclude that there is now considerable evidence that the West is taking seriously its own root problem of economic growth—the two-pronged inflationary pressures—and in attempting a basic solution of it.

X

Our speculative search for elements of convergence in the evolution of the three economic subdivisions of the contemporary world may now be concluded. The foregoing analysis reveals that a basic convergence of the world's economies toward certain common characteristics may be reasonably expected.

Let us summarize. The indicated convergence of the three economic subdivisions of the contemporary world encompasses the following interrelated similarities. First, the economies of the future will be characterized by an ever-wider *self-determination* of human needs. Second, production and related social institutions everywhere will increasingly be recognized and shaped as *instruments* for the satisfaction of self-determined human wants. Third, the criterion of choice between private goods for individual and family consumption and public goods for collective use will be the relative *merit* of each case, to be determined on the basis of comparative convenience and comparative cost. Fourth, in order to conform to the three preceding characteristics, production will be organized in *autonomous enterprises*, with various legal forms and blends of private and public ownership or lease of land and capital. The extent of independent management will depend on the degree to which efficient operation of an enterprise is conditional on its prompt responses to changes in technology and demand (when such changes are frequent and irregular, as they are increasingly bound to be in a self-determining society). Thus a further common characteristic of future economies will have to be a *price system* that reflects relative scarcities in relation to changing technology and self-determined aspirations.

These interrelated characteristics of the evolving convergence of the world's economies will form their common "grammar," as it were.[12] The rules of grammar are a necessary, although not sufficient, condition for meaningful communication. Communication requires style in addition to grammar. All people, speaking a language, must use the same grammar, but their styles may differ greatly. Similarly, all economies based on the principle of self-determination of human needs must use the common "grammar" consisting of the five characteristics discussed above. But the "style" of each such economy may vary greatly from that of the others. There is no need to stress that the various national and regional economies of the future are likely to continue to be different from one another in all their aspects except in the five essential characteristics in which they will eventually all share.

Such economic convergence of the world would reflect the *underlying evolution of attitudes* concerning the nature of man and society. Paradoxically, this less tangible evolution appears to be moving in two seemingly opposing directions. There has been a growing emphasis everywhere on man as an autonomous person, the ultimate source of all thought, work, and progress in society, and the actual beneficiary of all real progress. At the same time, there has been an appreciable increase in socialization. This paradox is becoming real enough in the Communist world and, to varying degrees, even in the West and in the developing countries. Yet, the paradox is disappearing with the growing realization that every form and instance of socialization increasingly requires justification in terms of its instrumental usefulness to man, even though conflicts about the allocation of burdens and distribution of benefits persist.

This evolution of attitudes concerning man and society has found its most comprehensive expression and formulation in the last encyclical letter of Pope John XXIII, *Pacem in Terris*. Although this statement is couched in terms of a social order to be striven for if peace is to be secured, it is addressed to all mankind and is based on the analysis of those essential characteristics common to all men. The universal acclaim that *Pacem in Terris* has received is the most convincing testimony to its general realism. If duly informed about its content and really free to voice their preferences, a vast majority of human beings would no doubt agree with its conclusions. Short of a universal referendum on the subject, this statement cannot, of course, be "scientifically" proved. Yet enough "sampling" has been done to make it strongly creditable.

Something extremely important is happening in our time. After more than a century of implacable conflict, the extremist ideologies of individualism and collectivism have capitulated to one another, as it were. Just as there never was an individualistic society, so there shall never be a collectivistic one. Their historical inapplicability upended the two ideologies. In their place, a universal *new attitude* is emerging in the West as well as in the East and in both the advanced and underdeveloped countries. This is the attitude of *personalism* as the *origin* of all human designs and works and the *finality* of all social arrangements. When the human person is so in the center of things, "socialization" assumes its natural, instrumental function in the service of man, and thus ceases to be the dreaded "road to serfdom." By the same token, individual initiative and personal choice come to be viewed as the mainsprings of social progress rather than being suspected as the sources of exploitation for the privileged few against the unfortunate many.

With the human person as the firm anchor of all social relationships—local, regional, national, and international—*justice* becomes the obvious criterion of all social arrangements and rearrangements. And since peace among men and nations is essentially the result of justice,[13] we may hope that *peace* will defeat the threat of nuclear annihilation.

Thus, there is an underlying link between the emerging economic convergence of the world and the hope for peace among men and nations.

EPILOGUE

In the spring of 1964, the Soviet-Chinese differences erupted into violent verbal exchanges in which Mr. Khrushchev personally took part during and after his visit to Hungary.* By non-Communist, Western standards open controversies of such scope and intensity are not easily composed. In fact, there are widespread expectations in the West that the estrangement between Moscow and Peking may be irreparable.

Such, however, need not be the logic of quarrels and insults among the Communists. Tito's party was expelled from the Cominform and the ensuing separation appeared complete and irreversible. Yet, for all intents and purposes, Tito has since been accepted back into the fold of the world Communist movement by all the Communist parties except the Chinese and their few satellites.

The evolving ideological and organizational differences in the world Communist movement may indeed turn out to provide a more flexible framework to accommodate a larger assortment of actual and potential Communists throughout the world. Thus "peacefully separated," all the world's Communists may continue to work, in a greater variety of ways, for what still are their essentially similar domestic and global objectives. For all of them, the Utopian Communist end may continue to justify using all the means short of those that would destroy their own end. When the Chinese Communists eventually come around to admitting that in the nuclear age war is such a means, their differences with Moscow may well be reduced to manageable proportions.

In the meantime, it is possible that the Moscow-Peking controversy may evolve or erupt into a more ominous form of "competitive coexistence" between the two Communist blocs that might force Moscow to revert to a more Stalinist posture at home as well as in relation to its satellites and the rest of the world.

Whichever way the controversy may turn, detour, or return, the West has no discernible reason to relax in anticipation of some favorable outcome that is not clearly in sight. Those who read such

* For documentation see consecutive reports and dispatches from Budapest, Moscow, and Washington in issues of *The New York Times* since April 5, 1964.

relaxing implications into Senator Fulbright's provocative speeches on American foreign policy in March and April, 1964, were carried away by wishful thinking.

If Milovan Djilas could comment on the evolving Soviet-Chinese controversy, he would be likely to view it from a longer perspective as a major manifestation of the same basic contradiction within the Communist system that has produced a growing variety of tensions inside the Soviet Union and within other Communist-dominated countries. These tensions are real. But they do not justify either adventurous responses or complacency on the part of the West. Rather, we should try to so influence these tensions that they will more certainly and effectively contribute to the evolution toward freedom, justice, and peace in the world.

APPENDIX A-1: COMPARATIVE RATES OF ECONOMIC GROWTH

In a paper prepared for the Subcommittee on Economic Statistics, the Central Intelligence Agency estimated Gross National Product (GNP) indexes for Western Alliance and Sino-Soviet Bloc for the period 1950–65. The following percentages of the average annual growth rate were calculated and projected for different countries in this survey:[1]

U.S.A.	3¼ for period 1950–59
	4¼ for period 1959–65
Europe–NATO nations	4¾ for both periods
Canada	3¾ for period 1950–59
	4¼ for period 1959–65
U.S.S.R.	7 for period 1950–59
	6 for period 1959–65
Europe–satellite nations	6½ for period 1950–59
	5½ for period 1959–65
China	9 for period 1950–59
	8 for period 1959–65

This study indicates that the margin that expresses the difference in the average annual growth rate between the two blocs will narrow somewhat during the 1960's. This conclusion has been partly proved by the subsequent official economic report from Moscow, which shows an appreciable decline in the rate of the Soviet economic growth. For example, the rate of growth of industrial labor's productivity in 1961 was estimated at 3.5 per cent, as against 6.4 in 1960 and 8 per cent in 1959. Retail sales increased 3.5 per cent through July, 1961, as against 9 per cent in 1960. Industrial production in the U.S.S.R. through July, 1961, has increased by 8.4 per cent, as against the average annual growth rate for 1950–59 of 10 per cent and the estimated 8.6 per cent for the period 1959–65.[2]

[1] See *Comparisons of the United States and Soviet Economies,* prepared by the Central Intelligence Agency in cooperation with the Department of State and the Department of Defense for the Subcommitte on Economic Statistics of the Joint Economic Committee (Washington, D.C., 1959), p. 48.

[2] For more details, see "Soviet Growth Slows," *The New York Times,* July 24, 1961.

The British economist Colin Clark opposes the view that Soviet economic development has proceeded at a faster rate than that of the West.[3] Clark admits that the Soviet rate of growth in two distinct periods had been higher than that of the United States, but maintains that on the average the real productivity of the Soviet economy grew only by 1.2 per cent per year for the period 1913–56. During the same period, the United States rate of productivity increase averaged 2.3 per cent annually. The two periods of exceptionally high rates of Soviet economic growth were the periods from 1933–37 and from 1948–53. Clark explained these two periods of exceptional growth by the recovery of the Soviet economy from the famine due to forced collectivization in the first of the two periods, and by the devastating destruction during World War II in the second.

Another important factor of economic growth is the rate of population increase. According to Mr. Clark, the rate of population increase in the Soviet Union (1.5 per cent per year) has lagged behind that of the United States (1.8 per cent per year).

From these two factors, Mr. Clark drew the conclusion that, barring exceptional circumstances, the existing gap between the overall performance of the two economies would not be narrowed. Without going into the merits of Colin Clark's statistics, we may bring out some shortcomings of his conclusions:

(1) Mr. Clark did not consider the percentage of the national product of the United States and the Soviet Union that is plowed back into production by way of investment. This percentage is considerably higher in the Soviet Union. (It is roughly about 30 per cent of the national product, while in the United States it is 17–20 per cent.)[4]

(2) In spite of the fact that the rate of productivity increase (as distinct from the rate of growth in GNP) has been higher in the United States than in the Soviet Union, the existing gap between the two economies would tend to be narrowed if our economy were to continue to operate considerably below its full capacity.

(3) The slower rate of population increase is a serious obstacle to the Soviet ambition to "catch up" with the United States, but there are indications that the Soviet Government is stepping up programs to foster the rate of population increase and that the Soviets are recruiting a larger percentage of population (74 per cent

[3] Clark, *The Real Productivity of Soviet Russia* (Washington, D.C.: Senate Internal Security Subcommittee, 1961).

[4] See *Comparisons of the United States and Soviet Economies,* Part I, p. 124.

as compared with 57.9 per cent in the United States) for their labor force.[5] In addition, if the Soviet Union ever succeeds in substantially improving the performance of its agriculture, it could then draw on substantial release of the rural labor force to be employed in nonagricultural production. While only 9 per cent of the American labor force is employed in agriculture, the corresponding percentage in the Soviet Union is about 49 per cent.

On the other hand, whatever various statistics may show concerning the comparative rates of growth, one must consider the following factors:

1. As a totalitarian dictatorship of world-wide ambitions, the Soviet Union may have a prestige interest in systematically overstating any statistics about its own economic performance.
2. Soviet calculations of their own economic growth omit personal and public (collective) services, which are least productive, while Western statistics on economic growth include all the branches of production.

In his most recent study,[6] Colin Clark gives the following data concerning the average rates of economic growth during 1950–57 in individual Western countries:

West Germany	10.9 per cent
Austria	6.4 per cent
Italy	5.6 per cent
France	4.7 per cent
Canada	4.7 per cent
United States	3.7 per cent
United Kingdom	3.2 per cent

The Working Party on Policies for the Promotion of Economic Growth of the Economic Policy Committee of the Organization for Economic Cooperation and Development estimated the rates of economic growth shown in the table on page 154.

In 1962–63, there were indications of a significant slowdown in the Soviets' rate of growth, due to their poor agricultural performance and, particularly, to their overextension in the military and space fields. According to one source, the Soviet rate of growth in 1962 was no more than 4.5 per cent, while in the same year the United States rate of economic growth climbed to 5.4 per cent and that of all the NATO countries taken together amounted to 4.8 per

[5] *Ibid.*, p. 79.

[6] Clark, *Growthmanship* (London: Institute of Economic Affairs, 1961), p. 41.

*Per Cent Increase in Total GNP**

Country	1950–55	1955–60	1960–62
Austria	7.0	5.2	3.4
Canada	4.6	3.2	3.9
France	4.5	4.2	4.7
Germany	9.0	6.0	4.5
Italy	6.0	5.9	6.7
United Kingdom	2.6	2.7	2.1
United States	4.3	2.3	3.5

* Source: OECD, *Policies for Economic Growth,* November, 1962, pp. 16 and 44.

cent.[7] According to this view, Khrushchev badly needs a basic *detente* with the West in order to be able to "get Russia moving again" on the path of economic growth and competition with the West. In another article, H. Schwartz sustains a very similar opinion.[8]

In January, 1964, the Central Intelligence Agency revealed that its latest information and analysis indicated that the rate of economic growth in the Soviet Union had dropped from its previous average of over 6 per cent in the 1950's to only 2.5 per cent in 1962 and 1963.[9] This spectacular decrease was due to the combined effects of the following factors: First, Soviet agricultural production was reduced substantially because of the accumulated inefficiencies of its organization and technology coupled with a bad winter and drought; second, while the Soviet GNP is less than 50 per cent of the American GNP, the Soviet Union had for years been using a larger amount of resources for military and space purposes. But resources that are invested in military and space production do not directly contribute to the growth of GNP, however great may be the political and psychological effects generated by such use of these resources.

[7] J. Alsop, "Getting Russia Moving Again," *The Washington Post*, July 26, 1963, p. A 17.

[8] "Economic Pressure Grows in the Soviet," *The New York Times*, July 28, 1963, Section 4, p. 4.

[9] Edwin L. Dale, "Sharp Slowdown in Soviet Growth Reported by C.I.A.," *The New York Times,* January 8, 1964, pp. 1 and 2. For a most comprehensive recent statistical estimate of the various aspects of the Soviet economic performance and a comparison with that of the United States, see U.S. Congress, Joint Economic Committee, *Annual Economic Indicators for the U.S.S.R.* (Washington, D.C., 1964).

These recent findings concerning the Soviet rate of economic growth appear to vindicate the earlier low estimates of the Soviet growth rate by Colin Clark. It must be remembered, however, that the CIA estimates of the Soviet economic growth for previous years were much higher than Clark's. Moreover, *Soviet* estimates of their own economic growth refer to our concept of GNP *minus* services, which would yield a higher *rate* of growth. Finally, from the Western point of view it is at least as important to realize that the Soviet Union is capable of continued competition in the military and space fields as it is to be aware of their declining current rate of growth in terms of the Gross National Product as we define it, which properly includes consumer services but measures the value of defense and space services in terms of their direct monetary costs only.

It was gratifying to know that while the Soviet economic growth in terms of our GNP concept amounted to only 2.5 per cent in 1963, our own real rate of growth in 1963 reached 5 per cent.[10] On the other hand, the fact that in the same year our unemployment still ranged between 5 and 6 per cent of the labor force was a clear reminder that, because of our high productivity, we need a still higher annual rate of growth if we are to have full employment.

[10] Edwin L. Dale, "Six Per Cent Growth Seen This Year," *The New York Times*, January 6, 1964, pp. 49 and 52.

APPENDIX B-1: THEORIES AND MODELS OF ECONOMIC DEVELOPMENT AND GROWTH

Since its formulation by the early British classical economists, economic theory has been concerned mainly with the analysis of more or less immediate aspects of demand and supply of individual products and their relative prices, as well as (at first implicitly and since J. M. Keynes explicitly) of aggregate demand for and supply of total production and the general price level. In this type of analysis the populational, cultural, sociological, political, and technological factors affecting wants and production were assumed constant or, if such changes were analytically considered as they were by Malthus and Ricardo, only their presumed ultimate effects on demand and supply were speculated about. Thus, for example, the combined Malthusian principle of population and the Ricardian principle of diminishing returns led to the conclusion of a stationary economy.

J. A. Schumpeter was the first economist in the classical tradition to broaden the framework of theoretical economic analysis by formally including in it the underlying changes in culture, technology, and organization. The result was his famous theory of economic development,[1] centered in the concept of innovation as the source of economic development whose agent is the entrepreneur.

Schumpeter's starting point is the stationary equilibrium concept of the classics, which Schumpeter called the circular flow of economic life. Schumpeter felt that the best way to evolve a theory of economic development was to start with the familiar stationary model that does not change as it flows through time. The circular flow of economic life is characterized by complete absence of entrepreneurial activity in its innovational sense. Hence, in the circular flow of economic life, there are no profits.

To explain the mechanism of development, Schumpeter relaxed the analytical properties of the circular flow. Now the entrepreneur changes the production function by introducing a new product or a new method of production, by finding a new source of supply or a new market, or by improving the organization of the firm. Here

[1] J. A. Schumpeter, *Theory of Economic Development* (Cambridge, Mass.: Harvard University Press, 1959).

lies, according to Schumpeter, the basic difference between economic growth and economic development. Economic growth means more of the same, whereas economic development denotes qualitative changes in the composition of input and output.[2]

A very special role was assigned by Schumpeter to credit creation. The prospective entrepreneur needs the financial ability to innovate. The importance of economic power for economic development was not observed by classical economists, and therefore they were not able to develop a complete theory of qualitative economic changes. For Schumpeter, economic power (ability to innovate) results from credit creation. Schumpeter discarded the Marxian concept of surplus value in the circular flow and introduced instead the role of credit, which, in his own words, is "the creation of new purchasing power out of nothing, which is added to the existing circulation."[3] This newly created means of payments makes it possible for the entrepreneur to bid away agents of production from their previous uses. In this lies the economic power of Schumpeter's entrepreneur.

II

Since the publication of Keynes's *General Theory*,[4] economists in the classical tradition became more concerned with the demand aspect of the growth problem, which, up to then, had been more or less taken for granted.[5] Thus, following the publication of Mrs. J. Robinson's *Essays in the Theory of Employment*,[6] R. F. Harrod[7] tried to discover the necessary and sufficient conditions for

[2] The reader should bear in mind, however, that the two terms are currently used interchangeably, except that "growth" is more often used in reference to advanced industrial countries and the word "development" is often reserved for the process of economic growth in underdeveloped countries. In either case, the actual process of expanding production over time is composed of both the "widening" and "innovating" elements.

[3] Schumpeter, *op. cit.*, p. 73.

[4] J. M. Keynes, *The General Theory of Employment Interest and Money* (London: Macmillan, 1936).

[5] At least it was assumed that it would automatically adjust, since it was believed that supply creates its own demand. J. A. Schumpeter was, of course, an exception.

[6] J. Robinson, *Essays in the Theory of Employment* (Oxford: Blackwell, 1937).

[7] R. F. Harrod, *Towards a Dynamic Economics* (London: Macmillan, 1954).

growth, when not only the supply side, but also the demand side were taken into analytical consideration.

Investment affects the economy in two ways. It increases the capital stock and hence output capacity of the economy (an aspect of investment which was largely disregarded in Keynes's theory), and, through the multiplier effect, investment expands the effective demand in the economy (the Keynesian aspect). While Harrod tried to discover the rate of growth of income (consistent with steady growth), E. D. Domar[8] attempted to establish the necessary rate of growth of investment to maintain "steady growth" in employment and income. Both approaches came to essentially the same thing.

If we define s as the average propensity to save (the savings income ratio), Cp as the incremental capital output ratio in an *ex-post* sense, and g as the rate of growth of income, Harrod's fundamental equation is: $g = s/Cp$. Now, the warranted rate of growth g_w is defined as that rate which leaves all parties satisfied that they have produced neither more nor less than the right amount. Hence, in a given economy at a certain time, if we have the existing savings income ratio s^* and the incremental capital output ratio Cp, we can find the warranted rate of growth, which will be $g_w = s^*/Cp$.

The limit to the rate of growth of an economy is given, over long periods of time, by the increase in population and technical progress. Should the actual rate of growth be higher than the warranted rate, the capital stock will be unduly depleted with resultant shortages in equipment. Thus, the economy will be stimulated to further growth. Therefore, instead of g approaching g_w, a cumulative divergence of the two rates will occur. If, on the other hand, the actual rate of growth is less than the warranted rate, there will be excess capacity, and again a cumulative divergence will occur between the two rates, with g departing farther and farther in the downward direction.

Both models may be rendered more realistic through the introduction of international trade, autonomous investment, and international movements of capital, without altering essentially any part of the argument. However, the argument rests, as Solow[9] has shown, on the assumption of fixed proportions in production, which essen-

[8] Evsey D. Domar, *Essays in the Theory of Economic Growth* (New York: Oxford University Press, 1957).

[9] R. Solow, "A Contribution to the Theory of Economic Growth," *Quarterly Journal of Economics*, LXX, 1956, pp. 65–94.

tially causes this divergence. The removal of this assumption, and its replacements by an assumption of variable proportions (factor substitutions), will prevent cumulative divergencies between the actual and the warranted rates of growth from developing.

A later elaboration of a basically similar model was undertaken by N. Kaldor.[10] Here, the savings income ratio is divided into two components, one for profit earners and the other for wage earners. Hence, for variations in income, savings will increase or decrease more rapidly than in the Harrodian function. Secondly, a technical progress function is introduced, which has one point of stable equilibrium, where the capital output ratio is constant. Also, because of the assumption about the shape of this curve, any increase in income will cause an increase in investment, which will further increase income, until the point of the constant capital output ratio is reached. Then, the capital stock and the level of income grow at the same rate. In addition, the model introduces population growth as a function of income. Naturally the buoyancy of investment and the expansion of population make the model tend toward explosive solutions.

However, the model will also yield a solution for stagnation. This will occur either if the technical progress function is suitably altered or if profits are lower than the minimum required to secure a margin of profit over turnover, below which the entrepreneurs would not reduce prices irrespective of the state of demand. For then the system will not generate sufficient purchasing power, and therefore employment will suffer. But these are special cases.

In Kaldor's own words, "the implications of our model in terms of Mr. Harrod's terminology could be summed up by saying that the system tends towards an equilibrium rate of growth at which the natural and the warranted rates are equal. . . ."[11] This is, in fact, the essence of the model: growth at equilibrium rates, and achieved by a special savings curve and a changing incremental capital output ratio. For consider the Harrod equation $g_w = s^*/Cp$, and let us denote the "natural growth values" with the subscript n; i.e., $g_n = s_n/Cp_n$. Now if the forces in the system are such that Cp approaches Cp_n and s^* approaches s_n, (or better if s^* is constant throughout and equal to s_n), then *a fortiori* g_w will tend toward g_n. In the Harrod model, cumulative divergencies occurred because the savings ratio and the incremental capital output ratio were fixed,

[10] N. Kaldor, "A Model of Economic Growth," *The Economic Journal*, LXVII (1957), 591–624.

[11] Kaldor, *op. cit.*, p. 612.

leading to excess capacity and further divergencies. Here this will not occur, partly due to the expanding population and partly because of the peculiar character of the technical progress function.

A second type of modification of the basic Harrodian model is provided by the model of R. A. Gordon.[12] He introduces the hypothesis, supported by empirical evidence, that there has been a secular trend for capital goods prices to increase faster than consumption goods prices. Thus, if we call P the weighted average of capital goods prices (P_k) and consumption goods prices (P_c), we can denote the ratio P_k/P by p'.

The secular rise in the ratio p' must be included explicitly into the growth equations, for obviously it will have an effect on the rate of growth. Allowing for this factor, the fundamental Harrodian equation becomes, $g = (1/Y)\ dY/dt = (1/p')\ s/v$.[13] Thus, through time the actual rate of growth will have a tendency to decline. The warranted rate of growth will be similarly affected. Further, in the basic Harrod model, equal rates of growth in investment and income are required. This is no longer true, if we allow $dp'/dt \neq O$, i.e., if the rate of change of p' through time is different from zero. For, the rate of growth of investment will be given by: $(1/I) \cdot (dI/dt) = (1/p')\ (s/v - dp'/dt)$, and this will be different from $1/p' \cdot s/v$ if dp'/dt is different from zero.

The inclusion of prices is certainly a welcome addition to the rather simple basic model. But the moment that explicit prices are introduced, can we continue to ignore the role of expectations and expected prices, and their effect, especially on investment? If expectations are important, then the model needs further alterations and complications to allow for these effects.

III

The Harrod-Domar-Kaldor-Gordon types of growth models are cast in terms of abstract macroeconomic variables. These theorems do not penetrate the generation and the operational background of their variables and are therefore not sufficient for shaping policies for economic development itself. Operational propositions of this latter kind must be couched in terms of more specific determinants

[12] R. A. Gordon, "Differential Changes in the Prices of Consumers and Capital Goods," *The American Economic Review*, LI (December, 1961), 937 ff.

[13] *Ibid.*

of the macroeconomic variables themselves. Two examples will illustrate the difference.

C. Furtado, a Brazilian economist, presented an operational view of economic development.[14] According to Furtado, the process of development consists of a series of changes in the manner and proportions in which the factors of production are combined with the aim of increasing the productivity of labor. The aim of the theory of economic development is to explain why the productivity of labor goes on increasing in an economy.

In developed economies, the process of development involves the introduction of technical innovations. In underdeveloped economies, there is a need for new combinations of existing factors at the existing technical level. In underdeveloped countries, there is always underemployment of the factors of production within the limits of known techniques because of the chronic scarcity of capital, which is the result of the lack of past savings.

The process of growth starts with an increase in productivity. The initial stimulus in underdeveloped countries must come from the outside because of the fact that in low productivity nations the satisfaction of elementary needs absorbs most of the productive capacity. Foreign trade is one way to provide initial stimulus.

An increase in productivity leads to an increase in real income (unless fruits of productivity increases are lost, due to cyclical unemployment, random factors such as adverse weather, or a fall in the terms of trade), first in the sector directly affected. This increase is absorbed by profits, which make possible the accumulation of capital. When the process of growth is consolidated and demand for labor increases, first wages and then consumption increase, and this will bring forth further new investment and further increases in productivity, and the process will become continuous.

However, a complication arises in underdeveloped countries because of the high marginal propensity to consume, which impairs saving. This must be corrected. Also, underdeveloped nations have a high marginal propensity to import, and therefore the process of growth will cause balance of payments difficulties. This difficulty may be met by modifying the structure of production to increase exports or substitutes for imports.

What Furtado attempted to do was to translate an essentially Solowian analytical model of growth into the underlying operational factors in newly developing countries. Another example of a

[14] C. Furtado, "Capital Formation and Economic Development," reprinted in *International Economic Papers,* No. 4 (1954), pp. 124–44.

more operational approach to economic growth by an economist associated with newly developing economies is that of R. Prebisch, the former Executive Secretary of the United Nations Economic Commission for Latin America.[15]

The Prebisch thesis focuses on the relationship between the developed industrial centers and the developing economies whose production is concentrated on raw materials, that is, the countries of the periphery. Prebisch analyzes the center-periphery relationship both statistically and theoretically and arrives at two major conclusions: (1) the traditional division of labor, in which Latin America was supposed to supply raw materials to the industrial economies of the center, no longer applies; (2) industrialization is an ineluctable need for Latin American economic development.

Assuming the necessary social and political development, Prebisch fixes his analysis of the Latin American periphery on the corresponding economic needs and concludes that for the periphery exports play a vital role analogous to that of capital investment for the industrial center. The periphery depends on exports to furnish the foreign exchange needed to purchase essential imports, and its exports are mainly primary products. The prices of these primary products, e.g., coffee, bananas, copper, are established competitively in the world market. They are subject to severe fluctuations, while the demand for the products themselves remains relatively inelastic. At the same time, the prices paid by the periphery for its imports of manufactured goods rise steadily. The result has frequently been continual deficits in the balance of trade and consequently stimulus to domestic inflation.

The growth of agricultural technology has not helped the fundamental imbalance between the center and the periphery. Indeed, it aggravates poverty in the latter by depriving the rural labor force of work and reducing world-market prices for the raw materials produced in greater abundance. The inability of the periphery to retain the fruits of its increased productivity is in contrast to the industrial center whose strong economic institutions raise wages and prices to absorb technological gains in productivity.

The solution for the economic development of the periphery in

[15] For a recent article showing the evolution of this "thesis" in detail and giving a rather complete bibliography, see Charles A. Frankenhoff, "The Prebisch Thesis: A Theory of Industrialism for Latin America," *Journal of Inter-American Studies*, April, 1962, pp. 185–206. For a less sympathetic view of Prebisch's thesis, see R. F. Gemmill, "Prebisch on Commercial Policy for Less Developed Countries," *The Review of Economics and Statistics*, May, 1962, pp. 198–201.

the face of a rapidly growing labor force and unfavorable prices for exports is industrialization. A slowly growing industrial complex will tend to absorb increments of the labor force at higher productivity levels and help to retain the benefits of increasing productivity through import substitution. The growth of industry will be coordinated with, and supported by, the application of new technologies to agriculture.

An essential corollary to the Prebisch theory of development for Latin America is the conscious evolution of regional free trade areas.

IV

Recently, an interesting attempt was made to construct a simple growth and development theory, which is analytically rigorous and yet is cast in terms of variables that are closely related to the operational realities of contemporary economies, whether they are industrially advanced or in the earlier stages of economic development. The proposition was presented to the annual meeting of the American Economic Association in December, 1961, by Professor J. M. Power.[16]

Power's theorem centers on the rate of new capital formation *in relation to* the evolving supply of other productive services, particularly labor. Power introduces three concepts of the rate of capital formation. The *actual rate* is that rate at which new capital formation takes place. The *warranted rate* is that rate of capital formation that would match the economy's saving capacity at full employment. The *natural rate* of capital formation, on the other hand, is that rate at which new capital formation would "match the rate at which labor is becoming available to combine with new capital, given techniques of production" (p. 40). This natural rate is positively related to the degree of capital intensity and labor-saving of new investment, on the one hand, and to the available supply of labor, on the other.

If the warranted and the natural rates of capital formation were the same, the problem of proper economic growth would reduce itself to the Keynesian problem of sufficient effective demand; the actual rate of capital formation would have to be kept just at the level of full employment saving capacity.

16 J. M. Power, "Labor Saving in Economic Growth," *The American Economic Review*, May, 1961, pp. 39–45.

Complications arise from *disparities* between the warranted and the natural rates of capital formation. If the *natural rate* of capital formation *exceeds* the latter's warranted rate, two kinds of disequilibria are possible. If the actual rate equals the warranted rate of capital formation, there will be unemployment, due to the fact that the technology of capital goods is excessively labor-saving in comparison with the relative abundance of the available labor supply. If, on the contrary, the actual rate of capital formation matches its natural rate, there will develop an inflationary situation of the excess demand variety.

Now, if the relationship is reversed, in the sense that the *warranted rate* of capital formation *exceeds* its natural rate, we are faced with a situation where the labor force grows slower than the saving capacity and where the technology of capital goods is not sufficiently labor-saving to offset the difference. If, in such circumstances, the actual rate of capital formation matches its natural rate, unemployment will develop, due to an insufficient aggregate demand. If the actual rate equals the warranted rate, however, the stage is set for inflationary pressures on the costs side, leading to inflation and unemployment at the same time. The unemployment that here is a concomitant of cost-push inflation (and/or, we should add, profit-squeeze) beclouds the basic underlying difficulty of this case, which is the scarcity of labor in relation to capital.

If the disequilibria due to the basic tendency for the *natural rate* of capital formation to *exceed* its warranted rate are to be overcome, the technology of capital goods should be reoriented toward more capital-saving and less labor-saving. This would tend to bring the natural rate of capital formation down to the level of its warranted rate. If, however, the rate of saving can be increased, this would tend to lift the warranted rate of capital formation closer to its natural rate. Some combination of the two types of remedies may constitute the most feasible basis for an equilibrating growth policy.

If actual disequilibria stem from the basic tendency for the *warranted rate* of capital formation to *exceed* its natural rate, then the remedial measures must be sought in an appropriate combination of more labor-saving investment and a lower rate of national saving.

In the *newly developing countries* the principal obstacle to the desirable convergence of the three rates of capital formation appears to lie in the tendency of the natural rate of capital formation to exceed its warranted rate. Capital formation tends to be too labor-saving relative to both the quantity and the quality of the available labor supply, largely because of the basic fact that technology of investment tends to outrun the development of corresponding human attitudes, aptitudes, and skills.

In the *advanced industrial countries*, on the other hand, the three rates of capital formation are in danger of divergence when technology of capital goods catches up with the growth of available labor supply, after most of the excess labor has already been syphoned out of agriculture. From that point on, "the frontiers of technology must be moved more rapidly in order to sustain the rate of growth." This analytical situation would seem to approximate the basic technological and structural characteristics of the *American* economy. *Western Europe*, except Italy, may also be approaching a similar technological-structural situation, although its agriculture, especially in Germany, still lends itself to much more intensive mechanization and extensive organization, which could release considerable labor supply for the nonagricultural sections of their economies.

The basic structural situation in the *Soviet Union* differs from the advanced Western economies: Its agriculture still employs almost one-half of the total labor force, and the Soviet economy as a whole can still continue to draw on a considerable technological backlog to be applied to production. On the other hand, the rate of innovation in the Soviet economy may be hampered by the institutional rigidity of what still is essentially a command-type of economy.

Power's model resembles W. Fellner's well-known theorem of "uninterrupted growth (dynamic equilibrium),"[17] which stresses the need that the incremental (marginal) capital output ratio multiplied by the rate of increase in output equal the rate of net savings and, as a supplementary requirement, that relative scarcities of the various productive factors be properly adjusted to the investment-saving equality condition. Fellner, however, went beyond a mere growth model, by incorporating into his theory, as additional corollaries, more specific requirements (gradualness of structural changes corresponding to a feasible degree of mobility of resources, compatible institutional arrangements, and monetary-fiscal policies) designed to prevent and to correct structural and cyclical obstacles to uninterrupted growth with full employment.

[17] W. Fellner, *Trends and Cycles in Economic Activity* (New York: Henry Holt, 1956), especially Part III.

V

The foregoing review of some of the more outstanding theories and models of economic growth reveals that only one of them, the first truly modern theory of economic development of J. A. Schumpeter, is explicitly based on the innovating ability and initiative of man. Later models and theories, at their best, *imply* this central human factor (this is true of the theory of W. Fellner, in particular), and, at their worst, rely on assumed mechanical relationships of some selected macroeconomic variables.

In advanced Western economies, the qualitative human growth factor may perhaps be taken for granted, because it is there, at least potentially. But in the newly developing countries, no such a tacit assumption is warranted. Their economic development and growth hinge on the awakening and cultivation of the human factor in its broadest sense, as we have stressed in the main text of this book. That is why Schumpeter still has an important message to convey even today.

APPENDIX C-1: THE CONCEPT OF HUMAN CAPITAL

In his presidential address to the American Economic Association, at St. Louis, December 28, 1960, Theodore S. Schultz said that he had been impressed by

> expressed judgments . . . by those who have a responsibility in making capital available to poor countries, about the low rate at which these countries can absorb additional capital. . . . This experience is at variance with the widely held impression that countries are poor fundamentally because they are starved for capital and that additional capital is truly the key to their more rapid economic growth. The reconciliation is . . . to be found in emphasis on particular forms of capital. The new capital available to these countries . . . is generally not available for additional investment in man. Consequently human capabilities do become limiting factors in economic growth.[1]

Schultz's work on the relationship between education and economic growth has been outstanding, but others have also written on the subject. A number of writers have suggested the thesis that education is a crucial variable in economic development. Among them are J. Viner ("Investment in Human Capital and Personal Income Distribution," *The Journal of Political Economy*, August, 1958, pp. 281–302); H. Villard ("Some Comments on Growth," *The American Economic Review*, March, 1961, pp. 123–26); B. A. Weisbrod ("The Valuation of Human Capital," *The Journal of Political Economy*, October, 1961, pp. 425–36); B. Horvat ("The Optimum Rate of Investment," *The Economic Journal*, December, 1958, pp. 747–67).

A very interesting paper on the subject of the role of education in promoting economic development has been submitted by Professor John Vaizey of the University of London. This paper, titled "The Strategy of Educational Development in Relation to the Economic Growth of Underdeveloped Countries," was read and discussed at the OEEC in Washington, D.C., Policy Conference

[1] T. S. Schultz, "Investment in Human Capital," *The American Economic Review*, March, 1961, p. 7.

for Economic Growth and Investment in Education, October 16–20, 1961.[2] Professor Vaizey started his paper with the statement that "any study of economic development in the less-advanced countries inevitably focuses attention on their human resources."

There are two points in Vaizey's paper which seem worth mentioning. First, he said that education has "a direct effect on economic growth through the supply of skilled man power, and a subtle and pervading influence on such matters as the attitude toward progress adopted by society" (p. 3), and, secondly, that "the chief merit of education as a means of economic development lies in the fact that it does not make heavy demands on the scarcer resources. . . . In fact, education is probably one of the easiest forms of development which can be undertaken by a poor country" (p. 5).

The last point made by Professor Vaizey needs to be qualified. It is true that some education can be carried on without much capital investment. But the process of educating a people is a complex and lengthy one, and a thorough contemporary education is also very expensive in terms of buildings, equipment, salaries, and scholarships.

The entire issue of *The Journal of Political Economy*, Supplement: October, 1962, is dedicated to a systematic analytical and statistical investigation of the various forms of investment in "human capital." One surprising piece of evidence suggests that even in the United States, the most capital-using economy in the world, "the contribution of education to economic growth between 1929 and 1957 exceeded that of physical capital" (T. S. Schultz, *ibid.*, p. 5).[3] Professor Schultz, the keynoter of the special Supplement, further suggested that "economic capabilities of man are predominantly a produced means of production" and that "the structure of wages and salaries is primarily determined by investment in schooling, health, on-the-job training, searching for information about job opportunities, and by investment in migration" (*ibid.*, p. 2).

[2] OEEC (Organization for European Economic Cooperation) was since then reorganized into OECD (Organization for Economic Cooperation and Development) with added American and Canadian membership.

[3] See Appendix F-1 for the implications of education concerning human know-how and know-what as the ultimate sources of productivity.

APPENDIX C-2: AUTONOMY AND DEPENDENCE OF ECONOMIC ANALYSIS

The growing use of economic analysis for purposes of detection, clarification, and solution of social problems raises anew the old question of the degree of independence of economic analysis as a scientific discipline in relation to the disciplines dealing with the psychological, cultural, political, philosophical, and theological aspects of the same complex social reality with which economic analysis is concerned.

As a separate scholarly discipline, economics alone can deal only with the specific problem of efficient use of human and material resources for the fulfillment of a preordered multitude and variety of changing human aspirations, be they individual wants, voluntarily associated objectives, or politically shaped societal goals.

Recent extension of the scope of economic analysis into the problems of economic growth and development has made a reconsideration of the nature of economic analysis more necessary than ever. When economists are enlarging the dimensions of their field of study by including in their analytical structures such broad human variables as the growth of population, cultural patterns, sociological developments, and political changes, it becomes obvious that they are dealing with factors which *in themselves* constitute substantial extraeconomic problems of their own, whose analysis and solution may involve also philosophical and even theological considerations, in addition to sociological, political, legal, and other social science analyses.

Even within the narrower compounds of more traditional economic analysis, the need for greater awareness of psychological, political, and ethical implications of economic analysis has recently been dramatized. In his celebrated critique of "conventional" economic theory, Professor Galbraith unwittingly provided an outstanding example of what one could, with some exaggeration, call the fallacy of "paneconomics."[1] Because the traditional economic

[1] J. K. Galbraith, The *Affluent Society* (Boston: Houghton Mifflin, 1958). The felicitous terminological distinction between "panethics" and "paneconomics" was introduced by Professor Josef Solterer of Georgetown University in his article "Quadragesimo Anno: Schumpeter's Alternative to the Omnipotent State," *Review of Social Economy*, March, 1951, p. 13.

theory of demand broadly implied that human wants were essentially independent of production and tended systematically to outrun production possibilities, while in our contemporary economy production obviously does influence wants through advertising and emulation, Galbraith suggests the far-reaching theoretical conclusion that in an advanced market economy (affluent society) demand is largely based on production-contrived "wants" and production therefore runs ahead of "real" human wants.

Galbraith's conclusion may serve as an example of misplaced economic theorizing. Instead of explicitly staying on the ground of *cultural-ethical criticism of a given structure of total demand* (too many "private" goods vs. not enough "public" goods), Galbraith wrapped his cultural-ethical judgment about a given historical-geographical structure of demand in the veil of a *new economic theory of demand* (namely, that beyond an unspecified level of satisfaction of a similarly unspecified variety of basic needs, wants cease to be genuine and depend on production; analytically, this makes demand depend on supply).

Galbraith's sweeping conclusion is not empirically derived but presupposes a basic psychological proposition—that man is a psychological *tabula rasa*—which proposition, in turn, further presupposes a peculiar metaphysical position concerning man's rationality and will, which Galbraith did not make explicit.

In a sense, the pretentious fallacy of "paneconomics" is worse than the naive opposite fallacy of "panethics." In this era of emphasis on sciences, mere ethical assertions without firm analytical and empirical connection with the facts of experience have little chance of exerting undue intellectual influence; a "panethical" self-styled "economist" would simply disqualify himself as a bona fide economist. The fallacy of "paneconomics," on the other hand, is not so readily detectable, because it is couched in technical terms of economic analysis. While simple "panethical" circumvention of economic analysis is unthinkable in reputable economic literature, constant efforts of self-criticism and mutual criticism are necessary if fallacies of "paneconomics" are to be avoided.

II

Here are some examples of how fallacies of "paneconomics" can invade economic analysis and its conclusions:

1. In the *theory of demand,* one must be careful not to interfere with the structure of human aspirations (individual, voluntarily associated, politically shaped) on grounds of economic analysis alone.

There is much room for psychological, cultural, political, and ethical examination and evaluation of human aspirations; but such considerations must be justified primarily within the substantive and methodological framework of corresponding disciplines that deal with human ends as such. Economic analysis itself can only attempt to explain what economic effects are likely to follow from given, proposed, or expected changes in the complex social structure of human aspirations.

2. In the *theory of production and market structures,* care must be exercised not to confuse abstract analytical models of traditional economic theory with *real* situations, which increasingly involve additional psychological, sociological and political considerations. Furthermore, it should be quite obvious, for example, that the abstract model of pure (let alone perfect) competition cannot any longer be interpreted as constituting an empirically relevant (unqualifiedly sufficient) *welfare* criterion with respect to production and distribution.[2] In addition, as Professor Baumol has recently shown by rigorous analysis, there are serious psychological, sociological, and economic deficiencies in the simple traditional assumption of straight profit-maximization as the ultimate criterion of output and price behavior of larger firms.[3] Careful distinctions and a cautious attitude are necessary in this area of economic analysis where a major analytical revision of considerable ethical implications is under way.

3. In the analysis of actual or potential *public policies for economic stabilization and growth,* the extraeconomic aspects of different policies should be made more explicit than they are usually made to be. Even though various possible public policies (fiscal, monetary, structural, functional) differ in feasibility and effectiveness with respect to the *economic* problem at hand, it is still necessary to keep in mind, and to point out, that these same policies also differ in their *political* and *ethical* implications, which makes it necessary that their choice be based on political and ethical comparisons as well as on economic analysis.[4]

4. In the *theory of economic development,* the cultural, politi-

[2] This point has long been forcefully emphasized by E. H. Chamberlin, *The Theory of Monopolistic Competition* (6th ed.; London: Oxford University Press, 1949), pp. 214 ff., and *idem, Towards a More General Theory of Value* (New York: Oxford University Press, 1957), pp. 92 ff.

[3] W. J. Baumol, *Business Behavior, Value and Growth* (New York: The Macmillan Company, 1959).

[4] The U.N. report on *National and International Measures for Full Employment* (Lake Success, N.Y.: United Nations, 1949) is an example of "paneconomics" in relation to public-policy recommendations.

cal, and population variables should never be analytically treated as if they were merely instrumental factors for economic effects, but should on the contrary be first recognized as constituting eminent problems of their own. Birth control, for example, may conceivably be treated in some circumstances as a convenient means of economic development, but it remains primarily an *end subject* of its own.

The naive fallacy of "panethics" (or "panpolitics") virtually eliminates economics as an analytical discipline, thereby missing those necessary insights that can be reached only by means of economic analysis. The more surreptitious propensity toward "paneconomics," on the other hand, arrogantly disregards moral philosophy (and theology) and even other social sciences. Both fallacies are clearly antithetical to the scope of economics as a specific discipline inquiring into the *complex end-means relationships* with which a variety of intellectual disciplines are concerned.

III

Within this analytical framework, the academic status of economics is quite clear. As a science dealing with the complex social relationships between scarce means and human ends, economics touches theology and philosophy, as well as other social sciences, on the ends side of its subject. As long as human ends are duly respected by the economist as subjects beyond the analytical power and reach of economics (just as the technology of scarce means in themselves is not an integral part of economics), economic analysis is an autonomous logical discipline beyond interference by theology, moral philosophy, and other social sciences.

From these distinctions it follows with utmost clarity that there is only one strict philosophical prerequisite imposed on an economist: Ability and willingness *clearly to distinguish between ends and means* at every stage of economic analysis, even when various ends appear as means in the context of economic activity and its analysis. This requirement is in perfect accord with the professionally established specific scope of economic analysis, which is to examine *relationships* between scarce means and human ends, not to pass on the technology of means or on value of ends.[5]

[5] This systematic delimitation of the analytical scope of economics has been quite generally accepted since the publication in 1932 of Lionel Robbins' *An Essay on the Nature and Significance of Economic Science*.

This special sensitivity to the basic subject of human ends is due to the realization that there are disciplines, such as theology, philosophy and politics, which are dedicated to a *systematic* analysis and evaluation of the ends of human nature and its existence within a social and historical framework. Because of this systematic aspect of ends, an economist cannot academically ignore them and leave them to the extrarational "value judgments"[6] or cover them up with the analytical cloak of his special discipline ("paneconomics" or "pan" extension of any other particular social science).

Just as the technological aspect of scarce means does not make economic analysis a branch of technology, so the theological-philosophical-political aspect of human ends does not make economics a subdivision of theology and philosophy. In the purely analytical sense, there can be no "Christian" economics, for example.

And yet there *is* "Christian" economics in a meaningful sense. It transcends the mere ability and willingness of the economic analyst always to distinguish clearly between means and ends as a prerequisite for bona fide economic analysis, which must steer clear of the two fallacies of "panethics" and "paneconomics." Although this prerequisite is both necessary and sufficient for a purely economic analysis, it is still quite logical to expect at least some economists to use their proficiency in economic analysis in the service of human ends *as they are clarified by rigorous theological, philosophical, and political analyses*. A "Christian" or "Western" economist in this more substantive sense will not only always sharply distinguish the ends from the means, as every economist should, but will also want to gain deeper insights into human aspirations and corresponding institutions, whether actual or projected, so that his economic analysis can trace economic implications and requirements in accordance with a systematically *clarified* order of ends.

This more substantive meaning of "Christian" or "Western" economics, is in due accord with the analytical scope of economics. As a social science, economic analysis must accept or assume *some* system of human ends. Now, *any* set of ends always has *systematic* aspects to be clarified. An economist wants to be *familiar* with these aspects through his own philosophical and political understanding or, in more complex cases, in consultation and cooperation with professional experts on ends. A "Christian" economist, for example, will strive to put economic analysis in the service of human existential ends as understood by Christian theology and

[6] The very term "value judgment" connotes positivistic downgrading of the subject of human ends and implies a nonsystematic, extrarational approach to it.

analyzed by rigorous philosophy, in which the moral theory of human behavior as well as social ethics are based on *systematic theories* of essence, existence, and knowledge (metaphysics and epistemology).

IV

At this point, the question arises as to the broad Christian position on human existential ends—i.e., to what extent is this position fundamentally *theological* and therefore Christian in the true sense of the term, and to what an extent is it only *philosophical* and therefore universal.

It is often said that there is little or no theology in the traditional Christian position on the subject of human ends as they are pertinent to the temporal affairs of man and society. Christian position on the subject of human existential ends is said to be reducible to the concept of the natural law, which, by definition, is a matter of purely rational perception of human nature.[7] But this epistemological position may be misleading, unless two clarifying qualifications are added.

The understanding of the natural law prior to Christian revelation—in Greek philosophy and Roman jurisprudence—did not encompass the unambiguous notion of the immortal human soul in the likeness of a personal God and therefore essentially and unconditionally transcending everything else in the world. In its full meaning, this notion of man is Christian by *revelation* and therefore theological in the sense of *sacra doctrina*, not merely as a *philosophica disciplina*, to use Schumpeter's distinction.[8] And this *theological* notion of man appears *essential* for a firm derivation of the concept of a human person as a morally self-determining being that, in consequence of the revealed supernatural essence of his soul, must never be denied, by institutional arrangements in the temporal societal order of things, the fundamental moral freedom of the fullest possible choice.

Historically, the full elaboration and elucidation of the substantive concept of natural law was the product of Thomistic philosophy. This philosophy was not only a *post hoc* to Christian

[7] H. A. Rommen, *The State in Catholic Thought* (St. Louis: B. Herder Book Co., 1945); and J. Messner, *Social Ethics* (St. Louis: B. Herder Book Co., 1949), exemplify this position.

[8] J. A. Schumpeter, *History of Economic Analysis* (New York: Oxford University Press, 1954), p. 8.

revelation, but was *primarily* a rational instrument of the evolving system of theology, conceptualized in a systematic philosophical framework. Although the neo-Thomistic renaissance has been an attempt at separating St. Thomas's philosophy from his theology, and recent efforts by Christian philosophers are more and more oriented in the hopeful direction of reconciling the Thomistic philosophical tradition with the modern and contemporary philosophical currents, we must still admit that at the bottom of *all* Christian-inspired philosophy there is to be found at least the benefit of a sort of theological "hindsight." It is difficult, therefore, to avoid the conclusion that, even in a purely epistemological sense, the natural law cannot be *fully* perceived and *clearly* understood without some implied help from revelation and theology.[9]

This theological-philosophical concept of human nature leads to very specific fundamental principles of societal metaphysics and social ethics. In accordance with the revealed essence of the human soul, the observable and inferable society-oriented aspect of human nature is logically subordinated to the primary moral independence of each man as an individual person. Society is only a means for the well-being of the autonomous human person, because there is no such thing as a societal "soul" destined for eternal life.

It follows that the concept of the common good (general welfare, public good, etc.) must be understood in the sense that it transcends the particular good of a *particular* person only because it must serve the good of *all* persons that constitute the society, including, for some purposes, those of future generations. Substantively, the common good consists in the historical implementation of such a measure of societal arrangements as are clearly beneficial to the utmost development of the spiritual and intellectual potentialities of the human person, and in the participation in the benefits (opportunities) that flow from such societal arrangements in proportion to the various personal needs as they are conditioned by the differences in environmental conditions of human existence. Only *such* societal arrangements are justified in the light of the essential Christian concept of human nature.

Everyone can see, for example, why the institution of the family

[9] This would seem to follow also from Gilson's persistent emphasis on the theological intention and orientation of the philosophy of St. Thomas, and Gilson's insistence that for epistemological and pedagogical reasons philosophical instruction in Catholic colleges ought not to be sharply separated from theology. See E. Gilson, *The Christian Philosophy of the Middle Ages* (New York: The Macmillan Company, 1955), particularly p. 366 ff.; and A. Pegis, *A Gilson Reader* (New York: Doubleday, 1957).

is essential, not only for the development but for the very existence of the human person. Similarly, anybody understands that mere coexistence of, let alone mutual interactions among, a multitude and variety of persons of a geographical-historical area require a minimum of compulsory rules of behavior. But the question of how extensive these rules need be is not self-evident. It is precisely because of historical and geographical differences in the actual conditions of human existence and in the corresponding societal arrangements, that it is indeed essential to be clear about the fundamental principles concerning the human person and society, of the instrumental character of societal arrangements, and particularly of the *subsidiary* nature of compulsory societal rules, emanating from the institution of government. In the Christian view, the institution of government is indeed essential for human existence, but it is always an essentially *limited* institution. The concept of an *essentially* limited government was not clear enough to Aristotle or to other pre-Christian philosophers, precisely because they did not have the revealed Christian notion of the human soul.[10]

V

The basic principles of societal metaphysics and corresponding ethics, as they result from the theological notion of the human soul, are very pertinent for economic analysis. In analyzing the various aspects of an economic system, a theologically and philosophically conscious economist will clearly want to examine its institutions and operation in the light of societal metaphysics and social ethics. In formulating economic problems and suggesting future policies, such an economist will want to be satisfied that his criticism and proposals not only conform to the requirements of the economic functions with which his analysis is concerned, but that they are at the same time compatible with the principles of societal metaphysics and social ethics. Without correct economic analysis, his criticisms and proposals would be merely "panethical" assertions. On the other hand, economists who are not consciously and systematically aware of the principles of societal metaphysics and social ethics, will not make the needed contribution either; their findings and recommendations will tend to be "paneconomic" or they will be based on nonsystematic assumptions concerning societal metaphysics and social ethics.

[10] See Rommen, *op. cit.*, particularly pp. 26, 159, 161, 163, 309.

Developed societies and their economies, for example, are evolving in the general direction of diversified pluralism. This historical pattern generates several typical problems. There are systematic organized group pressures; there is a tendency to emulate the pressured attainments and objectives of the most aggressive group; individual persons see their status increasingly determined by their group membership, rather than by their personal needs and merits; governments are in danger of being cornered into the position of a political service-arm of group coalitions. Each of these basic problems of contemporary pluralistic societies has its economic aspects and counterparts. These must be analyzed, and solutions must be sought that not only do full justice to the economic functions involved but will also prevent or minimize major deviations from the basic principles of societal metaphysics and corresponding social ethics.

To reach solid conclusions on social problems, analytical contributions of a variety of disciplines are required. Although each of them is analytically autonomous, their analyses always overlap and their conclusions should dovetail, because they all deal with the various *aspects* of the same complex social *reality*. The place of theology and philosophy in such cooperation is determined by the fact that there are basic insights concerning human existence in the social framework where help is needed from professional theologians and philosophers, not to devise specific policies, for which their professional knowledge does not qualify them, but to help illuminate the underlying human situations in the light of the revealed and clarified essence of human nature. This has been the essential scope of papal social encyclicals, of which John XXIII's *Pacem in Terris* is the most comprehensive and illuminating example.

APPENDIX D-1: ECONOMIC STRUCTURE AND DEVELOPMENT OF COMMUNIST CHINA[1]

Although the Soviet Union and Communist China share many profound common characteristics, there are a number of basic differences in their respective economies. The most obvious of these arise from the wide disparity in their economic foundations, the different stages of the two societies with respect to economic growth, the dissimilarities in institutional structures, and the deviation in their current economic policies.

Communist China started her industrialization program on an economic foundation far less favorable than did the Soviet Union. Even in aggregate terms, Chinese pre-Communist industrial output lagged well behind that of Russia in 1913. If calculated on a per capita basis, the situation would be much worse, since China's population was four times as large as Russia's at that time.[2]

Both China and Russia had an agrarian economy before their Communist revolution, yet the pressure of population on land was less serious in Russia than in China. The density of population measured by the number of people per unit of cultivated land is extremely high in China. One estimate puts the number of acres of cultivated land per head of population in China at 0.45 as against 2.01 in Russia.[3] The vast tracts of unused land enable the Soviets to plough up millions of acres of virgin land within a very short period. But China has far less scope for expansion. Moreover, Russia possesses more fertile natural resources than China. The following data may serve to illustrate these differences:[4]

	Mainland China	*Soviet Union*
	(in million metric tons)	
Coal reserves	265,000	1,200,000
Iron ore reserves	2,504	10,900

[1] The author wishes to acknowledge the help he received from Mr. Cheng Chu-yuan in the preparation of this appendix.

[2] Wang Hai-chi, *Economy of New Democracy* (Shanghai, 1950), p. 6. In Chinese.

[3] A. K. Chiu, "Agriculture," in H. F. MacNair (ed.), *China* (Berkeley, Calif.: University of California Press, 1946), p. 468.

[4] W. W. Rostow, *The Prospects of Communist China* (New York: John Wiley, 1954), p. 261.

The problems of higher density of population, less cultivated land, smaller coal and iron reserves, as well as less development of basic industrial output, has made it more difficult for China than for the Soviet Union to become an industrial power.

In 1955, six years after the complete Communist takeover, Communist China was less developed than Lenin's Russia had been in 1921, to say nothing of Stalin's Russia of 1929, when the First Soviet Five-Year Plan was launched. The Soviet economy is a major industrial economy, capable of generating and sustaining a more or less regular rate of growth. Assuming that the Communist Chinese will be successful in engineering the decisive transition to self-sustaining growth, they will still be at least two generations behind the Soviet Union in terms of the growth process.[5]

Although there is an analogy between the Soviet situation in 1928 and the Chinese position in 1952, Rostow pointed out that the 1929 Soviet economy was more favorable than the Chinese economy in 1952 with respect to the following additional points:

1. The Soviet Union had a balance between population and food resources capable of sustaining the masses even in a period when agricultural investment was neglected and peasant productivity damaged by Soviet political and social policies.

2. The Soviet Union enjoyed substantial Tsarist investment in housing and transport, which permitted the regime to minimize its investment outlays in these directions.

3. The Soviet Union also enjoyed a sizable pre-Bolshevik scientific and technical potential not yet applied to industry, which made for abnormally large increase in output as the result of industrial investment.

4. The Soviet Union had a backlog of unexploited rich natural resources, making for the abnormally large increase in output as the result of investment in minerals and certain other natural resources.

In Rostow's conception, Stalin's era is economically to be defined as the phase when these advantages were exploited with ruthless energy to push the nation from the intermediate industrial status, achieved in the years 1890–1917, to its mature industrial status of 1954.[6]

[5] W. W. Rostow, A *Comparison of Russian and Chinese Societies Under Communism* (Cambridge, Mass.: Center for International Studies, MIT, 1959), p. 4.

[6] *Ibid.*, p. 7.

China started her industrialization with a bare agricultural balance and had no real or potential reserves as Russia had enjoyed. According to a comparison of China's 1952 economy with Russia's of 1928, China still was behind. Some basic data can serve as an indication. The rate of industrial growth of the Chinese First Five-Year Plan (1953–57) was somewhat less than that achieved by Russia in her First Five-Year Plan (1928–32). Even after the First Five-Year Plan, China is still far behind Russia's level of production achieved by 1932 after its First Five-Year Plan. More importantly, China's achievements of 1957 compared unfavorably to the Soviet level even before the latter's First Five-Year Plan was inaugurated.[7]

II

The different stages of the two societies with respect to economic growth partly explain also different structures in the economic institutions of these countries.

The Chinese economy, in its present stage, is still an agrarian economy wherein 80 per cent of the population are peasants. But in the Soviet Union, only 49 per cent of the population is engaged in agriculture. The Soviet Government nationalized all land from its first beginnings, and has organized its peasant households within the mechanization program into *kolkhozi* and *sovkhozi*. In 1959, the Soviet Union had 6,500 state farms and 60,000 collective farms with 890,000 tractors. Communist China, since 1958, has reorganized her 120,000,000 peasant households into 24,000 rural communes, which are much larger in size than the Soviet collective farms but still less mechanized in production. By the end of 1959, China had only 40,000 tractors. The land in China belongs to the individual communes rather than to the state. The rural commune, when it was initiated in 1958, appeared as a comprehensive, all-round, all-inclusive, socio-economic unit, which could be considered as the embryo of the Communist goal of distribution according to need. It showed strong intent to abolish all private ownership, as well as the family system. But after three years of experiments, the regime has made a series of retreats: the system has swung full circle to a return to the pre-1957 conditions when peasants were

[7] Yang Chien-pai: "A Comparative Analysis of China's First Five-Year Plan and the Soviet Union's First Five-Year Plan," in *T'ung-chi kung-tso tung-hsin* (*Statistical Work Bulletin*) (Peking, August, 1955). In Chinese.

allowed to till their private plots and resume family life.[8] This resembles the situation in Soviet *kolkhozi.*

Both countries are subject to a central-planning system, but in recent years, the Soviet system has provided more leeway for consumer choice. The existence of private plots and their continuous development has enabled the Soviet peasant to provide more products for a free market. In Communist China, the critical shortage of foodstuffs and cotton goods forced the government to adopt a strict rationing system, covering all important necessities. Begun in 1953, the rationing system is still confronted with a serious situation. The free market, in its real sense, has been eliminated in mainland China.

III

The basic long-run economic policy set by Chinese Communist leaders is to become industrially self-sufficient within the period of three five-year plans (or by 1967). To attain this goal, China has adopted a policy similar to that of the Soviet Union, which involves industrial development at the expense of agricultural development. But since their economic foundation is different, the Chinese one-sided industrialization program has set up its own vicious circle in the economic development and brought about a great chaos throughout the whole country.

To break this vicious circle, Communist China has, since 1958, advocated a series of new policies to convert its abundant man power into capital. The most important way is to mobilize the entire farm labor force to engage in capital projects. Every year, about 100 million peasants were assigned to work in large-scale water conservation and forestation projects. Small workshops with indigenous methods and home-made tools were erected everywhere throughout the whole country. This new tendency was in contrast to the capital-intensive project conducted in the Soviet Union aiming at higher automation and modernization.

Due to the critical scarcity of materials and capital, the current Chinese policy has more use for political control and ideological indoctrination as its motivating forces for economic growth. In the Soviet Union, Khrushchev has in recent years turned more to "capitalist" devices, such as material incentive and increased supplies of consumer goods to stimulate the Soviet farmers and workers. These

[8] Cheng Chu-yuan, "The Changing Pattern of Rural Communes in Communist China," in *Asian Survey,* November, 1961.

differences in practical behavior are largely the reflection of the different economic foundations and different stages of economic growth of these two Communist powers.

IV

Recent consecutive attempts in the Soviet Union to reorganize the administration of their centrally planned economy along the tricky and treacherous lines of "centralized decentralization" have resulted in a surprising organizational similarity between the Soviet and Chinese Communist economies: "the Russians, like the Chinese, have centralized 'decentralization' at party headquarters," said a *New York Times* editorial on November 27, 1962.[9]

[9] For a detailed examination of the Chinese economy since the Communist takeover, see Cheng Chu-yuan, *Communist China's Economy 1949–1962*, (Jersey City, N.J.: Seton Hall University Press, 1963).

APPENDIX D-2: ECONOMIC SYSTEM OF COMMUNIST YUGOSLAVIA

The Communist regime was imposed on Yugoslavia after World War II in consequence of the Teheran and Yalta agreements between the Western Allies and the Soviet Union. In the years following the imposition of Tito's regime, the Yugoslav economy was a copy of the Soviet economy—cultural, geographical, natural, political, and economic differences notwithstanding. Tito wanted to impress Stalin by making the Yugoslav regime and economy as Leninist-Stalinist as were the Soviet regime and economy.

Tito's ambitions to be second to Stalin in the Communist leadership and to be given full control over the Balkans had, however, upset the ever suspicious Stalin. Early in 1948, Stalin attacked Tito for insubordination and ordered his expulsion from the Cominform. The Yugoslav Communists, expelled from the Soviet bloc, had to turn to the West for trade, aid, and protection against possible Soviet attack.

The ensuing years have witnessed slow but steady changes in the organization of the Yugoslav economy. In 1962, the organizational structure of the Yugoslav economy appeared to be quite different from the Soviet and satellite economies. The course of events has led Tito to realize that it is possible to include certain Western traits into the economy without endangering the dominant role of the Communist Party (The League of Yugoslav Communists).

Starting from the basic constraints that the means of production must belong to the state and that the Party must retain its control over the direction of economic development, the Yugoslav Communists began to search for a new, more efficient organization of the economy. The result was the rise of a Yugoslav brand of "socialist" economy. Its basic characteristics are as follows.

The general economic plan (social plan) is imposed by the central government. It determines the volume of investment and its distribution among the various *sectors* of the economy. The banking system is asked to distribute these centrally determined funds among *firms* in each sector. In distributing these centrally determined funds, the banks, as a rule, give preference to the firms that offer the most promising projects for the utilization of investment funds.

The firm in Yugoslavia is free to determine the quality and quantity of output to be produced and is also, in general, free to charge any price within the lower limit determined by the costs of production and the upper limit determined by the government. The firm is supposed to be managed jointly by the Workers' Council and a director appointed by the local government. The Workers' Council consists of 15 to 120 employees, depending upon the size of the enterprise. They are elected by the workers of the firm for a two-year period. Workers are paid wages from the "profit" of the firms in which they work. "Profit" in Yugoslavia differs from the concept of profit in the West. It is the difference between the total revenue of the firm and its costs of production, excluding the wage bill. Thus, workers' incomes change from month to month as does the "profit" of the enterprise. Therefore, the Workers' Councils are expected to press for investment in the most profitable (demanded) products within each industry.

In summary, the Yugoslav Government has retained full control over the course of economic growth of the country. It definitely controls relative growth *of each* industry. However, the regime has tried to refrain from administrative interference with the utilization of resources *within each* industry. The expressed hope of the government is that once the distribution of funds between industrial sectors is determined in accordance with the government's scale of preferences, the inelastic supply of funds, as officially allocated to each sector, should be used in accordance with the private scales of preferences as expressed by voluntary demands in the corresponding product markets.

To what extent this organizational structure of the Yugoslav economy is operative and effective depends on the answer to the following empirical questions:

1. To what extent are Yugoslav banks capable of assessing relative profitabilities of competitive investment projects by individual firms, and how well do they resist political and private pressures, influence-peddling, and briberies?

2. How effective and how efficient is the division of the managerial functions between the Workers' Council and the director of the firm?

3. Are directors of firms appointed in a genuinely open contest on the basis of their technical and managerial qualifications, or are they selected primarily by the political criterion of their relation-

ship with the Communist Party? Do they take orders from the Party?

4. Are Workers' Councils capable of efficient managerial decisions, and how well do they resist improper pressures from inside and outside the firm? How do they get along with the director?

5. How genuine are the nominations and elections of the members of Workers' Councils? Are nominations and elections just a smoke screen for Communist Party manipulations, as in U.S.S.R.?

Only a systematic investigation at the grass roots of the Yugoslav economic system could provide dependable answers to these empirical questions.[1]

There is another problem, both economic and political, which Yugoslavia faces. Constitutionally, Yugoslavia is a federation of six republics, each of which has great differences in nationalities, history, culture, and economic development. In fact, the northwestern republics, notably Slovenia, which had been associated with Western Europe throughout their history until World War I, have since been systematically exploited in favor of the southern republics with which they have little or no affinity. Can such a federal union be maintained under conditions of increasing economic and political self-determination? Will not Slovenia, which covers the immediate hinterland of Trieste, be increasingly attracted by the adjoining European community? To prevent such an attraction to the West, Yugoslavia will have to cease discriminating against its advanced northwestern republics. Here, then, is another powerful factor that will influence the future of the new economic and political system in Yugoslavia.

[1] For a systematic examination of the Communist economic system in Yugoslavia, see Svetozar Pejovich's unpublished doctoral dissertation, *Economic Systems and Development: The Case of Yugoslavia*, Georgetown University, Washington, D.C., 1962.

APPENDIX E-1: SELECTED BIBLIOGRAPHY ON INFLATION

Books

The American Assembly. *United States Monetary Policy*. New York: Columbia University Press, 1958.

The American Assembly. *Wages, Prices, Profits, and Productivity*. New York: Columbia University Press, 1958.

BACH, G. L. *Inflation, A Study in Economics, Ethics, and Politics*. Providence, R.I.: Brown University Press, 1958.

BOMBACH, GOTTFRIED (ed.). *Stabile Preise in wachsender Wirtschaft*. Tuebingen: J. C. B. Mohr, 1960.

BURNS, ARTHUR F. *Prosperity Without Inflation*. New York: Fordham University Press, 1957.

CHAMBERLIN, EDWARD H. *The Economic Analysis of Labor Union Power*. Washington, D.C.: American Enterprise Association, 1958.

FELLNER, WILLIAM, *et al. The Problem of Rising Prices*. Paris: OEEC, 1961.

FRIEDMAN, MILTON (ed.). *Studies in the Quantity Theory of Money*. Chicago: University of Chicago Press, 1956.

HABERLER, GOTTFRIED. *Inflation, Its Causes and Cures*. Washington, D.C.: American Enterprise Association, 1960.

HANSEN, ALVIN H. *Economic Policy and Full Employment*. New York: McGraw-Hill, 1947.

HANSEN, BENT. *Inflation Problems in Small Countries*. Cairo: National Bank of Egypt, 1960.

HARROD, ROY. *Policy Against Inflation*. New York: St Martin's Press, 1958.

KAPLAN, A. D. H., DIRLAM, JOEL B., and LANZILLOTTI, ROBERT F. *Pricing in Big Business*. Washington, D.C.: The Brookings Institution, 1958.

MEADE, J. E. *The Control of Inflation*. Cambridge, Mass.: Cambridge University Press, 1958.

MEANS, GARDINER. *Administrative Inflation and Public Policy*. Washington, D.C.: Anderson Kramer Associates, 1959.

Moulton, Harold. *Can Inflation Be Controlled?* Washington, D.C.: Anderson Kramer Associates, 1958.

OECD. *Policies for Price Stability*. Paris: 1962.

Paish, F. W. *Studies in an Inflationary Economy, The United Kingdom, 1948–1961*. London: Macmillan Co., 1962.

Slichter, Sumner H. *The American Economy, Its Problems and Prospects*. New York: Alfred A. Knopf, 1948.

Thorp, William L., and Quandt, Richard. *The New Inflation*. New York: McGraw-Hill, 1959.

Weintraub, Sidney. *A General Theory of the Price Level, Output, Income Distribution and Economic Growth*. Philadelphia: Chilton, 1959.

Wilson, Thomas. *Inflation*. Cambridge, Mass.: Harvard University Press, 1961.

Articles

Alhadeff, D. "Credit Controls and Financial Intermediaries," *The American Economic Review*, September, 1960.

Bowen, W. "Cost Inflation vs. Demand Inflation," *Southern Economic Journal*, January, 1960.

Bronfenbrenner, M., and Holzman, F. D. "Survey of Inflation Theory," *The American Economic Review*, September, 1963. (With an extensive bibliography.)

Chandler, L. "The Impact of Low Interest Rates on the Economy," *Journal of Finance*, June, 1951.

"Creeping Inflation," *Monthly Review, Federal Reserve Bank of New York*, June, 1959.

Galbraith, J. K. "Market Structure and Stabilization Policy," *Review of Economics and Statistics*, May, 1957.

Gallaway, L. "The Wage Push Inflation Thesis," 1950–57, *The American Economic Review*, December, 1958.

Gavy, G. "Structural Aspects of Money Velocity," *The Quarterly Journal of Economics*, February, 1959.

"Growth Without Inflation in Britain," *Monthly Review, Federal Reserve Bank of New York*, July, 1959.

Holzman, F. "Inflation: Cost Push and Demand Pull," *The American Economic Review*, March, 1960.

"Inflation and Economic Development," *Monthly Review, Federal Reserve Bank of New York*, August, 1959.

Kessel, R., and Alchian, A. "The Meaning of the Inflation-Induced Lag of Wages Behind Prices," *The American Economic Review*, March, 1960.

KESSEL, R., and ALCHIAN, A. "Effects of Inflation," *Journal of Political Economy*, December, 1962.

LANZILLOTTI, R. "Price Objectives in Large Companies," *The American Economic Review*, December, 1958.

LERNER, A. "On Generalizing the General Theory," *The American Economic Review*, March, 1960.

MACHLUP, F. "Another View of Cost-Push and Demand-Pull Inflation," *Review of Economics and Statistics*, May, 1960.

MACK, R. "Inflation and Quasi-Elective Changes in Costs," *Review of Economics and Statistics*, August, 1959.

MARGET, A. "Inflation: Some Lessons of Recent Foreign Experience," *The American Economic Review*, May, 1960.

PESEK, B. "A Comparison of the Distributional Effects of Inflation and Taxation," *The American Economic Review*, March, 1960.

PHILIPS, A. W. "Employment, Inflation, Growth," *Economics*, February, 1962.

SAMUELSON, P., and SOLOW, R. M. "Analytical Aspects of Anti-Inflation Policy," *The American Economic Review*, May, 1960.

SEERS, DUDLEY. "A Theory of Inflation and Growth in Under-Developed Economies, Based on the Experience of Latin America," *Oxford Economic Papers*, June, 1962.

SELDEN, R. "Cost Push vs. Demand Pull Inflation," *Journal of Political Economy*, February, 1959.

SINGH, MANMOHAN. "Monetary Policy in an Inflationary Economy: A Case Study of the British Experience, 1951–57," *The Indian Economic Journal*, VII, 1959–60.

SLICHTER, S. "Wage-Price Policy and Employment," *The American Economic Review*, May, 1946.

SMITH, W. "The Discount Rate as a Credit Control Weapon," *Journal of Political Economy*, April, 1958.

SMITH, W. "Financial Intermediaries and Monetary Controls," *The Quarterly Journal of Economics*, November, 1959.

SOLO, R. "A Comparison of the Distributional Effects of a Mixed Economy," *The Canadian Journal of Economics and Political Science*, November, 1959.

STERDY, A. "A Note on Interest Rates and Demand for Money," *Review of Economics and Statistics*, March, 1959.

WOLOZIN, H. Inflation and Price Mechanism," *Journal of Political Economy*, April, 1958.

Zebot, C. "Toward an Integrated Theory of Inflation in the United States," *Weltwirtschaftliches Archiv*, December, 1961.

Congressional Studies

Administered Prices: A Compendium on Public Policy, Subcommittee on Antitrust and Monopoly of the Committee on Judiciary, U.S. Senate, 1963.

Administered Prices, Hearings, Subcommittee on Antitrust and Monopoly of the Committee on Judiciary, U.S. Senate, 1957–59.

Eckstein, O., and Fromm, G. *Steel and the Post-War Inflation*, Study Paper No. 2, Joint Economic Committee, 1959.

Employment, Growth, and Price Levels, Hearings, Joint Economic Committee, 1959.

Government Price Statistics, Hearings, Joint Economic Committee, 1961.

Harris, S. *The Incidence of Inflation or Who Gets Hurt?*, Study Paper No. 7, Joint Economic Committee, 1959.

Houthankker, H. *Protection Against Inflation*, Study Paper No. 8, Joint Economic Committee, 1959.

Kuh, E. *Profit Markups and Productivity*, Study Paper No. 15, Joint Economic Committee, 1959.

Leiserson, M. *A Brief Interpretive Survey of Wage-Price Problems in Europe*, Study Paper No. 11, Joint Economic Committee, 1959.

Redford, E. *Potential Public Policies to Deal With Inflation Caused by Market Power*, Study Paper No. 10, Joint Economic Committee, 1959.

Schultze, C. *Recent Inflation in the United States*, Study Paper No. 1, Joint Economic Committee, 1959.

Schultze, C., and Tryon, J. *Prices and Costs on Manufacturing Industries*, Study Paper No. 17, Joint Economic Committee, 1959.

Wilson, T. *An Analysis of the Inflation in Machinery Prices*. Study Paper No. 3, Joint Economic Committee, 1959.

APPENDIX F-1: PRODUCTIVITY CONCEPTS AND MEASUREMENTS

In terms of the frequency of its current use, both scholarly and popular, the concept of productivity is second only to the concept of economic growth. It is one of those terms which is used without much concern about its precise meaning. What does productivity really mean? The general idea is simple enough. What we are after is some indicator as to how successful we are in economizing the scarce means, including man's own effort and time, for the satisfaction of our growing needs and wants.

This preliminary clarification of the concept of productivity immediately raises the crucial point. Since man's creativity is not miraculous in a supernatural sense, *improvements in productivity* are limited to the sphere of *substitution*. Analytically, two types of substitution may be distinguished. Substitution of inputs that are becoming relatively less scarce for those getting scarcer, and of more "creating" inputs for less "creating" ones. The effectiveness with which an economy keeps substituting resources in accord with their changing relative scarcities depends on how various markets and other allocative mechanisms register changing scarcities, and how technology keeps adapting relatively more abundant resources for new productive uses. Substitution of more "creating" inputs for less "creating" ones, on the other hand, is even more dependent on the pace of quality improvements. This is the main form of increasing productivity.

II

There is one "input" which differs essentially from all the others in its impact on productivity. This is the unembodied human know-what and know-how from which all improvements ultimately spring. *Scientific discoveries* about the working of physical and human nature *and their inventive applications* to physical and organizational technology may be very scarce as to their origin; they are always scarce also as to their "numbers." However, any particular discovery or invention, *once made,* ceases to be scarce unless its scarcity is deliberately and effectively contrived. Thus, *existing* discoveries and inventions become *free agents* capable of enhancing existing productivities in various segments of the economy.

This peculiar nonscarcity condition is not strictly universal, of course. In addition to various forms and degrees of contrived scarcities of existing discoveries and inventions, there are *two* further *limitations* of their nonscarcity aspect. Scientific discoveries and applicable inventions cannot be assimilated by just anybody, but only by those who have sufficiently mastered the corresponding disciplines to be capable of receptive assimilation of their findings. Assimilation of inventive applications has also another limitation. Their use as effective inputs often presupposes complex and costly physical investments.

Except for these limitations, however, it is true that the existing human know-what and know-how are by their very nature free goods available to all takers. Evolving human know-what and know-how are thus the mainspring of increasing "creativity" in the productive processes: Productivity improvements are ultimately reducible to human know-what and know-how. This conclusion indicates the problem of how productivity is to be measured.

If all the inputs were tangible and measurable in correct value terms, and if there were no inputs with zero value (price), the "total factor productivity"[1] formula (output/inputs ratio) would then yield unity value by definition ($O/I = 1$). The formula yields higher values either because some of the measurable inputs are left out or because inputs are undervalued or output overvalued or, finally, because there are intangible "inputs" which are not fully reducible to economic value terms (prices) because they are at least partly free goods. This is precisely and exclusively the *residual* aspect of the human know-what and know-how.

[1] The term "total factor productivity" is used by J. W. Kendrick (*Productivity Trends in the United States,* National Bureau of Economic Research, Number 71, General Series, 1961) to denote the productivity concept which includes all measurable inputs. However, Kendrick's "total factor productivity" measure relates output to direct labor and capital inputs only. For a provocative as well as systematic examination of the concept and measurement of productivity antedating the recent comprehensive study by J. W. Kendrick, see I. H. Siegel, *Concept and Measurement of Productivity,* Bureau of Labor Statistics, U.S. Department of Labor, 1952, and *idem,* "Conditions of American Technological Progress," *The American Economic Review,* May, 1954, p. 177.

III

On this conceptual basis, what would be the corresponding productivity measure? If one is to measure progressive improvements in man's ability to produce more per unit of productive effort and scarce resources used, the productivity measure would have to be the ratio of output to *all* the scarce things and services contributing to production *except* for the intangible and free human know-what and know-how, the increase in which such a complete productivity measure would then exclusively and exactly reflect.

However, just as there is no perfect price-level index, so there is no perfect productivity yardstick. Government productivity statistics are still based on the output-per-manhour measure, which relates output to the direct labor input alone. A great step forward in approximating a truer productivity measure has been made with the publication of J. W. Kendrick's recent work on productivity.[2] This study represents an attempt at both conceptual clarification and statistical computation of alternative productivity measures. Kendrick has added to the usual labor-productivity yardstick a separate capital-productivity measure, and has developed a combined labor-capital productivity formula.

One could misinterpret Kendrick's reasoning to the effect that productivity analysis is concerned with *physical* volumes of output and input. But Kendrick's output and input measures are economic *value-quantities* because "relative prices are necessary to aggregation."[3] Now, prices are indices (however imperfect) of relative scarcities of the goods that are so priced. And scarcity in its economic significance is fundamentally the ratio of human needs and aspirations to the available supply of things and services capable of producing the corresponding goods. This ratio cannot be measured without resorting to meaningful prices as effective exchange values in terms of money. It is for this conceptual reason that a meaningful measure of productivity can emerge only from comparing the economic value of output with the economic value of the corresponding inputs, both subject to familiar, although unfortunately rather arbitrary, corrections for price-level changes.[4]

[2] Kendrick, *op. cit.*

[3] *Ibid.*, p. 9.

[4] Because the concept of productivity requires for its measurement economic value comparisons, it is truly coextensive with the notion of "productive efficiency," which Kendrick relates to market structures. *Ibid.*, p. 18.

IV

Since Kendrick's broadened productivity measure is still limited to direct labor and capital inputs only, the term "total factor productivity" is not a truly descriptive one. Clearly, between measurable labor and capital inputs in Kendrick's sense, and the unembodied ultimate human know-what and know-how in the sense of this appendix, there must be other scarce and contributing inputs that, no matter how difficult to measure, may yet be susceptible to being singled out with sufficient precision to establish a basis for their measurability in value terms. Organizational factors, both private and public, that are observably institutionalized and contributive to the nation's productive performance, come to mind as subjects for further analytical and statistical enlargement of the productivity concept and measurement. Even if some of these additional factors may not be susceptible to being imputed as measurable inputs to individual firms and industries, they should at least be added as *macro*-inputs when the productivity of the economy *as a whole* is being assessed.[5]

Since human economic progress ultimately hinges on the widening of human know-what and know-how, efforts toward a fuller "total factor productivity" measure should aim at as complete as possible an enumeration of all the additive inputs, private as well as public (collective). Only then will the resulting productivity value, on the right-hand side of the equation, approximate an index of human productive "creativity," which is a residual function of the degree of accumulation of the ultimate, unembodied know-what and know-how as the truly creative *free* agents in the service of production.

Such a comprehensive productivity yardstick would be most useful for the newly developing countries. The yardstick would focus directly on their fundamental development problem, thus stimulating their efforts toward a systematic increase of widespread know-what and know-how as the mainspring of their economic betterment.

For purposes of a wage and price policy consistent with noninfla-

[5] The July–August, 1963, issue of *Business in Brief* (No. 51, pp. 6–7) of the Chase Manhattan Bank summarizes from recent studies of the productivity concept its following constituent (contributing) elements (in addition to the quantities of labor and capital): More efficient use of materials, economies of scale, better allocation of labor and capital, formal education, on-the-job training, intensity of work, and, as the residual catchall, "the quality of capital and other factors."

tionary economic growth along the full-employment path of industrially advanced Western economies, a combined labor-capital productivity measure is the appropriate one, provided that "labor" and "capital" inputs are valued in prices that reflect all the costs of production, including all taxes. In other words, labor and capital can appropriate the entire productive income of the society only if they pay for all the associated productive services and for all the nonmarketable public services the society wishes to have.

APPENDIX F-2: INDIVIDUALISM AND PLURALISM

The insight which we have today in the philosophical, sociological, political, and economic background of Galbraith's concept of "countervailing powers" is due largely to the work of Professor G. Briefs of Georgetown University.[1] Briefs made a general analysis of the nature of pluralism and came to the conclusion that pluralism represents the second stage of individualistic liberalism. This conclusion stems from Briefs's analysis of the basic tenets of individualistic liberalism, which he lists as follows: self-determination, self-responsibility, self-interest, and competition. Pluralistic groups, Professor Briefs finds, have accepted these same principles in their own associated behavior.

Once he arrived at this conclusion, Professor Briefs had to ask himself: Why did the individualistic society of the nineteenth century evolve into the pluralistic society of today?

The causality of these changes Professor Briefs saw in the people's behavior at the lowest margin of ethics. He called it "marginal ethos," meaning by that the existential embodiment of ethical principles and attitudes.[2] He said that the error of the British classical system was in its assumption of a *constant* marginal ethos. For, once people are told and taught to follow their self-interest through competition, their social and economic power being unequal, the marginal ethos is bound to *decline*. Those who get hurt in the process will realize that they should organize in order to increase their social and economic power to influence the course of events. In that way, the first labor unions and business associations were born.[3]

[1] The starting point in Professor G. Briefs's thesis, which he fully developed in subsequent years, is his article "The Roots of Totalism," published in *Thought*, March, 1944.

[2] See G. Briefs, "The Ethos Problem in the Present Pluralistic Society," *Review of Social Economy*, March, 1957.

[3] The rise of business associations is analyzed by Professor Briefs in his article "Cartels, Realism or Escapism" in the *Review of Politics*, January, 1946. The rise of trade unions he analyzed in his monograph *Unionism Reappraised* (Washington, D.C.: The American Enterprise Association, 1960).

Once these pluralistic groups are well established, they themselves accept the four basic tenets of classical liberalism; and, being in competition with each other and having no "invisible hand" around to guarantee the equality of power, the marginal ethos, whose decline individuals hoped to reverse by organizing themselves, will be once again exposed to submarginal pressure. Thus it would not be too long before the government would have to step in, not only to regulate the social and economic life, but to participate actively in shaping its outcome. Once this happens, whatever the intentions, the power of the government will tend to increase, leading possibly to a complete government control either in the name of one or some of the groups as their political arm, or by virtue of its own strength.

The transference of the original canons of the traditional individualism to the contemporary group-pluralism of Western societies, has been exemplified in the controversy about the former Labor Secretary Arthur Goldberg's "Chicago Speech." In an address to the Executives' Club in Chicago, on February 23, 1962, Secretary Goldberg made the following statement:[4]

> The government must have better responsibility in the areas of collective bargaining. I do not mean by this that the government should dictate terms of settlement or impose them, because I don't think a third party can provide the answer to the decision the parties should make. That is why I am against compulsory arbitration as a general principle. . . . I think government has the obligation to define the national interest and assert it when it reaches important proportions in any area of our economy . . . is not an easy program because what we are saying to private groups is that you have a responsibility, a public responsibility, that no longer can this be resolved just on a clash of self-interest. That the clash of self-interest which is still necessary must be accompanied by a sense of public interest.

Spokesmen for both organized labor and business registered similar disagreements with Goldberg's position.[5] One rather typical view, expressed by "a source close to the steel industry,"[6] was very characteristic of the unchanged individualistic philosophy of contemporary economic groups: "From a broad philosophical viewpoint, most businessmen feel that in a competitive system you

[4] Quoted from the U.S. Labor Department's news release on the subject, February 23, 1962, pp. 14–15.

[5] See reports on various reactions to Secretary Goldberg's views in *The New York Times*, February 27–28, and March 1, 1962.

[6] *Ibid.*, February 28, p. 19.

serve the national interest in pursuing your private interest.[7] Organized labor's version of the argument usually emphasizes "freedom of collective bargaining."

Another business spokesman, T. L. Block, Chairman of the Inland Steel Company, on the other hand, supported Secretary Goldberg's position. "I heartily endorse Mr. Goldberg's concept," said Block. "It is the Government's function to elucidate the national objectives. . . . Those guidelines should be taken into account in collective bargaining. . . . Each side has to represent its own interest, but neither side must be unmindful of the needs of the nation. Who else can point out those needs but the government?"

Block's view was clearly still a minority position. It will be only when this evolving philosophy becomes widely shared by both business and labor that contemporary group pluralism will have overcome its individualistic legacy, thereby eliminating the danger that Briefs pointed out.

[7] *Ibid.*

APPENDIX F-3: NATURE OF EXCESSIVE UNEMPLOYMENT SINCE 1957[1]

Two essentially distinct theories have been advanced purporting to explain the pattern of unemployment experience since 1957. On one side are the proponents of insufficient-aggregate-demand theories; on the other are those seeking to explain the recent high levels of unemployment by citing significant structural changes that have occurred in the economy during this period. Others occupy a position somewhere between these two points of view. Before setting out the fundamental theoretical properties of each view, a summary of the employment, unemployment, and labor-force experience since 1957 is in order.

Since 1957, employment has increased an average of only 0.9 per cent per year, while the labor force has grown at an average of approximately 1.04 per cent per year. Occupations such as farmers and farm laborers, craftsmen and foremen, operatives, and laborers, except farm and mine, experienced an absolute decrease in employment since 1957. The decline in employment in these unskilled and semiskilled occupations was more than offset by increases in skilled, professional, and service occupations. Nevertheless, not only has employment declined in the unskilled and semiskilled occupations, but unemployment rates in these occupations have increased both absolutely and relatively.[2] Unemployment has increased markedly in certain durable goods industries, in transportation, construction, and mining. The over-all rate of unemployment has averaged 6.0 per cent or more for each year for the past six years.

After each of the three business cycles since 1951, the unemployment rate reached progressively higher levels. The unemployment rate of the 1951–53 recovery period was 3.1 per cent, it increased to 4.3 per cent in the 1955–57 period, and went to 5.5 per cent in the recovery year, 1962; it was 5.9 per cent in November 1963. Furthermore, between 1957 and 1962, long-term unemployment (fifteen weeks or over) increased by 100 per cent, and unemployment last-

[1] The author wishes to acknowledge the assistance of Mr. Richard Lurito in the preparation of this appendix.

[2] U.S. Department of Labor, *Manpower Report of the President* and *A Report on Manpower Requirements, Resources, Utilization, and Training* (Washington, D.C.: March, 1963), p. 11.

ing six months or longer increased by nearly 150 per cent. Given this unemployment background, the two theories mentioned were advanced to explain the rising levels of unemployment.[3]

Both the insufficient-aggregate-demand and structural-change theories recognize that a certain rate of unemployment is generated by "frictional" factors. Frictional unemployment results from the seasonal nature of work in many occupations, changes in the composition of final demand, technological change, migration of industry, and freedom of workers to change jobs and to enter and leave the labor market. However, it is agreed that the high rates of unemployment since 1957 cannot be attributed solely to these frictional factors.

Although there exist variations in the theoretical properties of insufficient-aggregate-demand explanations of recent unemployment experience, at the heart of such theories is the contention that the high levels of unemployment since 1957 are explainable by traditional supply-and-demand analysis. Unemployment, it is argued, is high because the rate of growth of final demand has been low relative to the actual and normal rate of growth of potential supply made possible by increases in capital stock, human capital, labor force, and productivity. The insufficient-aggregate-demand theory views employment and, given the labor force, unemployment as variables dependent upon the level of national income. The problem of high unemployment can be alleviated by implementing policy measures designed to increase the rate of growth of the aggregate final demand and, in turn, the rate of growth of national income.[4]

Given this point of view, it is not surprising that the major policy remedy advanced to relieve the problem of unemployment should be a downward revision in the tax-rate structure for individuals and corporations. In the 1963 Economic Report of the President, it is argued that such a tax revision would "enlarge markets for consumer goods and services and translate these into new jobs, fuller work schedules, higher profits, and rising farm incomes. . . ."[5]

[3] *Ibid.*, p. 3. For a systematic survey of statistical and theoretical aspects of U.S. employment problems, see *Hearings, Measuring Employment and Unemployment* (Washington, D.C.: Joint Economic Committee, Congress of the U.S., 1963).

[4] See *Higher Unemployment Rates, 1957–60: Structural Transformation or Inadequate Demand* (prepared by the staff of the Joint Economic Committee), November, 1961.

[5] p. xv.

II

Opposing the insufficient-aggregate-demand theory are the views of those seeking to explain the recent high levels of unemployment by isolating certain structural changes that have taken place in the economy. However, the views held by proponents of structural-change theories are not nearly so homogeneous as those held by advocates of insufficient-aggregate-demand theories. This may explain why structural-change theories have gained less currency than the opposing views. The general view of one segment of those supporting the structural-change position can be summarized as follows: Unemployment, since 1957, has remained at high levels in the face of sufficient over-all final demand forces. The factors which explain the high levels of unemployment are: (1) acceleration in technological change, (2) the adversely changing impact of technological advances on the demand for unskilled and semi-skilled workers, and (3) the declining mobility of labor. Studies have been made aimed at demonstrating that these structural factors do not, in fact, explain the unemployment experience since 1957.[6] Whether the tests used to isolate the assumed effects on unemployment are statistically or conceptually valid is moot; the controversy in this area continues.

Another variant of the structural-change hypothesis has been advanced by Clarence Long. This view of recent high levels of unemployment turns around the concept of "hard-core" unemployment. Hard-core unemployment is that type of unemployment that is difficult to eliminate by customary economic measures. It consists of (1) structural-geographical unemployment, and (2) institutional unemployment.

Structural-geographical unemployment may be defined as unemployment resulting from "deep-seated and relatively permanent changes in the quality and location of the demand for and supply of labor."[7]

The two most incisive studies of structural-geographical unemployment are by Clarence Long[8] and the Bureau of Labor Statistics.[9] Professor Long argues that the lack of labor mobility in "de-

[6] See *Higher Unemployment Rates, op. cit.*

[7] See *Unemployment: Terminology, Measurement, and Analysis* (Washington, D.C.: Subcommittee on Economic Statistics of the Joint Economic Committee, Congress of the United States, 1961), p. 81.

[8] C. Long, "A Theory of Creeping Unemployment and Labor Force Replacement," *Review of Social Economy*, March, 1961.

[9] Study Paper No. 23, on the *Structure of Unemployment in Areas of Sub-*

pressed areas" is evidence of structural-geographical unemployment. Two basic causes of labor immobility are cited: (1) the lack of adequate skill, which prevents the unemployed workers in declining industries from migrating in search of other jobs, and (2) the relatively high wages in their existing trades. To quote Professor Long, "high hourly and daily wages make it possible for coal miners to stay on in mining industries as long as they can get one or two days of work a week."[10]

The paper prepared by the Bureau of Labor Statistics gives the following data concerning structural-geographical unemployment. First, unemployment in depressed areas "accounted for 1.1 million or nearly one third of total unemployment in the Spring, 1959,"[11] and, second, 45 per cent of unemployment in the depressed areas were adult men between twenty-five and sixty-four—in other words, the heads of families. Third, unemployment in depressed areas accounted for more than 40 per cent of the very long-term unemployment (over one-half year) in the country. Fourth, the paper lists fifty-eight "depressed areas" like Charleston in West Virginia, Joliet in Illinois, Scranton in Pennsylvania, etc.

Institutional unemployment is the second type of hard-core unemployment. An analytical explanation of this type of unemployment has also been dealt with in Professor Long's paper. His explanation amounts to the following. The legal and/or social minimum wage is higher than the productivity of certain groups of unskilled workers. Hence, the possibility of their employment does not depend on the customary economic measures but on their learning new or improving existing skills. In other words, those workers whose productivity lags behind the minimum wage cannot be employed in the short run.

The insufficient-aggregate-demand theorists counter by maintaining that postwar unemployment has been due to the unavailability of jobs. They admit that labor-market frictions exist, but maintain that such frictions can be reduced by public and private policies aimed at the development of new skills among displaced workers.[12] In this area, however, disagreement is reduced to terminological differences. The character of basic remedies appears to be rather similar in both views.

---

stantial Labor Surplus, prepared by the Bureau of Labor Statistics, Department of Labor, for the Joint Economic Committee, January, 1960.

[10] *Ibid.*, p. 15.

[11] *Ibid.*, p. 61.

[12] See *Higher Unemployment Rates*, especially pp. 77–79.

Still another structural change hypothesis has been advanced.[13] The essence of this view is that the factors which impede or stimulate economic growth have an "independent" existence; they are not simply dependent upon functions of other economic variables. This is in sharp contrast with the national-income approach, in which the level and rate of growth of income are functionally related to and interrelated with the level and rate of change in investment and consumption. In this scheme, employment and, given the labor force, unemployment are simply a result of the level and rate of change of income.

The alternate hypothesis focuses attention on the investment variable, and in particular on that part of it which can be considered as "autonomous." Autonomous investment is independent of economic parameters, at least in the shorter run, and is not likely to be steady—that is, to proceed at an even pace. Innovations and related adjustments often "cluster" in time and create the need for rearrangements and/or changes in the economic pattern hitherto followed. The level and rate of change of national income, therefore, cannot be presumed to be steady or even. From this point of view, it is not possible that national income can be made to grow steadily at about the rate at which the labor force grows. This is because the character and rate of autonomous investment produces structural changes that often cannot be assimilated quickly or easily into the economic system. Structural changes, in turn, may result in rising levels of unemployment. At the same time, institutional rigidities affecting the labor force may be one of the handicaps that hold down autonomous investment, or investment generally.

In the alternate scheme, then, the two key forces behind the level and rate of growth of national income are the rate and character of autonomous investment and the length of time needed for the economy to adjust to the rate and character of autonomous investment.

The character of autonomous investment may pose problems requiring a considerable degree of physical and entrepreneurial skills. These skills may or may not be available when and where they are needed. More significantly, the character of autonomous investment may involve technological change resulting in shifts in the composition of the employment mix. Such shifts are seen in the

[13] See Henry W. Briefs and Joseph L. Tryon, "U.S. Economic Growth: Issues and Prospects," in *National Security: Political, Military, and Economic Strategies in the Decade Ahead* (New York: Frederick A. Praeger, 1963), pp. 833–73.

decreasing demand for the kind of unskilled and semiskilled occupations mentioned above, along with an increase in demand for higher skilled and professional people, who may not be in sufficient supply. The character of autonomous investment may also involve changes in organizational and/or market structures. Not only does autonomous investment result in change of this sort, but it may create uncertainties of investment plans. In addition, time is needed before investment opportunities can come to fruition in the form of investment programs. Unemployment can result during such a transitional period.

As mentioned, the rate of autonomous investment is itself uneven. There is a strong presumption that in the 1957–62 period, the over-all rate of autonomous investment has been sluggish. Consequently, the rate of growth of national income has been correspondingly slow. Since the rate of autonomous investment is uneven, there is no reason to assume that the economic system will always fluctuate around a growth rate compatible with full employment.

In periods of low rates of autonomous investment, coupled with the kind of "autonomous" investment that results in technological change and resultant adjustments up and down the matrix of economic relationships, it can be expected that unemployment will rise and become a problem.

In this view, policy measures aimed at accelerating the rate of growth of national income through tax revision may or may not prove successful. Even though national income may be stimulated, there is no guarantee that the underlying difficulties resulting from the character and rate of autonomous investment will be cured; if they are not cured, unemployment may continue to plague the economy. Thus, specific and flexible policies aiming at stimulating the flow of autonomous investment are indicated.

APPENDIX F-4: COMPARISON OF PROFIT MARGINS AND WAGE RATES, 1948–62

The following statistics clearly indicate the direction in which profit *margins* (and the rates of other nonlabor income) and wage *rates* (not including the cost of the various fringe benefits) have been moving since 1948. The figures are self-explanatory.

TABLE 1: Average Gross Hourly Earnings of Production Workers in Manufacturing: 1948–63

1948	1.33	1956	1.95
1949	1.38	1957	2.05
1950	1.44	1958	2.11
1951	1.56	1959	2.19
1952	1.65	1960	2.26
1953	1.74	1961	2.32
1954	1.78	1962	2.39
1955	1.86	1963	2.46

Sources: *Employment and Earning Statistics*, U.S. Department of Labor, 1961, p. 32; *Economic Report of the President*, January, 1962, p. 239, January, 1963, p. 204, and January, 1964, p. 240.

TABLE 2: Behavior of Profit Margins: 1948–63

(Profit Margin on Sales before Taxes, Manufacturing)			
1948	11.1%	1955	10.2%
1949	9.3	1956	9.7
1950	12.6	1957	9.3
1951	12.2	1958	7.4
1952	9.2	1959	8.8
1953	9.2	1960	7.9
1954	8.4	1961	7.7
		1962	8.2
		1963 (3rd qu.)	8.3

Sources: O. Eckstein, in *The Relationship of Prices to Economic Stability and Growth*, Compendium, Joint Economic Committee, 85th Congress, 2nd Session, 1958, pp. 370–71; *Quarterly Financial Report for Manufacturing Corporations*, Federal Trade Commission and Securities and Exchange Commission; and *Economic Report of the President*, January, 1964.

TABLE 3: Gross Profit and Interest of Corporations as a Percentage of Corporate Gross Product

1929	1939	1948	1962*
22.0	15.6	21.5	16.0

* Annual rate based on data for first six months. Source: *Survey of Current Business*, November, 1962, p. 27.

Commenting on these and related findings, an article in *Survey of Current Business* stated that "the share of total corporate output returned to capital in the form of profits declined by one-fourth over postwar years . . . after payment of taxes [it] dropped two-fifths."[1]

TABLE 4: Factor Shares in Productivity Gains: 1948–57

Private Domestic Economy	
Labor share of total productivity gain	121.8%
Capital share* of total productivity gain	–21.8%

* "Capital Share" contains all the conventional categories of nonlabor income. Source: J. W. Kendrick, *Productivity Trends in the United States*, p. 129.

[1] "Corporate Profits and National Output," *Survey of Current Business*, November, 1962, p. 23.

APPENDIX F-5: ADMINISTERED PRICES, STEEL, AND INFLATION

The grand jury indictment of a large segment of the American steel industry in April, 1964, to the effect that between 1955 and (at least as late as) 1961, they had conspired to fix the "extras" on top of the basic price for carbon steel sheet, prompted widespread speculation as to whether this collusion, if so proved in court, might not explain our "creeping inflation" and unemployment since 1957, thereby disproving the theory of "administered prices" as the generally accepted explanation of it.

One advantage of this reasoning is that it has substituted an apparently easy answer for one that was not so easy to comprehend and still less easy to serve as the basis for a corrective public policy. However, the new conspiracy theory for our lagging rate of economic growth overlooks that individual firms, even in a very competitive industry, may be motivated toward a similar pricing behavior when they are all under a common pressure. Just like commonly experienced and protracted demand increases will elicit similar price responses on the part of all firms in the affected industry, so will commonly experienced and protracted cost increases.

Now, it is a matter of public record that the steel union pressures for wage increases, beyond real productivity improvements, did not wait for the first collusive steel-price increase since 1955.[1] To the extent that wage increases had preceded steel-price increases, it really does not matter a great deal whether the subsequent steel-price increases resulted from collusive price-fixing or were "administered" through the customary procedure of price leadership. This remains true even if it is shown that steel-price increases in fact exceeded steel-wage increases. The crucial point is that wage increases in the postwar period used to be systematically in excess of real productivity improvements[2] and that, round by round, they in fact preceded the subsequent price increases.[3]

[1] See on this O. Eckstein and G. Fromm, *Steel and the Postwar Inflation*, Study Paper No. 2, Joint Economic Committee (Washington, D.C., November 6, 1959).

[2] See on this O. Eckstein and G. Fromm, *op. cit.*, and W. Fellner, *et al.*, *The Problem of Rising Prices*, pp. 45–65 and 451–88.

[3] See J. K. Galbraith, "Market Structure and Stabilization Policy."

Even if conspiratory price-fixing in the steel industry is proved and, hopefully, prevented in the future, there will continue to be a systematic downward rigidity of steel prices, as well as of other prices, and even further increases in them if wages (including all the fringe benefits) should continue to exceed real productivity improvements.

The fact that steel prices increased considerably more than other industrial prices appears like a prima-facie indication that there may have been price-fixing collusion in the steel industry. This, however, does not mean that noncollusive "administered prices" in steel would have stayed put, let alone decreased, in face of above-productivity wage and other cost increases.

Thus, whatever the outcome of the judicial case pending against the eight steel companies may be, the problem of "administered prices" competing with administered wages will remain one of the basic problems of the American economy. The anti-inflationary "Guideposts" and an accompanying strengthening of the collective bargaining procedure are as important now as they were before the antitrust case concerning the "extras" in the price of carbon steel sheet. In view of the expected spending effects of the massive tax reduction enacted early in 1964, consistent application of the Guideposts will be more important than ever if we are to avoid a revival of inflation and its negative effects on our balance of international payments, employment, growth, and income distribution.

APPENDIX G-1: COMPARATIVE PUBLIC AND PRIVATE INDEBTEDNESS

The following tables offer unmistakable evidence in support of two facts that characterize our economy: (1) To be in debt is apparently a very natural thing for *every* sector of the economy. (2) Of the total debt of all the public and private sectors, the Federal debt has *grown* the *least* since World War II and has actually *decreased* relative to the value of total national production and income, whereas the indebtedness of all the other sections has been *increasing* in relation to their respective income levels.

Data on tables are taken from *U.S. Income and Output* and *Survey of Current Business.*

TABLE 1: Increases in Net Public and Private Debt
(billions of dollars)

Year	Federal	State and Local	Corporate	Noncorporate
1946	229.7	13.6	93.5	60.6
1961	248.1	65.0	311.5	312.3

TABLE 2: Federal Debt (Held by Public) as Per Cent of GNP

Year	Per Cent
1946	97.4
1961	41.1

TABLE 3: State and Local Debt as Per Cent of GNP

Year	Per Cent
1946	6.5
1961	12.5

TABLE 4: Corporate Debt as Per Cent of Net Income (Product) Originating in Corporate Business

Year	Per Cent
1946	108.3
1961	135.4

TABLE 5: Individual and Noncorporate Debt as Per Cent of Net Income (Product) Originating in Individual and Noncorporate Sectors

Year	Per Cent
1946	106.3
1961	343.9

APPENDIX G-2: POSTWAR INFLATION IN THE UNITED STATES

Inflation in the United States since the end of World War II was due at first to the consumption component of aggregate demand. Consumer expenditures amounted to 97 per cent of disposable income in 1947, but were later reduced to 94.5 per cent for the period 1948–50, and 92.5 per cent for the period 1951–57.[1]

Why did the consumption component increase so sharply in immediate postwar years? The reason for that was rather simple: "By the end of the war there had accumulated a tremendous amount of pent-up consumers' demand, and an unprecedented amount of liquid assets to make this demand effective."[2] The inflationary boom lasted until the second part of 1948. The main characteristics of this first postwar boom were: (1) a seemingly insatiable demand for consumers' goods, (2) increase in private investment, (3) increase in exports, (4) decrease in government expenditure, (5) rise in prices. Wholesale prices increased by 60 per cent, and retail prices went up by about 35 per cent.

After a mild and short recession in 1949, a new short boom got under way in 1950 and was intensified by the outbreak of the Korean War in June of that year. During the beginning stages of the Korean War, speculative buying and hoarding by both producers and consumers, followed by a substantial increase in government expenditures (about 23 per cent of the GNP in 1953), pulled prices up. Consumption averaged about 94 per cent of disposable personal income in this second postwar boom. Prices and wages started moving up, but were checked by government controls. Controls on installment credit and mortgage credit were also imposed. Taxes (personal as well as corporate) were increased. Early in 1951, price and wage controls were introduced after the consumer price index had increased from 102.8 in 1950 to 111.0 in 1951. The result was

[1] See Department of Commerce, "Economic Growth and Progress," *U.S. Income and Output, 1958* (Washington, D.C.: Government Printing Office, 1959), pp. 1–26.

[2] R. Gordon, *Business Fluctuations* (New York: Harper & Row, 1961), p. 468.

that wholesale prices declined somewhat over the period 1951–52 (114.8 in 1951 to 110.1 in 1953) while the consumer price index stayed relatively stable.

The 1953 downturn was 13 months long, and a new upswing got under way in the fall of 1954.

Apparently, the inflationary pressures in the period from 1946–54 originated on the demand side. However, demand pressures were not the only source of our earlier postwar inflation. Cost-push was also present, but it was overshadowed by demand pull. There is no major quarrel among economists as far as the analysis of the causes of inflation in the period 1946–54 is concerned. However, differences of opinion do exist concerning the explanation of the causes of inflation after the recession of 1954.

The "Chicago School" stresses the monetary factor. One of its members, R. Selden, wrote "that the role of costs in this inflationary episode has been greatly exaggerated."[3] A similar view was expressed by A. Hansen, who stated that the inflationary pressures in 1955–57 were caused by an excessive investment in plant and equipment.[4] In this period the wholesale price index increased from 93.2 in 1955 to 99.0 in 1957. During the same period, consumer prices rose from 93.3 in 1955 to 98 in 1957.

On the other hand, a number of economists—e.g., the late S. Slichter, Galbraith, Means, Moulton, Weintraub—maintained that the main cause of the inflationary pressures after 1954 is to be found on the cost side (whether in a form of wage or profits or other costs push).

An extensive study titled *The Problem of Rising Prices,* written by six prominent European and American economists, among them W. Fellner, and published by the Organization for European Economic Cooperation in 1961, confirms both demand-pull and cost-push explanations. According to this authoritative study, the period of 1955–57 was predominantly characterized by a demand-pull type of inflation, while price increases after 1957 were attributed to the wage push.

According to J. W. Kendrick, labor's share of the total productivity gain over the 1948–57 period was 121.8 per cent while capital's share was —21.8 per cent. This comprehensive statistical

[3] "Cost Push Versus Demand-Pull Inflation, 1955–57," *The Journal of Political Economy*, February, 1959, p. 2.

[4] "A Neglected Factor in Inflationary Pressures, 1955–57," *Review of Economics and Statistics,* May, 1959, pp. 184–85.

finding is indicative of a persistent wage-push element in the postwar inflation in the United States.[5]

In the period 1957–62, slow but steady inflation continued in the consumer goods markets and the labor market, while the wholesale price index has shown a remarkable stability.

Consumer price index rose from 98.0 in 1957 to 106.7 in 1963. The average wage rate in manufacturing industries has increased from $2.05 in 1957 to $2.46 in 1963, an increase of 18 per cent.[6]

Unemployment of manpower and capital goods has also shown an upward trend. From 4.3 per cent of the labor force unemployed early in 1957, the rate of unemployment has averaged 6.0 per cent in the ensuing years. Unused manufacturing capacity has been, on the average, 5 per cent higher than in the years preceding 1957.

Slowly creeping inflation, followed by an increase in the rates of unemployment of labor and capital in the period 1957–62, has been due to a combination of factors, such as an increase in wage rates in excess of the rate of productivity improvements and demand shift accompanied by relative monetary restraints and absence of an active fiscal policy.

[5] See Kendrick, *Productivity Trends in the United States* (New York: National Bureau of Economic Research, 1961), p. 129.

[6] *Economic Report of the President*, January, 1964, p. 240.

APPENDIX G-3: WHAT COMPETITION CAN AND CANNOT DO

When economists speak of competition, they usually refer to theoretical models concerning the structure, functioning, and effects of various markets with respect to such economic variables as prices, inputs, outputs, productive efficiency, and supply-demand adjustments under static or dynamic assumptions. For the purposes of this discussion, however, it seems useful to start from a more fundamental and broader concept of competition, briefly to explore its general meaning with respect to human activity and the life of society, and only then to branch off into more specific meanings and forms of competition as it affects those aspects of individual activities and social processes that we analytically refer to as economic.

In its generic meaning, competition may best be thought of as the process of social change to the extent that it is generated by pluralistic and autonomous human action aiming at, and productive of, results which society may voluntarily accept as improvements over that which is already in existence and use. So understood, competition is obviously the social product of one of the most spontaneous traits of human nature that knows no absolute institutional barriers. In this fundamental sense, we could speak even of some competition among slaves, or of competitive elements in the Soviet system.

A social system, or even an organization, with such a completely harmonious and perfectly complementary division of abilities, functions, and performance as to exhibit no parallelism and progressive substitution is inconceivable. There is no human mastermind and engineering genius that would be able to predetermine how the yet unfolded human potentialities could be developed, socially distributed, and used to their full capacity on the basis of some "scientific" once-and-for-all decision, independent of comparative experience, multiform experimentation, and differential improvements.[1] In these elements of its operation, competition is an axiom of human existence in society and a *sine qua non* of civilization. With respect to competition in this, its deepest meaning, there is no unresolved question as to the "whether" or "why" of it, but only as to "how much" competition is desirable and in what ethological atmosphere and institutional framework it can best perform its social function. Furthermore, if competition in this sense is a prerequisite of civilization and the motive force of its development, there can be no a priori reason for the absence of competition as such in any sphere of human endeavor and social life, including their economic aspects.

The *economic* aspect of life concerns decisions, actions, and social processes that are related to the use of limited human and material resources for the satisfaction of the changing and expanding aggregate of asserted (or expected) individual wants and recognized social ends.[2] Continuous *improvement* in the use of such resources is therefore a generally understood *necessity*, although its historical-geographical realization has by no means been even. Consequently, we find some measure of competition built into economic processes of all times and places, and we find it as a spontaneous feature of economic history. Economic competition does not have to be legislated into operation, although it may be politically helped.

On the other hand, political compulsion appears to be a prerequisite if economic competition is to be checked effectively. This seems to be true even with respect to apparently nongovernmental limitations on competition stemming from monopolistic restric-

[1] The Latin verb *competere* developed from *petere cum,* i.e., to strive for or to seek (something) in conjunction (not cooperation) with (others). This seems to point to the underlying idea of our generic concept of competition, namely the notion of social improvement through interpersonal (or intergroup) challenge, comparative ability, effort, and performance. Competition thus reflects the inherent human imperfection (in isolation) in its historical striving toward "perfection" through mutual interplay or interaction (in society). The same goes for the French word *concurrence.*

[2] This is a modification of Robbins' definition of economics as the science which studies "human behavior as a relationship between ends and scarce means which have alternative uses." (L. Robbins, *An Essay on the Nature and Significance of Economic Science* [2d ed.; London, 1946], p. 16.) The advantage of the modification is twofold. First, the modified definition covers (explicitly) both the static and *dynamic* (changing, expanding, expected . . . wants) dimensions of the economic aspect of life and, second, it distinguishes between *individual* wants and *social* ends as the two distinct and historically competing categories of resource-use.

tions. A few broad historical examples will illustrate the point. Collective monopolies of the late medieval closed-shop guilds could not have developed had the guilds not possessed political power. Commercial monopolies of the mercantilist era also were government-protected. And contemporary monopolies, such as really do exist beyond the actual reach of competition, are likewise sheltered by virtue of some specific government measures designed to protect their exclusive supply positions.

When government withdraws its protective political hand or does not extend it beyond the original boundaries, later outgrown, competition invariably invades or reinvades the field. Such, for example, was the genesis of the domestic system that emerged outside the politically protected and economically closed guild-towns on the eve of the mercantilist era. Again, the victory of economic liberalism in Europe, in the course of the eighteenth and nineteenth centuries, gradually ended mercantilist monopolies simply by withdrawing political privilege. In our own time and country, the complete (political) monopoly of atomic energy is slowly, but surely, giving way to competitive research and development for the production and use of nuclear power on the fringes of its still protected secrecy.

These broad historical examples serve to illustrate our starting proposition that there are spontaneous elements of competition in the very nature of human arrangements, particularly economic, and that some measure of competition appears to be essential for human welfare. This much, but not more, will therefore be assumed to constitute "perennial and universal" competition. Beyond this basic assumption, philosophically derived and historically illustrated, the full meaning and specific effects of economic competition can be assessed only by specifying its analytic forms and their operational framework. In this study we want to establish how economic liberalism interpreted competition, and we will examine the extent, forms, and effects of economic competition as it has developed under the impact of liberal ethos.

II

Under the influence of a combination of intellectual, technical, political, and accidental factors operating in the Western world in the course of the eighteenth and nineteenth centuries, competition came to be extolled and promoted not only as one integral aspect of human action in society, which it always had been to some extent, but as a seemingly all-inclusive and anodyne social mechanism. Adam Smith's "system of natural liberty," which laid the logical foundations for all the subsequent movements, systems, and theories of economic competition, claimed for competition the following potentiality:

> All systems either of preference or restraint . . . being . . . completely taken away, the obvious and simple system of natural liberty establishes itself of its own accord. Every man, as long as he does not violate the laws of justice, is left perfectly free to pursue his own interest his own way, and to bring his industry and capital into competition with those of any other man, or order of men. The sovereign is completely discharged from . . . the duty of superintending the industry of private people, and of directing it toward the employments most suitable to the interest of the society.[3]

Except for the ambiguity in the meaning of the clause concerning the nonviolation of "the laws of justice," Smith's "system of natural liberty" appears to be completely self-contained and self-sufficient.

It should be recalled, however, that Adam Smith was not an anarchist. He never questioned the *raison d'être* of government. But much of the favorable interpretation as well as criticism of Smith's doctrine ignored the full meaning of his position with respect to the role of government in the "system of natural liberty." Also, Adam Smith was criticized as if he had devised his "system of natural liberty" in an historical vacuum. I submit that for a correct understanding of both the logical and historical import of Smith's "system of natural liberty" we must consider it, first, in the context of the functions that he assigned to the government and, second, against the background of his criticism of the practices of mercantilistic economic policies.

In a "system of natural liberty," the government, according to Smith, had three broad functions to perform. Let us again have the author speak for himself:

> According to the system of natural liberty, the sovereign has only three duties to attend to, three duties of great importance, indeed, but plain and very intelligent to common understanding; first, the duty of protecting the society from violence and invasion of other independent societies; secondly, the duty of protecting, as far as possible, every member of the society from the injustice or oppression

[3] Adam Smith, *Wealth of Nations* (Harvard Classics ed.; 1909), p. 466.

> of every other member of it, or the duty of establishing an exact administration of justice; and thirdly, the duty of erecting and maintaining certain public works and . . . institutions which it can never be for the interest of any individual or small number of individuals, to erect and maintain because the profit could never repay the expense to any individual or small number of individuals, though it may frequently do much more than repay it to a great society.[4]

Against the historical background of stifling mercantilistic restrictions and regulations it is understandable why Smith hoped that within a "system of natural liberty" of his time the competitive market mechanism would do most of the job of social welfare and that the subsidiary functions of government, which he listed as second and third in order, would not have to be numerous and extended. On the logical plane, however, it is equally obvious that Smith's three functions of government are very flexible and capable of application to, and explanation of, most differing historical situations.

There is little, if anything, in the reality of economic policies of most contemporary Western nations that could not be accounted for on the basis of Smith's doctrine of government functions in a "system of natural liberty." Although he attempted to enumerate specific instances of government intervention,[5] Smith did not set up a taxonomic list of public measures that would exhaust his three government functions. Clearly, "injustice" and "oppression" as well as "public works and institutions," which in Smith's system constituted justification for government intervention, are abstractions that provide ample room for any kind and number of historical cases. Nonmarket activities as well as market phenomena may constitute, or result in, "injustice" or "oppression." "Public works and institutions" may be schools or hospitals, roads, and parks, TVA or the Atomic Energy Commission, public relief or social insurance, and so on, provided there is a recognized social need for them but inadequate private interest in "erecting and maintaining" them. What particular instances are so considered and dealt with depends on a society's understanding of its own social reality and its ends and the corresponding classification of malfunctioning both in the market and outside it. Whatever the degree of social understanding and the extent of classification, Adam Smith cannot be invoked in favor of nonintervention when instances of "injustice"

[4] *Ibid.*, pp. 466–67.
[5] *Ibid.*, pp. 468 ff.

or "oppression" and of the absence or inadequacy of private interest in the presence of recognized cases of public need are found.[6]

III

Criticism of Adam Smith is on firmer ground when directed not against his "system of natural liberty" in elusive broad principle, but against his *analysis* and findings concerning the working and effects of the market mechanism under competitive conditions. Smith's economic theory was to determine what specific functions, within the "system of natural liberty," could be entrusted to the competitive market mechanism alone. But his analysis erred in the direction of exaggerated determinateness and self-sufficiency of economic competition.

In Smith's system, the market was exempt from government intervention to the extent that free competition, according to his analysis, was believed to work in the best possible social interest. However, as a genuine scholar, Smith must have been aware that his was not the last word as to the empirical findings on, and analytical elaboration of, free competition. We may therefore enlarge the scope of our remarks at this point so as to encompass some of the most relevant results of economic analysis of the competitive system since Adam Smith.

Until the relatively recent theories of "monopolistic," "imperfect," and "workable" competition,[7] economic theory was es-

[6] Professor Goetz Briefs recalls that the early liberal concept of "justice" was a narrow and negative one in the legalistic sense of government protection of personal integrity and private contracts and did not include the concept of social justice in a broader and positive sense. However true this is in general with respect to the historically prevailing liberal ethos and conceptually, but not politically, even of J. S. Mill (J. S. Mill, *On Liberty* [World Classics ed.; 1924], p. 15), in the *Wealth of Nations* I do not find conclusive textual evidence that Adam Smith used such restrictive interpretation. We may grant to Smith at least the benefit of the doubt and interpret his "justice," "injustice," "oppression," and "public works and institutions" in a flexible, somewhat pragmatic sense.

[7] It is unfortunate that analytical terminology concerning competition has not yet been uniformly systematized. Almost every major author has a competitive terminology of his own (for a survey of conflicting competitive terminology, see F. Machlup, *The Economics of Sellers' Competition*, [Baltimore, The Johns Hopkins Press, 1952], pp. 79 ff.), but the following terms are generally accepted and understood: "Free competition" was used by Adam Smith, his classical followers, and neoclassical economists, including Alfred Marshall. Although the concept was never clearly defined in its analytical properties, it is understood that "free competition" meant any market situation free of mo-

sentially Smithian in its conclusions and differed from Smith mainly in analytical refinements brought about by marginalism, the general equilibrium approach and the subsequent neoclassical synthesis.[8]

---

nopoly and with freedom of entry; "imperfections" or "frictions" as to the mobility and divisibility of factors and in regard to the knowledge of market conditions were recognized but analytically ignored. "Perfect competition" was first used by Cournot and later became the standard assumption of marginalist and general equilibrium theories. In addition to freedom from monopoly and (usually) of entry, this competitive model assumes also perfect mobility and divisibility of the factors and also perfect knowledge of market conditions. "Pure competition" is analytically associated with Chamberlin's theory of monopolistic competition. It differs from the concepts of "free" and "perfect" competition in that it assumes only the absence of monopoly without any additional requirements. "Monopolistic competition" is analytically a blend of elements of "pure" competition and monopoly; it denotes competition among limited "monopolists" (differentiated but substitute products). "Imperfect competition" came into prominence and systematic use with Mrs. Robinson's book on the theory of it. But the meaning of this concept is still contested between those who use the term simply as an alternative for Monopolistic Competition and those who, like Chamberlin, see it as denoting only various degrees of deviation from analytical requirements of Perfect Competition in regard to mobility, divisibility, and knowledge.

All these analytical concepts refer to competition in a static sense. There is no established terminology for the dynamic concept of competition. Terms like "workable" or "active competition" have a dynamic connotation, but their analytical properties have not been precisely defined, although they have been amply described by J. M. Clark, the author of this term, in "Toward a Concept of Workable Competition," *American Economic Review*, June, 1940, p. 241, and in "Competition and the Objectives of Government Policy" in E. H. Chamberlin (ed.), *Monopoly, Competition and Their Regulation* (London: Macmillan, 1954), p. 317, and several other sources.

[8] In addition to the major turning points in the development of the competitive economic theory, which are discussed on the following pages of the appendix, there are, to be sure, *other* more or less significant differences in the development of classical and neoclassical economic analysis. Classical economists, for example, lacked a theory, but not the concept, of demand and therefore centered their explanation of economic value in cost elements, thus implying proportionality between physical productivity and economic utility. Furthermore, Adam Smith believed in a progressive improvement of living standards (even with an expanding population) through a growing division of labor and technological advances. Malthus and Ricardo, on the other hand, diverged from the optimism of Adam Smith in regard to economic progress in that they assumed, in conjunction with the Malthusian law of population, nature to be rather rigidly subjected to the pressure of the law of diminishing returns. Thus, they postulated a historical development toward stationary conditions. And this postulate may be held responsible for the later analytical prevalence of equilibrium analysis at the expense of analytical consideration of economic dynamics. But post-Ricardian English and Continental classical economists returned, at

According to the classical tradition in economic theory, free competition assures the lowest possible prices and costs as well as optimum structure, qualities, and quantities of production. Any temporary deviation from these optima soon would be corrected by the forces of competition. Competition also would effect "justice" in income distribution. Under free competition the prices of productive services, just as the product-prices themselves, were supposed to conform to the corresponding social values of the productive contributions by the various productive factors.[9] Furthermore, it was assumed that the functioning of the competitive-market mechanism, by securing the flexibility of all prices, including interest rates, in the direction of their "normal" levels, would result also in full employment. Thus the competitive-market mechanism was credited with simultaneous and interrelated achievements of correct composition and efficient production of outputs, of just distribution of income, and of the highest possible level of total production and employment.

This picture of universal harmony and happiness was questioned first by Malthus who pointed to the possibility of a deficient aggregate demand, thus casting doubt upon the self-sufficiency of the

---

least temporarily, to the original Smithian optimism. When the marginalists developed the missing theory of demand (which has since been questioned, modified, and remodified), it soon became apparent that they only analytically elaborated and theoretically integrated the utility concept which Adam Smith and his classical followers sensed and whose origin goes far beyond Smith to scholastic economists. R. de Roover, "Monopoly Theory prior to Adam Smith," *Quarterly Journal of Economics*, November, 1951, pp. 492–524; "Scholastic Economics: Survival and Lasting Influence from the Sixteenth Century to Adam Smith," *Quarterly Journal of Economics*, May, 1955, pp. 161–90; "Joseph A. Schumpeter and Scholastic Economics," *Kyklos*, X, 1957, pp. 115–43. Finally, when Marshall joined classicism and marginalism in his neoclassical synthesis, the new integrated theory was in its essence not strikingly different from the conclusions reached by Adam Smith, a fact which Marshall himself was the first to acknowledge (see A. Marshall, *Principles of Economics* [8th ed.; London, 1920–48], p. 626).

[9] It should be noted that the ethical connotation (assumption of automatic justice) of functional income distribution under competitive conditions is actually stronger in some neoclassical and modern formulation of the theory than it was in the classical tradition. Cf. J. B. Clark, *The Distribution of Wealth* (New York, 1899), especially pp. 243 and 324; A. C. Pigou, *Economics of Welfare* (4th ed.; London, 1932), especially p. 133; Joan Robinson, *The Economics of Imperfect Competition* (London, 1933), pp. 282–83; G. F. Bloom, "A Reconsideration of the Theory of Exploitation," *Quarterly Journal of Economics*, May, 1941, pp. 413–42.

competitive-market mechanism in relation to full employment.[10] The classical tradition did not accept this first analytical criticism of its market theory, but the Malthusian doubt soon helped to mark the beginning of the growing "underworld" of Socialist dissenters. It took more than a century before Keynes analytically elaborated the original Malthusian doubt and incorporated the possibility of a deficient aggregate demand as an integral part of modern economic theory.[11]

Another departure from the Smithian competitive harmony was John Stuart Mill's assertion of the dichotomy between the laws of production and those of distribution.[12] The latter were declared as being both susceptible to, and partly in need of, interference from outside the competitive-market mechanism.[13] This distinction provided a welcome rationalization in favor of developing labor unionism and growing social legislation. However, as to its repercussion on nondistributive aspects of economic processes and achievements, this assertion of functional independence of the distributive side of economic life still belongs among the problem areas of theoretical economics where analysis has been inconclusive to this day.[14]

When Alfred Marshall, in his neoclassical synthesis, redefined the economic theory of free competition, another limitation of the competitive-market mechanism was clarified *analytically*. Free competition does not guarantee the *reality* of "normal"[15] prices and corresponding outputs, but only a more or less long-run *tendency*

[10] T. R. Malthus, *Principles of Political Economy* (New York: A. M. Kelley, 1951), pp. 6–7, 31–33, and elsewhere.

[11] Keynes very generously acknowledged the Malthusian origin of the idea of deficient effective (aggregate) demand. J. M. Keynes, *The General Theory of Employment, Interest and Money* (London: Macmillan, 1949), p. 32, and more particularly on pp. 362–64. In Schumpeter's opinion, Keynes's acknowledgment was too generous, because beyond an intuitive *idea* Malthus had little *analysis* concerning the insufficiency of effective demand as an explanation of unemployment. See J. A. Schumpeter, *History of Economic Analysis* (London and New York: Oxford University Press, 1954), p. 623. For opposite opinion cf. P. Lambert, "The Law of Markets Prior to J. B. Say and the Say-Malthus Debate," *International Economic Papers*, No. 6, 1956, pp. 7–22.

[12] J. S. Mill, *Principles of Political Economy* (5th London ed.; New York: D. Appleton, 1900), pp. 257–58.

[13] *Ibid.*, Book IV, Chap. vii, and Book V.

[14] Cf. footnote 40 below.

[15] Marshall was also aware that even a perfect functioning of the competitive-market mechanism with its "normal" effects would not necessarily yield ethically acceptable results (Marshall, *op. cit.*, p. 29). This explicit admission amounts to an implicit relativism with respect to the entire metaphysical "substructure" of classical and neoclassical economics.

in their direction, depending on the varying degrees of temporal disparity between the interrelated changes in demand and supply; the actual market prices and outputs may never be "normal" or even in temporary equilibrium. With Marshall, the competitive-market mechanism lost its original analytical simplicity and determinateness. Another gap was thus opened in economic theory for noncompetitive arrangements or even nonmarket interventions to deal with short-run disequilibria and with nonrealized "normal" tendencies.[16]

The time seemed now to be ripe for a fresh look at the whole structure and functioning of the market mechanism. More than a century of economic liberalism and modern industrialism resulted in structural changes that seemed to be pointing in the direction of increasing interest groupings and concentration of production, on the one hand, and of expanding markets, on the other. While the latter development was made possible by great advances in transportation and communication and favored competition, increasing importance of groups and concentration of production in large plants and big firms appeared as a tendency away from it in the direction of oligopoly and, in small national markets, sometimes even in the direction of virtual monopolies.[17] However, Schumpeter's dynamic analysis pointed to new dimensions of innovating competition, both actual and potential, from which even (static) monopolists may not escape.[18] Innovating competition typically

[16] Marshall himself contributed to the exploration of these and other welfare problems. His surplus (producers' and consumers') analysis (*op. cit.*, Appendix K) was his pioneering methodological contribution to what with Pigou became known as "welfare economics" in a technical sense (on the assumption of *given* wants). Marshall's celebrated case of taxing increasing costs industries and subsidizing decreasing costs industries (*op. cit.*, pp. 390–94) is a master example of application of his surplus methodology. But Marshall also went beyond the purely *technical* welfare economics into the sphere of *general* welfare considerations on *ethical* assumptions concerning ends (*op. cit.*, Book I, Chaps. 1, 2; Book III, Chap. 6; Book VI, Chap. 13).

[17] This would seem to explain the fact of a *relatively* much larger industrial concentration in European economics and to point to the corresponding "demonopolizing" potentialities of European integration. (See, e.g., Prof. Zeuten's remarks on this point at Talloires in 1951, *op. cit.*, p. 501; Cyril A. Zebot, "Some Economic and Ethical Aspects of the Schuman Plan," *Review of Social Economy*, March, 1953, pp. 6 ff.; Tibor Scitovsky, "Economies of Scale and European Integration," *American Economic Review*, March, 1956, pp. 71–79.)

[18] Joseph A. Schumpeter first developed his dynamic theory of a competitive economy in his *Theorie der wirtschaftlichen Entwicklung* (Leipzig, 1912; its English translation, *The Theory of Economic Development*, was published in 1935). An attempt at detailed empirical verification of the theory was made

starts as nonprice competition in costs and quality but evolves into price competition when imitation develops from innovation. Temporarily sheltered monopolylike profits from innovation thus came to be viewed as the very vehicle of economic progress. Possible loss in short-run efficiency and equity may be more than compensated for by the gain in the long-run progress of general welfare. This dynamic reinterpretation of competition came to be largely accepted at a time when growing pessimism as to the realism of traditional competitive assumptions threatened to destroy all faith in the mechanistic simplicity of the economic theory of classical origin.

Chamberlin added yet another reassuring element. On the surface, his static theory of monopolistic competition[19] had a pessimistic connotation because it emphasized the ubiquity of monopolistic elements in all markets. In its essence, however, Chamberlin's analysis revealed competition as crossing (at least potentially) all traditional industry and product-boundaries[20] and thus, by implication, confirmed Schumpeter's dynamic theory.

The Great Depression and the appearance of Keynes's *General Theory* shifted the interest from micro- to macroeconomics. Key-

---

in Schumpeter's monumental work on *Business Cycles: A Theoretical, Historical and Statistical Analysis of the Capitalist Process*, 2 vols. (New York: McGraw-Hill, 1939); finally, the theory was restated and brought up to date in a broader social context in Schumpeter's *Capitalism, Socialism and Democracy* (3d ed.; New York: Harper & Bros., 1950), Part II.

[19] E. H. Chamberlin, *The Theory of Monopolistic Competition* (Cambridge, Mass.: Harvard University Press, 1933).

[20] In the logic of Chamberlin's theory, the traditional competitive requirement of "freedom of entry" assumes a new dimension. As competition among the existing firms becomes interproluct or "interindustry" (assuming conventional industry divisions) competition, freedom of entry (potential competition) becomes the opportunity to enter the market with a new product. Practical significance of this conceptual shift lies in the growing reality of multiproduct firms. An established modern firm may more readily have financial, technological, and managerial requisites to enter new markets by adding new products to its existing product line or substituting them for the previous ones. By not depending on the establishment of new *firms* but only on the addition of new *products*, freedom of entry, as a powerful stimulus to competitive market behavior, may be an easier requirement to fulfill, especially in the areas of production where fixed investment is large and highly expert management is needed. For a recent discussion of this aspect of "workable" competition, see R. M. Robertson, "On Changing Apparatus of Competition," *American Economic Review*, May, 1954, pp. 51–62, and R. B. Heflebower, "Toward a Theory of Industrial Markets and Prices," *American Economic Review*, May, 1954, pp. 120–39.

nes's analytical victory over the so-called Say's Law (the assumption of an automatic full-employment equilibrium) overshadowed the other problems of competition. Except for his advocacy of combined fiscal and monetary controls as instruments for full employment, Keynes was very classical in his continued confidence in competition to take care of the other aspects of economic welfare. But post-World War II economic growth, accompanied by an interacting demand-and-cost inflation, soon proved Keynes's analysis and policies insufficient for coping with the problem of dynamic economic stability for the solution of which they had been designed. This led to a revival of interest in the unresolved problems of microeconomics. It was at this juncture that Galbraith appended a new optimistic footnote to the prevailing, but temporarily interrupted, analytical trend toward "workable competition." His concept of "countervailing power"[21] is pictured as lending support to the diminishing forces of competition among producers—support, coming from the opposite side of the market in a growing number of oligopolistic situations. Although the theory has not been enthusiastically accepted, admittedly it is not without merit.[22]

IV

The classical model of free competition had the advantage of a simple analytical determinateness. But it is equally obvious that

[21] J. K. Galbraith, *American Capitalism—The Concept of Countervailing Power* (Boston: Houghton Mifflin, 1952; 2d ed., 1956).

[22] Criticism of Galbraith's theory was expressed in most of the published reviews of his book, but its breadth was particularly evident from the session of the Annual Meeting of the American Economic Association in 1953 that dealt with Galbraith's new theory (*American Economic Review*, Papers and Proceedings, XXIV, 1954, pp. 1–34). Galbraith was varyingly vulnerable on three broad counts. First, he erected his magnificent structure of "countervailing" forces in the American economy on a rather scanty and insecure empirical foundation. Second, he exaggerated the practical relevance of the static oligopolistic model (on the supply side of the market) for the American economy and underestimated the aspects of "workable" competition. Third, Galbraith admitted the ineffectiveness of the "countervailing" mechanism in inflation, but did not give sufficient consideration to the thesis that the dynamics of growing group pressures is inherently inflation-generating. In defense of his theory, Galbraith introduced, among other arguments and concessions, the rather modest, albeit interesting and relevant, welfare criterion of "minimization of social tension" as the mainstay of his theory (*ibid.*, p. 3). In other words, the alleged social mechanism of "countervailing" forces is not claimed to be (at least not primarily) a factor of *economic* (scarcity-reducing) welfare, it is now being rationalized as a *sociological* and *political* stabilizer.

this competitive model was defective.[23] It fell short of explaining the competitive reality either statically or dynamically. To this extent the prevailing competitive attitudes, molded by the traditional competitive doctrine,[24] were not analytically founded.

In virtually assuming away all the manifold inequalities of competitive ability and economic mobility on both sides of the market,[25] by disposing of them in the catch-all analytical footnote on market "imperfections" or "frictions," the competitive model failed to register substantial "deviations" in the operation of the competitive-market mechanism. In the historical economic reality, the ubiquitous "friction" caused considerable competitive waste in production and possibly even more competitive disparities in distribution. Recurring general depressions were only the most visible manifestation of the inherent limitations of economic competition.

On the other hand, the traditional competitive model also failed to discern the implications of economic progress. For more than a hundred years, the prevailing economic theory ignored the struc-

23 The modern theoretical counterpart of the classical concept of "free competition is Chamberlin's construct of "pure competition." The concept has its *analytical* usefulness along with the opposite construct of "pure monopoly," but both of them are being rejected as *welfare* criteria. The analytical usefulness of these constructs is in that real market structures are mixtures (blends, compounds) of elements that can be isolated only in separate theoretical constructs. But the very fact that real market structures are inseparably compounded of both competitive and monopolistic elements (as well as of various degrees of "imperfection" as to factor divisibility and mobility and knowledge of market conditions) logically precludes a meaningful use of such elemental analytical constructs (perfect competition, pure competition, pure monopoly) as *welfare standards* for measuring, evaluating and "reforming" existing market structures. This Chamberlinian distinction between the analytical usefulness of elemental market constructs and their inherent essential deficiency as welfare standards received broad international recognition at the Talloires Conference in 1951 (see Chamberlin [ed.], *op. cit.*, especially pp. 493–540).

24 By "traditional competitive doctrine" we mean Adam Smith's "system of natural liberty," not in all its logical implications as set out in this appendix, but as interpreted by French optimists (Say and Bastiat) and vulgarized by the so-called Manchester School. This interpretation and vulgarization of economic liberalism stressed Smith's optimistic outlook as against Malthus-Ricardo's pessimism and de-emphasized the role of government. Similar popularizers of *laissez-faire* (a term Smith never used) were instrumental in shaping competitive attitudes in other countries of Europe and the United States (E. J. Carey in U.S.A., the so-called Paris Group toward the end of the nineteenth century in France, and L. von Mises with his European and American pupils in our own time).

25 This abstraction was carried to the extreme in the general equilibrium theory. Under its influence, which completely dominated especially the "new welfare economics," the needed *analytical* consideration of the multiform "imperfections" and "frictions" in a competitive economy was further delayed.

tural changes following from the expanding economies of scale. And until Schumpeter, Chamberlin, and J. M. Clark, economic theory did not show, even by implication, the competitive aspects of the growing "monopolistic" features of Western economies.

As already mentioned, in economic theory much of this has by now been corrected. Contemporary economic analysis is less simple and symmetrical in its variables, less definite and determinate in its conclusions, but it is more representative of economic reality. By and large, we know today what may be legitimately expected from the spontaneous working of the competitive-market mechanism and what can be achieved only from without. But we should not assume that these analytical advances have all been adequately absorbed into the prevailing contemporary ethos patterns (attitudes). This obviously is not yet the case.[26]

On the basis of the analytical ground surveyed in this appendix, we can now set up an elementary device that will permit a rough comparison of competitive realities with the corresponding competitive attitudes. We can arrange the major analytical findings concerning the workings of the competitive-market mechanism in a sort of "balance sheet," summing up the chief credits and debits, achievements and shortcomings, potentialities and limitations of competition as it has developed from economic liberalism.

V

Economic competition that received its historical impetus from economic liberalism has resulted in the following principal achievements and potentialities:

1. Free competition *generalized* and *expanded* the old institution of *the market* as the evaluating catalyst between production and consumption beyond all historical barriers. Competition thus made possible the fast-growing division of labor of a mechanical age by providing for its coordination into a largely spontaneous system of economic cooperation. As a result, the technical effectiveness of modern specialization has been turned into a workable economic efficiency.[27]

[26] For a systematic examination of the contemporary ethos of American businessmen, see F. X. Sutton, *et al.*, *The American Business Creed* (Cambridge, Mass.: Harvard University Press, 1956). A similar study of the contemporary ethos patterns of other significant segments of the American society, such as union labor, farmers, and so on, is equally needed if we are to be in a position to appraise fully the contemporary ethos tendencies.

[27] This over-all achievement is of course subject to certain limitations, as recorded on the debit side of the "balance."

2. Competition among producers has been the most effective and reliable force working in the direction of *lower costs* and *prices* as well as *larger outputs* of individual products.

3. To the extent that buyers have been capable of assessing product qualities, competition among producers also must be credited as having been the strongest *stimulus to product-quality improvements*.

4. Competition has vastly *expanded* the *range of product choice* by the consumers and has, to that extent, further increased general welfare opportunities.

5. To the extent that Schumpeter's dynamic theory of competition is valid,[28] competition among fewer, but financially, managerially, and technologically bigger and more adaptable (to changes in technology and in demand) firms has been the chief source of *economic progress* through the competitive process of multiform innovation and imitation.

6. To the extent that interarea or intertemporal comparison of economic aggregates is logically possible, there seems to be little doubt that on a purely *quantitative* level of *historical comparison* the societies in which economic competition has prevailed have so far achieved unmatched diversity and the highest comparative aggregates of both per capita production and civilian consumption.[29]

7. As a social system of *decentralized* decision-making, the competitive-market mechanism has acted as an effective instrument for social distribution and dispersion of *power* and *influence*. In this sense, the prevalence of competition in the era of economic liberalism not only benefited production, but also laid the sociological and economic foundations for historical expansion of individual liberties and for political democracy.

[28] Its validity presupposes a potentially broad basis on both sides of the market so as to turn a firm's *possibility* for innovation into an active *incentive* to undertake it. For more detailed and up-to-date examination of dynamic aspects of competition, see, in addition to the references given in other parts of this appendix, W. Fellner, *Competition Among the Few* (New York: A. M. Kelley, 1949), especially Ch. 11; and P. Hennipman, "Monopoly: Impediment or Stimulus to Economic Progress?" in E. H. Chamberlin (ed.), *op. cit.*, pp. 421–58; and W. Baumol, *Business Behavior: Value and Growth* (New York: The Macmillan Company, 1960).

[29] The main difficulties of such comparison lie in the geographical and historical differences in market structures, tastes (ends), and income distribution —the chief factors that influence the valuation of the products involved. For a technical discussion of this problem, see T. Scitovsky, *Welfare and Competition* (Chicago: Richard Irwin, 1951), pp. 70–82, where detailed bibliography on the subject will also be found. Cf. also W. Froehlich, "Moral Judgments in Income Concepts," *Review of Social Economy*, March, 1955, pp. 1–19.

With variations of time and place, the competitive beliefs and attitudes stemming from economic liberalism overreached the actual achievements and potentialities of the competitive market mechanism. In the course of its operation, economic competition has revealed the following major shortcomings:

1. The competitive market does not provide for the satisfaction of *collective needs* whose satisfaction comes through indivisible demand and may require compulsion in production. These must be determined and their satisfaction secured from outside the competitive-market mechanism on a community basis or through political action.[30]

2. The competitive market does not avoid, or compensate for, the *social costs* incurred in the provision of privately produced and privately acquired products.[31] These costs too must be handled outside the competitive-market mechanism on a community basis or through political action.

3. Due to many and substantial differences in starting position, competitive ability, and economic mobility between persons and social groups, the competitive market does not guarantee *equal opportunity* for economic action and the corresponding *equitable satisfaction* of individual needs and wants. Distributive justice too must be helped from without the competitive-market mechanism through collective bargaining or through political action.[32]

4. The competitive-market mechanism is not by itself capable of guaranteeing the *quality* of many *products* because the consumers

[30] This category of competitive limitation was, as it is pointed out above, recognized by Adam Smith as the third function of government in a "system of natural liberty." However, Smith was not definite as to the application of this function, and competitive ethos patterns have differed as to its extent. For a special case of this general category, see point 6 below.

[31] The problem of social costs was first dealt with analytically by H. Sidgwick in his *Principles of Political Economy*, 1883, pp. 406–10. A. C. Pigou later elaborated on this point within his system of "welfare economics" (*Wealth and Welfare*, 1912; *Economics of Welfare*, 1920). For an expanded, more recent treatment of this problem, see J. R. Hicks, "Foundations of Welfare Economics," *Economic Journal*, December, 1939, pp. 696–712, especially p. 704.

[32] This limitation of competitive potentiality assumes particular importance for countries of "retarded" (preliberal) civilization where there usually is a vast difference between the advantageous starting position and business acumen of a dynamic minority, on the one hand, and the almost complete competitive ineptness of a vast majority, on the other. Many of the historical shortcomings and injustices in the earlier stages of economic liberalism, particularly in Europe and Latin America, as well as those of the more recently and partially introduced economic liberalism in newly developing countries can be traced back to this condition.

are inherently unequal with the producers in their ability to assess product-quality.[33] Consumer quality protection, too, requires measures taken from outside the competitive market.[34] This is also true of the "excessive," that is, useless or even detrimental, dimension of product differentiation whose elimination also requires noncompetitive cooperation.[35]

5. Another shortcoming of the competitive economy stems from the very competitive condition that individual producers make and execute their production and investment plans in isolation. This competitive condition is bound to *magnify* the unavoidable social waste of general as well as sectorial *overinvestment* and *underinvestment* resulting from the imperfect knowledge of future demand, which is, of course, characteristic of all economic systems where goods are not produced on order.[36]

[33] For an analytical examination of the product-quality problem in relation to buyers, see T. Scitovsky, "Ignorance as a Source of Oligopoly Power," *American Economic Review*, May, 1950, pp. 48–53.

[34] This competitive shortcoming is really only a special case of the limitation discussed under point 3 above. By failing analytically to consider the fact that the average consumer could not possibly be an equal expert with his business counterparts in every market, while at the same time convincing the producer and trader of the automatic social justice of competitive results, the original competitive doctrine invited, and competitive reality forced, competitive lowering of individual ethical standards in business practices. Submarginal practices would thus tend to depress the previous marginal ethos until the competitive reaction would start hurting the self-interest of the submarginal offender. Competitive ability and mobility at the margin of various economic activities may always be presumed to be insufficient to deter submarginal behavior. Historically, such submarginal practices and pressures obtained not only in retail markets but also in business relations between producers of various groups of unequal mobility and business acumen, particularly in broad areas of labor-management relations. In an interesting article in *Social Order* (January, 1956, pp. 13–20), Professor G. A. Briefs analyzed and illustrated such submarginal pressures in the earlier stages of belated economic liberalism in Middle Europe. E. H. Chamberlin did the same thing for the American economy in *Toward a More General Theory of Value* (New York: Oxford University Press, 1957), p. 133.

[35] An interesting British example of this kind of noncompetitive cooperation was cited by Mrs. J. Robinson at the Talloires Conference in 1951 (*op. cit.*, p. 513).

[36] This and other limitations of economic competition were examined in some detail at the Talloires Conference, especially by K. Rothschild, "The Wastes of Competition," in E. H. Chamberlin (ed.), *op. cit.*, pp. 301–14. The postwar French system of national investment programming by means of "indicative planning" is usually justified on this ground. Through its method of cooperative disclosure of investment plans with voluntary but financially induced compliance in implementing them, economic growth is believed to be fostered and balanced in the proximity of the potential trend line of economic expansion.

6. Due to the ethological fact that particular interest is the prevailing motive force in a competitive-market economy, the competitive-market mechanism directs investment from the viewpoint of the *present and limited future.*[37] To the extent that for the benefit of society a more distant future is to be taken into account in economic decisions, such considerations too must be brought to bear on economic decisions from outside the competitive market.[38]

7. The competitive-market mechanism cannot guarantee a *dynamic full-employment stability* of the economic system. Freely fluctuating, or even controlled, interest rates do not necessarily equate savings and investment at the proper level and time. Dynamic economic stability (growth) too must at least partly be sustained, or restored, from outside the competitive market by noncompetitive cooperation, specific monetary and fiscal policies, and, in emergency situations, also by means of direct controls.

8. Finally, *in terms of values,* the attitudes in a competitive society, in which particular interest is the prevailing motive force, are likely to be unsympathetic to values that transcend the self-centered or group-oriented interest. For such values to hold their own in a society whose economic activities are motivated and executed by vigorous competition and group rivalry, special educational and political efforts must constantly be made to counteract the spontaneous corrosion of such values by competitive attitudes and pressures.[39]

[37] The first to make this point analytically was H. Sidgwick in his *Principles of Political Economy,* 1883, pp. 412–13.

[38] This limitation of competitive potentialities is particularly relevant for underdeveloped countries with respect to the need for initial priority to be given to the provision of investment in "social" capital and long-range economic development. Paradoxically, this same competitive limitation returns to its initial significance in countries of the highest industrial development with respect to their social need for conservation of gradually dwindling natural resources and for urban redevelopment. Analytically, however, it is very difficult to effect a clear welfare gradation between "limited future"-type and "more distant future"-type investments. Onesidedness can be on either side. Thus, for example, both the recent practice of, and literature on, economic development tend to neglect benefits that economic development can derive from a fuller use of market forces. (Cf. P. T. Bauer, "The Economic Development of Nigeria: A Reply," *Journal of Political Economy,* October, 1956, pp. 435–41.)

[39] This value-effect of economic competition is, in a sense, the most significant one. For it raises the arch-problem of the common good. Inasmuch as the common good exceeds the simple summation of individual and group interests, the problem arises as to how this dimension of the common good is to be actualized. The usual answer, pointing to the government as the caretaker of such "transcendental" aspects of the common good, only shifts the location

VI

Such, approximately, is the balance of efficiency and deficiency of economic competition. The items on the *credit side* of the "balance sheet" register real and potential accomplishments of economic competition. By contrast, they may be used as standards by which to evaluate the extent to which noncompetitive attitudes in varying degrees held back and, in many parts of the world, still (or again) are holding back the *welfare potentialities* of economic competition.

The items on the *debit side* of the competitive "balance sheet," on the other hand, represent the shortcomings of economic competition. They can thus serve as indicators of the extent to which the competitive ethos patterns that had developed from the original economic liberalism overreached the *analytical realism* of economic competition. Actual disparities have differed in time and place and presumably persist in varying degrees to our day.

A comparison of various contemporary societies by reference to the competitive "balance sheet" would reveal to what extent they have either neglected (suppressed) or overextended (exaggerated) the elements of perennial competition. The results would indicate the nature and extent of the problem of ideological *readjustment* by individual societies.[40] Such readjustment, if it were to lead to

---

of the problem but does not solve it. The problem boils down to the question as to whether vigorous economic competition and increasing group influences leave in a majority of citizens a *strong* and *active enough motivation* for those aspects of the common good that transcend (or even go partly against) their respective individual and group interests. Our own difficulties in matters of adopting and pursuing an effective foreign policy, providing for sufficient educational facilities and opportunities, holding a firm line against inflationary pressures, developing a rational farm policy, etc., offer a good indication of the very pertinent nature and vast dimensions of this problem. The problem is not an insoluble one, but it requires more analytical and practical attention than it usually is receiving.

[40] Individual items in the "balance sheet" are, of course, not entirely independent of each other. An action that may be viewed as effecting an improvement with respect to one particular item, may indirectly affect some other item in an unintended way. The most obvious example of such interdependence is the relationship between income distribution and productive efficiency. But economic science has not been able to determine and measure the exact form of this relationship, which, moreover, obviously depends on a number of psychological and other factors whose impact on the interdependence is subject to variation in time and place. Similar undetermined relationships exist among other items of the "balance sheet." While inexactly known interrelatedness of the various items in the "balance sheet" diminishes the latter's immediate use-

properly combined social and distributive justice as well as efficient production and balanced economic growth, would have to result in attitudes that would lead to an adequate integration of a competitive-market mechanism with noncompetitive forms of cooperation, and of the two with supplementary government policies.

The West is learning this lesson. While competition is being stressed and strengthened by such recent developments as the European Economic Community and general liberalization of international trade and payments, a series of major cooperative arrangements are in the process of vigorous development:

1. After having eliminated all quantitative restrictions to intra-Community trade (except in agricultural products) and reduced mutual tariffs by 60 per cent, the European Community has been working toward the coordination and unification of its various national policies concerning social security, taxation, transportation, and economic growth, possibly including some form of coordinated investment programming along the lines of the French "indicative planning." As these complementary, competitive-cooperative arrangements are taking place and are being institutionalized, the Community is thereby progressing toward an ever-closer political union despite General de Gaulle's opposition to an ultimate federal solution. Even the determination to secure eventual British membership in the Community seems to have survived de Gaulle's veto of British entry in January, 1963.

2. The European Economic Community and the United States have engaged in the "Kennedy Round" of across-the-board tariff reductions of up to 50 per cent, which would greatly liberalize all world trade. Should Great Britain join the Community in the meantime, such tariff reductions could go as high as 100 per cent on some commodities.

3. The United States and Western Europe have embarked on cooperative "incomes policies" to eliminate the causes of inflation and unemployment that stem from the processes of collective income distribution and related price administration. These policies aim at approximating such a wage and price behavior as would result from a smoothly working competitive price mechanism freed of "frictions" that breed inefficiency and injustices. In addition to this competitive objective of the evolving "incomes policies," these cooperative arrangements are competitive also in that they differ in

fulness for practical purposes of policy, its usefulness as a guide to further analytical effort is thereby only increased.

scope and form. While the American "guideposts," for example, are comprehensive but flexible and rely on voluntary compliance, the "incomes policies" of the various European countries are more detailed and involve more administrative compulsion.

4. In the United States two recent cooperative developments of major proportions have been under way: the new American fiscal policy for economic growth, and President Johnson's "unconditional war on poverty." These developments show that while cooperative arrangements in the United States are usually slower in developing than elsewhere in the West, their gradualness bespeaks caution lest institutional and political cooperation *supplant* rather than *supplement* the time-tested American principle of economic competition.

5. Beyond the West itself, an expanded dimension of help to the newly developing countries was emphasized during the recent United Nations Conference on Trade and Development in Geneva in the spring of 1964. Instead of relying excessively and onesidedly on direct foreign aid, the developing countries should seek mutual cooperation through regional common markets of their own, lower tariffs for their exports, and possibly some form of financial compensation when the prices of their exports register sizable declines in relation to the prices of their imports.

These are examples of recent cooperative arrangements within and among the nations in the West and the developing parts of the world. In the field of international payments a variety of cooperative arrangements has already evolved since World War II. These arrangements are under constant review for further improvement and extension. But their objectives are clear cut: Freely convertible currencies at stable exchange rates and with sufficient international liquidity for expanding world trade and investment.

NOTES

Chapter 1

1. In his first postwar broadcast to the Soviet people, Stalin declared that "this war, like the last, was the inevitable result of the development of world economic and political forces on the basis of monopoly capitalism which breeds crises, and therewith breeds wars," *The New York Times*, February 10, 1946, p. 30. In assessing this statement, *The New York Times* editorial remarked that "the basis of the policies of the United States and other Western nations during and after the war has been the assumption that they . . . could live in peace and cooperation with Russia," *The New York Times*, February 11, 1946, p. 28.

This speech by Stalin was the first official pronouncement of the future Soviet policies, and, as *The New York Times* editors rightly assessed, "coming from Stalin they are both gospel truths and directives for action for Russia and for communists everywhere." See also "The Sino-Soviet Economic Offensive through 1960," *Intelligence Report* (No. 8426, Department of State), March 21, 1961, p. 1.

2. Winston Churchill in the address at Fulton, Missouri, said that "a shadow has fallen upon the scenes so lately lightened, lighted by the Allied victory. . . . From Stettin in the Baltic to Trieste in the Adriatic, an iron curtain has descended across the continent," *The New York Times*, March 6, 1946, p. 4.

3. See chap. 4, pp. 39–40.

4. The text of the Soviet Communist Party Draft Program, *The New York Times*, August 1, 1961.

5. See "OAS Study Finds Red's Subversion from Cuba Rising," *The New York Times*, June 6, 1963, pp. 1 and 14.

6. Text of Kennedy's address offering " 'Strategy of Peace' for Easing Cold War," *The New York Times*, June 6, 1963, pp. 1 and 14.

7. Recently, there has been considerable decline in the Soviet economic growth. See Appendix A-1.

8. For the Soviet Economic Offensive, consult U.S. Department of State, *The Communist Economic Threat*, 1959, especially pp. 9–11; Robert L. Allen, *Soviet Economic Warfare* (Washington, D.C.: Public Affairs Press, 1960), especially chaps. 9–15; M. S. Handler, "Reds' Foreign Aid Put at 3 Million," *The New York Times*, March 5, 1961; U.S. Senate Committee on Foreign Relations, *Hearings on International Development and Security* (Washington, D.C.: U.S. Government Printing Office, 1961), Part I, pp. 176–77; U.S. Congress, Joint Economic Committee, *Dimensions of Soviet Economic Power* (Washington, D.C., 1962).

9. See the article "Only Idiots Like War, Khrushchev Asserts," in *The Evening Star* (Washington, D.C.), April 6, 1964, p. 6. There are, of course, many

other aspects of the Soviet strategy on our own shores. See *The New York Times*, July 26, 1961, p. 26.

10. A very good analysis of historical and ideological factors that have triggered economic growth in the U.S.A. and Western Europe was written by Walter Prescott Webb, "Ended: 400 Year Boom—Reflection on the Age of the Frontier," *Harper's Magazine*, October, 1951, pp. 23–33. See also Walter Prescott Webb's "Windfalls of the Frontier," *Harper's Magazine*, November, 1951, pp. 71–77.

11. In regard to this point, we should remember the following three factors which helped Soviet economic development: (a) a complete absence of any regard for the human costs of forced and rapid industrialization; (b) availability of technology already tried and applied in the West; (c) the degree of civilization inherited by much of the Soviet urban population from their pre-Bolshevik generations was high enough to permit application of the existing technology. According to W. W. Rostow, the Russian "take-off" was actually well under way even before the end of the last century. See W. W. Rostow, *The Stages of Economic Growth: A Non-Communist Manifesto* (New York: Cambridge University Press, 1960), p. 95.

12. See Appendix A-3.

13. For recent change, see chap. 3, p. 22.

14. This is even the case in Pakistan, doubtlessly a loyal ally of the West. See speech of Pakistan President Mohammed Ayub Khan before the Joint Session of the U.S. Congress on July 12, 1961.

15. See H. T. Oshima, "Share of Government in Gross National Product for Various Countries," *The American Economic Review*, June, 1957, pp. 381–90. One exception appears to be Burma, where General NeWin, Chairman of Burma's Revolutionary Council, recently began (January 1, 1963) nanationalizing branch after branch of the Burmese economy and announced his aim of total nationalization. See International Monetary Fund, *International Financial News Survey*, March 22, 1963, pp. 86–87.

16. See Appendix A-1.

Chapter 2

1. For reference, see chap. 1, footnote 11.

2. For other approaches to the subject, see Appendix B-1.

3. It has been either explicitly or implicitly acknowledged by a number of writers (M. Dobb, G. Johnson, J. Solterer, T. S. Schultz, H. Villard, W. Fellner, etc.) that capital-output ratio has been surprisingly constant. For newest reference, see T. S. Schultz, "Investment in Human Capital," *The American Economic Review*, March, 1961, pp. 3–5.

4. J. K. Galbraith, *The Affluent Society* (Boston: Houghton Mifflin, 1958).

Chapter 3

1. Rostow, *The Stages of Economic Growth*, pp. 38, 44–45.

2. *Ibid*., pp. 134–42. For a comparison of the rates of population increases in underdeveloped areas today and in the Western World during the period

1650–1900, see *Demographic Album of the United Nations* and J. R. Hicks, H. Hart, and J. Ford, *The Social Framework of the American Economy* (New York: Oxford University Press, 1945), chap. 4. See also "India's New Plan," *The New York Times,* August 10, 1961, p. 26; and "Mankind Continues to Grow," *The New York Times,* August 16, 1961, p. 30.

3. The concept and importance of "human" capital was analyzed by a number of economists: T. S. Schultz, *The American Economic Review,* March, 1963, pp. 1–17; B. Horvat, "The Optimum Rate of Investment," *The Economic Journal,* December, 1958, pp. 747–67; J. Viner, "Investment in Human Capital and Personal Income Distribution," *The Journal of Political Economy,* August, 1958, pp. 281–302; H. Villard, "Some Comments on Growth," *The American Economic Review,* March, 1961, pp. 123–26. See also Appendix C-1.

4. See Appendix H-2.

5. For statistical data on educational facts in underdeveloped countries, see UNESCO's annual reports: *Basic Facts and Figures,* and *The International Yearbook of Education.*

6. Thus, for example, *The New York Times* of November 12, 1962, in a dispatch from Moscow, reported from the Soviet newspaper *Sovietskaya Rossiya* of November 11, unbelievable examples of misinvestment (of about $660 million) in useless new plants and equipment in the Kuznetsk Basin of the Soviet Union.

7. On India's relative position among the underdeveloped countries, see in particular J. K. Galbraith, *Economic Development in Perspective* (Cambridge, Mass.: Harvard University Press, 1962).

8. On the significance of extraeconomic considerations for economic analysis, see Appendix C-2.

9. M. Frankel, "U.S. May Reject Neutrals' Plea," *The New York Times,* September 6, 1961, p. 5.

Chapter 4

1. Rostow, *The Stages of Economic Growth,* p. 11.

2. For this Canadian case, see *ibid.,* p. 69.

3. See references to Malenkov's speech of August, 1953, and N. S. Khrushchev's speech on farm policy delivered a month later, in Harry Schwartz, *Russia's Soviet Economy* (Englewood Cliffs, N.J.: Prentice-Hall, 1954), p. 125.

4. Rostow, *op. cit.,* p. 136.

5. The difference between "totalitarian" and "autocratic" is not always remembered. Totalitarian means extending central political control over the entire *range* of the society. Autocratic refers to the nonelective and nonresponsible *method* of exercising totalitarian control.

6. Professor Goetz Briefs comments that it is not the state that is totalitarian, that "only the ruling party is. . . . The State strictly speaking, is a mere instrument, a technical device for the exercise of the political decisions made by the party. . . . The totalitarian regime is the reservation of the State for the exclusive purposes and ends of the One party in command of all power." See G. Briefs, "The Roots of Totalism," *Thought,* March, 1944, pp. 61–62.

7. There are some exceptions. (1) Family plots on collective farms, which cannot be larger than three acres. In irrigated regions, the upper limit on the maximum amount of such plots is less than half an acre. See Naum Jasny, *The Socialized Agriculture of the USSR* (Stanford, Calif.: Stanford University Press, 1949), p. 314; and H. Schwartz, "Private Farming Big Aid to Soviet," *The New York Times*, November 28, 1960, p. 63. (2) Manifestations of black markets in both the process of production and the final distribution.

8. See H. Schwartz, *op. cit.*, pp. 489–93, and Franklyn Holzman, *Soviet Taxation* (Cambridge, Mass.: Harvard University Press, 1955), especially chap. 6.

9. See chap. 9 on Soviet price system.

10. See the text of Soviet Party Draft Program, *The New York Times*, August 1, 1961.

11. This conclusion is implied in President Kennedy's address to the nation on the Berlin issue of July 25, 1961, and was voiced in various congressional comments on the address.

12. U.S. Congress, Joint Economic Committee, *Comparison of the United States and Soviet Economies* (Washington, D.C.: Government Printing Office, 1959), Part I, pp. 95–121.

13. Rostow, *op. cit.*, 136.

14. Milovan Djilas, *The New Class* (New York: Frederick A. Praeger, 1957).

15. Karl Marx and Friedrich Engels, *Communist Manifesto*, trans. by S. Moore (Chicago: H. Regnery, 1955), Part I.

16. To the best of my knowledge, the phrase "dictatorship of the proletariat" was mentioned for the first time in Karl Marx's *Critique of the Gotha Program*, but the concept of it had already been introduced in the *Communist Manifesto*.

17. Andrei Vyshinsky, *The Law of the Soviet State*, trans. by Hugh W. Babb (New York: The Macmillan Company, 1948), chap. 1, sections 2–3.

18. Djilas, *op. cit.*, p. 55, and Articles 4–6 in the Soviet Constitution where it is said that all means of production in the U.S.S.R. are state property. Having this in mind and combining it with Article 126 of the Constitution, which has already been mentioned, and Vyshinsky's statement (in *The Law of the Soviet State*) that "the dictatorship of the Proletariat is authority unlimited by any statutes whatever," one gets a clear-cut picture of the supremacy of the Party and its will.

19. See "Text of Statement by Leaders of 81 Communist Parties After Meeting in Moscow," *The New York Times*, December 7, 1960, pp. 14–17, and the text of the 1961 Soviet Communist Party Program, *The New York Times*, August 1, 1961.

20. See Rostow, *op. cit.*, pp. 4–16.

21. C. L. Sulzberger appears to agree that this concept is more in the nature of wishful thinking than a realistic appraisal of the future course of the Soviet socio-economic development. Sulzberger said that "recently we began to speculate whether in approaching our productive standards the Soviet Union might also approach our political methods through gradual embourgeoisement. Such an idea is probably wishful thinking." See C. L. Sulzberger, "Applying Hindsight to Foresight," *The New York Times*, August 9, 1961, p. 30.

22. A vivid picture of deeply rooted and widespread intellectual ferment

among the educated strata in the Soviet Union was presented in five articles by H. E. Salisbury, on his return trip to the Soviet Union, in the *The New York Times*, February 5–9, 1961. In his article of February 6, we read that "the strongest and deepest tendencies in Soviet society appear today to be firmly oriented toward Western and liberal ideals. With few exceptions, the leaders of Soviet thought in all the more advanced areas of human knowledge are more attracted to ideals of humanistic nature than to the conventional materialism of thought." Recently, antitotalitarian intellectual revolt and ferment have spread even to Czechoslovakia, the most docile and conformist of the Soviet satellites. See, on this, "Easing of Curbs Stirs Cultural Revolt in Prague," *The New York Times*, June 13, 1963, p. 7.

23. Some of the extraideological factors from *within:* their own scientific research, technological inventions and applications, development and allocation of resources, organizational problems, psychological phenomena, religious factors, etc; and the entirely non-Marxian reality of national characteristics.

24. Some of the extraideological factors from *without:* Western military strength, technological advances, economic successes, political integration; gradual consolidation of new nations; the "why" of the Berlin Wall; actual and potential communications with the West, etc.

25. *The New York Times* of November 12, 1962, reported that "Thousands Quit Work in Siberia over Low Wages and Bungling."

26. See V. Gsovsky, "Elements of Soviet Labor Law," *The Monthly Labor Review* (U.S. Department of Labor), March, 1951, p. 3.

27. David Granick, *The Red Executive: A Study of the Organization Man in Russian Industry* (New York: Doubleday, 1960).

28. See H. S. Levine, "The Central Planning of Supply in Soviet Industry," *Comparison of the United States and Soviet Economies*, p. 174.

29. See J. Berliner, "The Informal Organization of the Soviet Firm," *Quarterly Journal of Economics*, August, 1952, pp. 347–49.

30. See U.S. Congress, Joint Economic Committee, *Soviet Economic Growth: A Comparison with the United States* (Washington, D.C.: Government Printing Office, 1957), p. 27.

31. Galbraith, *Economic Development in Perspective*, p. 66.

32. See *Pravda* of February 28, 1958, p. 1, and March 1, 1958, pp. 1–3, and J. Miller, "The Reorganization of the MTS," *Soviet Studies*, July, 1958, pp. 84–89.

33. This proposal of Khrushchev was carried out in a short time. MTS were renamed RTS (Repair Tractor Stations), their duties now being to serve as repair centers and distributive agencies for new tractors. Those collective farms that were unable to pay for the tractors, were granted special long-term credit for this purpose.

34. Such a change (from Kolkhozi to Sovkhozi) would make the former (within cooperative farms) pressures for farmers' participation in the management of the farms now (in state farms) illegal.

35. Djilas, *op. cit.*, p. 53.

36. On February 14, 1957, Khrushchev submitted a report on the decentralization, and the corresponding "thesis" appeared on March 30, 1957. See "Tezisi Doklada N. S. Khrushcheva," *Pravda*, March 30, 1957, pp. 1–4.

37. See O. Hoeffding, "The Soviet Industrial Reorganization of 1957," *The American Economic Review*, May, 1959, pp. 70 and 74.

38. *Comparison of the United States and Soviet Economies*, pp. 68–69.

39. See "Soviet Tightens Output Controls," *The New York Times*, July 24, 1961, p. 1.

40. See "Russians Complete Formation of 17 Major Economic Regions," *The New York Times*, February 24, 1962, p. 1.

41. See *The New York Times*, March 29, 1962, p. 3.

42. See *The New York Times*, November 12, 1962, p. 1.

43. *The New York Times*, November 25, 1962, p. 16.

44. H. Schwartz makes the point that the Soviet Government, in its disposition of the country's resources and their output, gives top priority to "national survival and ideological aggrandisement." This sounds misleading because it implies that the Soviet Government works for the vital interests of the Soviet people. In actuality, the Soviet *Government* uses the resources and production of the Soviet people for *its* own self-perpetuation and Communist global expansionism. See also on this *Comparison of the United States and Soviet Economies*, p. 253.

45. How absurdly fictitious these boasting claims and promises are can be readily seen from the following simple facts and calculations. In 1955, Khrushchev assured the Soviet people that by 1960 they would have as much meat and butter per capita as the American people. But in 1962, with Soviet incomes far below those in the United States, meat was selling for about $2 a pound and butter for almost as much. (*The New York Times*, June 4, 1962, p. 28.) According to a study by the director of statistical research of the European Economic Community, Soviet industrial production (not their agriculture) in 1972 will only equal the American industrial production of 1956. International Monetary Fund, *International Financial News Survey*, June 15, 1962, pp. 1–2.

46. See the Soviet Communist Party Draft Program of 1961.

47. Djilas, *op. cit.*, p. 63.

48. For a growing official awareness of this in the West, see the U.S. note to the Soviet Government on Berlin, *The New York Times*, July 17, 1961, and President Kennedy's speech of July 25, 1961, reported in full in *The New York Times*, July 26, 1961.

49. See *The New York Times*, January 19, 1958, p. 9.

50. See *The New York Times*, August 16, 1961, p. 35.

51. See, on this, the report from Moscow by Seymour Topping in *The New York Times*, June 5, 1963, p. 5, where it is said that "the Soviet leadership seems to have become more sensitive to world public opinion than in the past. Western analysts recently have noted that in some instances foreign reactions have exerted a moderating influence in domestic affairs."

52. It may be interesting to compare the actual share of public goods in the national product in some representative advanced and underdeveloped societies. According to Oshima, *op. cit.*, the postwar average percentage of government receipts to gross domestic product varied as follows: United Kingdom, 35; Netherlands, 31; New Zealand, 30; United States, 25; Brazil, 18; Indonesia, 15; Mexico, 10; India, 8. Assuming a rough correspondence between government receipts and expenditures and between the latter and public goods, it would follow from this comparison that, on the whole, economically advanced societies have a considerably higher degree of centralization than underdeveloped countries.

Chapter 5

1. Rostow, *The Stages of Economic Growth,* p. 91.
2. *Ibid.,* p. 92.
3. *Ibid.,* p. 91.
4. Galbraith, *The Affluent Society,* p. 146.
5. *Ibid.,* pp. 152–53. Bracketed sentences were added for greater clarity.
6. *Ibid.,* p. 155.
7. A careful reading of Vance Packard's *The Hidden Persuaders* (New York: David McKay Co., 1957) reveals that even this comprehensive indictment of modern advertising (in its broadest meaning) clearly implies that the effectiveness of advertising depends on the pre-existence of inherent aspirations; that advertising has an informative core; and that it is selective and competitive in its operation. See also George Katona, *The Powerful Consumer: Psychological Studies of the American Consumer* (New York: McGraw-Hill, 1960).
8. See in particular Thorstein Veblen, *The Theory of the Leisure Class* (New York: The Modern Library, 1934).
9. For more on this, see chap. 8, pp. 96–97.
10. Wassily W. Leontief, *Structure of the American Economy, 1919–1939* (New York: Oxford University Press, 1951). For a concise presentation and critical evulation of the subject, see D. Evans and M. Hoffenberg, "The Interindustry Relations Study for 1947," *Review of Economics and Statistics,* May, 1952, pp. 97–142.
11. See Alvin Hansen, *Economic Issues of the 1960's* (New York: McGraw-Hill, 1960), pp. 91–92.
12. Hansen calls for a working balance between the free enterprise and social controls but is not clear as to what are the limits of the proposed balance (*ibid.,* chaps. 7–8).
13. According to a recent study by Gunnar Myrdal for the Fund for the Republic (*The Role of Government in the Economy*), two-fifths of the American population may be classified as poor, or at least "nonaffluent." One-fifth are officially recognized as "falling below the poverty line," while another fifth or more do not show to any substantial degree in the abundance commonly assumed to characterize American society. See R. McGill, "Our Non-Affluent Two-Fifths," *The Washington Evening Star,* January 29, 1963, p. A-17. Subsequently, Mr. Myrdal published his views on the problem of poverty in the United States in *Challenge to Affluence* (New York: Pantheon Books, 1963). As it turned out, Myrdal's work prepared the way for a major new public policy by President Johnson, his "unconditional war on poverty." The new policy was first explained in the January, 1964, *Economic Report of the President,* pp. 55–84. In a special message to Congress on March 16, 1964, President Johnson detailed the beginnings of a systematic antipoverty program and asked for an appropriation of $1 billion for fiscal year 1965.
14. In November, 1961, The First Ministerial Council of the OECD set as a common target for 1960–70 a growth of real GNP of 50 per cent. To make this possible, it was calculated that the United States must develop a minimum annual rate of economic growth of 4.5 per cent. See OECD, *Policies of Economic Growth,* November, 1962.
15. From 1953 to 1959 (inclusive) the over-all price level increased by 14 per cent in the United States, by 15 per cent in Germany, and by 34 per cent in France. During the same period, the GNP of the United States increased

by approximately 23 per cent, that of Germany by 42 per cent, and of France by some 30 per cent. During 1961–62, consumer prices rose in the United States by 2.2 per cent, in Germany by 8.6 per cent, and in France by over 10 per cent. During the same two years, the United States GNP rose by less than 7 per cent, the German GNP went up by 9 per cent, and that of France by 9.5 per cent. It should also be added that, since 1957, unemployment in the United States has been well above 4 per cent (5.9 per cent in November, 1963), while unemployment in Germany and France has been negligible. Thus the relatively lower rate of inflationary price increases in the United States was associated with a lower rate of economic growth and a much higher rate of unemployment. With a better growth rate and full employment, inflationary pressures in the United States should be expected to increase, creating in their wake, as even a cursory comparison of the French and German experiences suggests and our analysis will show, another drag on economic growth.

Chapter 6

1. See Appendix F-1.

2. For an excellent analysis of the repressed inflation, see Thomas Wilson, *Inflation* (Oxford: Blackwell, 1961), chap. 6. The United States experience with repressed inflation during World War II was described and explained by J. K. Galbraith, "The Disequilibrium System," *The American Economic Review*, June, 1947, pp. 287–302.

3. The important problem of quality changes and their introduction in the indexes was widely discussed by the Price Statistics Review Committee and its consequent commentators. See U.S. Congress, Joint Economic Committee, Subcommittee on Economic Statistics, *Government Price Statistics* (Washington, D.C.: Government Printing Office, 1961), pp. 533–34, 588–90, 608–11.

4. The effects of inflation have been dealt with by a number of economists; to mention some: H. Wolozin, "Inflation and Price Mechanism," *The Journal of Political Economy*, October, 1959, pp. 463–75; W. Martin, Jr., "Comments on Employment, Growth and Price Levels," *Monthly Bulletin*, Federal Reserve Bank of New York, February, 1960; Gottfried Haberler, *Inflation, Its Causes and Cures* (Washington, D.C.: American Enterprises Association, 1960), pp. 46–54; S. Harris, *The Incidence of Inflation or Who Gets Hurt?* (Study Paper 7, Joint Economic Committee [Washington, D.C.: Government Printing Office, 1959]).

5. *Business Conditions*, Federal Reserve Bank of Chicago, November, 1961, pp. 7–9.

6. There are, in fact, only a few markets where price response to changes in demand or supply is automatic, immediate, and full. See, on this, chap. 7, pp. 73–74.

7. See A. C. L. Day and Sterie T. Beza, *Money and Income* (New York: Oxford University Press, 1960), pp. 322–25, for a somewhat similar view of indirect effects of inflation.

8. See chap. 7, pp. 74–77.

9. For the inflationary redistribution of income see G. L. Bach, "Inflation in Perspective," *Harvard Business Review*, January–February, 1958, pp. 99–110; H. Aujac, "Inflation as the Monetary Consequence of the Behavior of

Social Group," *International Economic Papers*, No. 4, pp. 104–24; F. Holzman, "Income Determination in Open Inflation," *Review of Economics and Statistics*, May, 1956, pp. 150–58.

10. Qualitative distortion of economic growth in consequence of inflation is even greater in newly developing countries. See on this A. A. Shaalan, "The Impact of Inflation on the Composition of Private Domestic Investment," *Staff Papers*, International Monetary Fund, July, 1962.

11. One of the latest articles by Professor Slichter on the subject was "Slow Inflation: Our Inescapable Cost of Maximum Growth Rate," published in the *Commercial and Financial Chronicle*, March 26, 1959. For an elaborate refutation of Slichter's thesis, see A. Marget, "Inflation: Some Lessons of Recent Foreign Experience," *The American Economic Review*, May, 1960, pp. 205–11.

12. For a historical development of the doctrine of "forced saving" that was formally elaborated by F. A. Hayek in his "A Note on the Development of the Doctrine of Forced Saving," *The Quarterly Journal of Economics*, XLVII, 123, see Gottfried Haberler, *Prosperity and Depression* (Cambridge, Mass.: Harvard University Press, 1958), pp. 42–45.

13. See A. Hansen, "Inflation and Growth," in *Stabile Preise in wachsender Wirtschaft* (Tübingen, 1960), pp. 181–85. Hansen says that in underdeveloped countries the flow of voluntary saving is not adequate and needs to be supplemented by forced saving. This, of course, implies inflation. Hansen himself is aware of this when he says that the question for underdeveloped countries is to find that "degree of inflation" which is "optimum for development" (p. 184).

14. R. Harrod, "Inflation in Dynamic Theory," *Stabile Preise in wachsender Wirtschaft*, pp. 167–79.

15. *Ibid*., p. 177.

16. See chap. 7, footnote 2.

17. See Hansen, "Inflation and Growth," p. 181.

Chapter 7

1. This is another way of saying that the amount demanded at each price of the particular good is determined by the price elasticity, cross-elasticities, and income elasticity of demand for that good.

2. It should be noted, however, that a change in the price of the particular good brings about a change in *quantity* demanded, demand schedule remaining unchanged. On the other hand, a change in income or in prices of other goods may bring about a shift in the demand *schedule* of the good considered.

3. See chap. 6, pp. 64–65.

4. See chap. 6, p. 61.

5. There is one exception. Various "transfer payments" are by definition independent of the participation of their beneficiaries in the process of current production. Such "transfer payments" represent *redistribution* of income after it has been functionally distributed to the various participants in production. Examples of private "transfer payments" are charitable contributions, whereas government "transfer payments" are made up of such categories as veterans' benefits, public relief, social security benefits, etc.

6. The amount of money-income increase consumed by income recipients

will depend on their "*marginal* propensity to consume." It can be reasonably assumed that with two exceptions (the lowest income groups and government) the "marginal propensity to consume" of all other consumer units is less than one, i.e., that they save part of their income increases.

7. This is, of course, due to the fact that those who save and those who invest are usually different persons influenced by different reasons. Therefore, intended saving does not automatically equal planned investment. On the basis of this fact, some Swedish economists (e.g., G. Myrdal and B. Ohlin) worked out a theory of the business cycle. See Haberler, *Property and Depressions*, pp. 131–32, which was followed by the new "general theory" of the economy as a whole by John M. Keynes, *The General Theory of Employment, Interest and Money* (London: Macmillan, 1936).

8. An unsuccessful innovation financed through bank credit would appear as an inflationary trigger of this kind.

9. For further analysis of inflation caused by the shift in the composition of aggregate demand, see Charles Shultze, *Recent Inflation in the United States* (Study Paper I, Joint Economic Committee [Washington, D.C.: Government Printing Office, 1959]).

10. With the exception of "transfer payments" that are financed out of tax revenues. See chap. 3, and Zebot, "Toward an Integrated Theory of Inflation in the United States," *Weltwirtschaftliches Archiv*, December, 1961, pp. 351–71.

11. In pronounced and protracted inflation, money tends to lose its normal function as a desirable store of value for liquidity purposes. This may happen also with respect to money substitutes, with the exception of well-selling shares of capital stock. In such circumstances, the liquidity function of money reverts to stockpiling of inventories of price-leading materials and products.

12. For the possibility that the liquidity preference proper (for speculative purposes) be satisfied through holdings of a variety of very liquid money substitutes, see J. Gurley, *Liquidity and Financial Institutions in the Postwar Period* (Study Paper 14, Joint Economic Committee [Washington, D.C.: Government Printing Office, 1960]); "The Scarcity of Money," *Monthly Letter*, First National City Bank of New York, February, 1960, pp. 20–23; W. Smith, "Financial Intermediaries and Monetary Controls," *The Quarterly Journal of Economics*, November, 1959, pp. 535–53.

13. See "Saving Institutions and Monetary Policy," *Monthly Review*, Federal Reserve Bank of Richmond, August, 1961, p. 2.

14. See chap. 6, pp. 59–64.

15. Oligopoly theory has long been suggesting considerable rigidity of individual prices relative to changes in demand. See P. Sweezy, "Demand Under Conditions of Oligopoly," *The Journal of Political Economy*, August, 1939, pp. 568–73. J. K. Galbraith, "Market Structure and Stabilization Policy," *Review of Economics and Statistics*, May, 1957, Part II. Department of Labor, Bureau of Labor Statistics, prepared for U.S. Congress, Joint Economic Committee, *Frequency of Change in Wholesale Prices, A Study of Price Flexibility*, (Washington, D.C.: Government Printing Office, 1959). U.S. Senate, Committee on the Judiciary, Subcommittee on Anti-trust and Monopoly, *Hearings, Administered Prices* (Washington, D.C.: Government Printing Office, 1957–1960), Parts I, IX, and X. William Baumol, *Business Behavior, Value and Growth* (New York: The Macmillan Company, 1960), Part I. Henry Briefs, *Pricing Power and "Administrative" Inflation* (Washington, D.C.:

American Enterprises Association, 1962). U.S. Senate, Committee on the Judiciary, Subcommittee on Antitrust and Monopoly, *Administered Prices: A Compendium on Public Policy* (Washington, D.C.: Government Printing Office, 1963).

16. The logical beginning toward an understanding of "administered prices" is to start off with P. Sweezy's concept of "kinked-demand curve" under conditions of noncollusive oligopoly. The concept of kinked-demand curve modified the traditional theory of market prices assumed to be spontaneously determined by the market supply and demand and to be promptly and fully sensitive to demand changes. The kink (convex to the origin) on the curve was supposed to impart the idea that, in the context of close interdependence of oligopolistic firms, the prevailing price becomes sticky because of the uncertainties about the reaction on the part of other firms to a price change by any one firm.

17. Gardiner Means, *Industrial Prices and their Relative Inflexibility* (Washington, D.C.: Government Printing Office, 1935), p. 1.

18. See J. M. Blair, "Administered Prices: A Phenomenon in Search of a Theory," *The American Economic Review*, May, 1959, pp. 431–50.

19. G. Ackley, "Administered Prices and the Inflationary Process," *The American Economic Review*, May, 1959, pp. 419–30.

20. Blair, *op. cit.*

21. R. F. Lanzillotti, "Pricing Objectives in Large Companies," *The American Economic Review*, December, 1958, pp. 921–40.

22. Baumol, *op. cit.* Part I.

23. The reason is, of course, public opinion, which is still more sensitive to product-price increases than to factor-price rises.

24. See Galbraith, "Market Structure and Stabilization Policy," Parts II–III; Blair, *op. cit.* The same idea has been implied in Lanzillotti's "target return" (Lanzillotti, *op. cit.*,), and Baumol's "minimum profit" hypothesis (Baumol, *op. cit.*, p. 49).

25. A significant demand shift for the firm's product, assuming an unchanged method of production, may *force* the firm to increase its price if production cost will be rising.

26. According to many economists, the American inflation of 1955–57 was due primarily to an investment boom. See A. Hansen, "A Neglected Factor in Inflationary Pressures, 1955–57," *Review of Economics and Statistics*, May, 1959, pp. 184–85; W. Fellner, M. Gilbert, B. Hansen, R. Kahn, F. Lutz, and P. deWolff, *The Problem of Rising Prices* (Paris: Organization for European Economic Cooperation, 1961), pp. 33–44.

27. In addition to direct government purchases of goods and services, government transfer payments help to finance parts of the nongovernmental components of aggregate demand. Although government transfer payments do not appear directly in the GNP account, their consideration in conjunction with the aggregate demand is justifiable on the ground that the propensity to spend of those who receive such transfer payments and of those from whom money has been taken through taxes to make transfer payments possible may not be the same.

28. These four components of aggregate demand represent the revenue side of the national product and income account. The left-hand side of the account is made up of all the cost of production elements, including business transfer payments.

29. See Appendix H–2.

30. For Great Britain's inflation, see James E. Meade, *The Control of Inflation* (New York: Cambridge University Press, 1958); Roy Harrod, *Policy Against Inflation* (New York: St Martin's Press, 1958); M. Singh, "Monetary Policy in an Inflationary Economy—A Case Study of the British Experience, 1951–1957," *The Indian Economic Journal*, July, 1959, pp. 28–44; Thomas Wilson, *Inflation* (Cambridge, Mass.: Harvard University Press, 1961).

31. See chap. 5, pp. 56–58.

32. For an empirical indication of the downward inflexibility of prices, see Charles Shultze and Joseph Tryon, *Prices and Costs in Manufacturing Industries* (Study Paper 17, Joint Economic Committee [Washington, D.C.: Government Printing Office, 1959]).

33. See chap. 6, p. 60.

34. See Shultze, *op. cit.*, chap. 5, n. 9.

35. See chap. 6, p. 61.

36. See Meade, *op. cit.*, pp. 7–9; M. Clement, "The Quantitative Impact of Automatic Stabilizers," *Review of Economics and Statistics*, February, 1960; and U.S. Congress, Joint Economic Committee, Subcommittee on Economic Statistics, *Government Price Statistics*, Part II, pp. 576–77 and 686.

37. In addition to the already mentioned references on this point earlier in this chapter, see Shultze, *op. cit.*, chap. 5, n. 9.

38. This, of course, can be deduced from the first assumption.

39. For a comprehensive analysis of the Soviet price system, see chap. 9.

40. For a statistical corroboration of this statement, see Shultze and Tryon, *op. cit.*

41. For an analysis of inflation triggered by increased aggregate demand and propagated by the cost-oriented prices in administered sectors, see Robert Solo, "Inflation in the Context of a Mixed Economy," *The Canadian Journal of Economics and Political Science*, November, 1959, pp. 471–86.

42. See chap. 7, pp. 72–73.

43. See chap. 7, pp. 79–80.

44. These elements of inflationary pressures from the production side are somewhat deceptive. Some economists have not realized the difference between cost-push as an independent *trigger* of inflation and cost-push as a propagating force of demand-pull inflation. As an example of a complete disregard of cost-push as an independent trigger of inflation, see Day and Beza, *op. cit.*, chaps. 20–21.

45. See Keynes, *op. cit.*, p. 296; also, A. Lerner, "On Generalizing the General Theory," *The American Economic Review*, March, 1960, pp. 121–43.

46. See Keynes, *op. cit.*, pp. 301–2.

47. See U.S. Congress, Committee on Judiciary Hearings, *Administered Prices*, pp. 32–74, 74–128, 4897–4923, 4926–48; see also Shultze, *op. cit.*

48. See his "Inflation: Cost-Push and Demand-Pull." *The American Economic Review*, March, 1960, pp. 20–42.

49. See particularly Sidney Weintraub, *A General Theory of the Price Level, Output, Income Distribution and Economic Growth* (Philadelphia: Chilton Co., 1959); and Harold G. Moulton, *Can Inflation Be Controlled?* (Washington, D.C.: Anderson Kramer Associates, 1958).

50. See Haberler, *Inflation: Its Causes and Cures*.

51. See Milton Friedman, "The Quantity Theory of Money—A Restatement," in M. Friedman (ed.), *Studies in the Quantity Theory of Money*

(Chicago: University of Chicago Press, 1956); R. Selden, "Cost Push vs. Demand Pull Inflation," *Journal of Political Economy,* February, 1959; and H. Levinson, *Postwar Movement of Prices and Wages in Manufacturing Industries* (Study Paper 21, Joint Economic Committee [Washington, D.C.: Government Printing Office, 1960]), p. 21. For a broad reference on varieties of cost push, see C. A. Zebot, *Weltwirtschaftliches Archiv.*

52. Taxes on business property, as well as excise and specific sales taxes, are also cost elements and may be construed as remuneration for the public order and other public services, without which production would not be possible or could be much costlier.

53. L. Morrissey presented a good summary of both the current U.S. Treasury policy regarding depreciation accounting and the general problem of depreciation of capital goods. See L. Morrissey, *The Many Sides of Depreciation* (Hanover, N.H.: Dartmouth College Press, 1960).

54. See W. Hogan, S.J., and F. Koelble, "Economic Depreciation and Employment in the 1960's," *Thought,* Winter, 1960, for a numerical estimate for the American economy.

55. See chap. 6, pp. 67–68.

56. Accelerated depreciation in the United States was instituted first during World War II, then during the Korean War, and finally, was written into the Revenue Code in 1954. (For details see L. Morrissey, *op. cit.,* pp. 8 ff.) A further liberalization of depreciation allowances was permitted in 1962.

57. Joseph Schumpeter said that "inflation comes through the payroll." See his *Capitalism, Socialism, and Democracy* (New York: Harper & Bros., 1950), p. 391.

58. See Baumol, *op. cit.,* Part I; Blair, *op. cit.,* pp. 435–48.

59. G. A. Briefs made the following point: "Collective bargaining can achieve effects which individual bargaining, even when based on great skill, cannot. Individual bargaining can raise the wage to the equilibrium point, but not beyond. Can collective bargaining transcend the equilibrium level? . . . Undoubtedly unions can press demands beyond the equilibrium point in their particular market." See Goetz Briefs, *Unionism Reappraised* (Washington, D.C.: American Enterprises Association, 1960), p. 13.

60. See on this chap. 2, p. 11.

61. Briefs, *Unionism Reappraised,* especially chaps. 1–2.

62. Bismarck's "social policy" in Germany; a series of papal social encyclicals (*Rerum Novarum,* 1891; *Quadragesimo Anno,* 1931; and *Mater et Magistra,* 1961) and the resulting Christian social action; cooperative movement, etc.

63. On this point, see G. Briefs, "Employment in the Dynamic American Economy," *Congressional Record,* August 8, 1961, pp. 13, 929.

64. Trade unions had to choose between the Marxian approach aiming at the revolutionary change of the economic system and the approach whereby their aim would be to improve the living conditions of the workers from within the system itself.

65. For a good insight into the rise of Gompers, and his work, see the book written by Gompers' secretary and associate, F. C. Thorne, *Samuel Gompers—American Statesman* (New York: Philosophical Library, 1957).

66. See Appendix G-1.

67. See chap. 8, pp. 113–14.

68. S. Melman attempted to show a positive correlation between Gompers'

slogan and productivity improvements. He maintained that productivity is a derived effect of the wage-push and the cost-minimizing labor-saving countermoves of management. See S. Melman, "Industrial Productivity," *Scientific American*, July, 1955.

69. This aspect of union wage philosophy is drastically implied in the following recent statement by an AFL–CIO official: "One of the errors in public thinking is that labor wages affect the price. They affect the price only if the company is *close to the margin* of profit, which has not been the case since World War II." (*Economic Intelligence*, December, 1961, p. 2; italics added.)

70. This fact was analyzed by John Dunlop. See his "The Task of Contemporary Wage Theory," in John Dunlop (ed.), *The Theory of Wage Determination* (New York: St Martin's Press, 1957), pp. 3–30, especially pp. 16–20. Wilson (*op. cit.*, pp. 234–59) also mentioned the fact that wage gains of some workers will be quickly emulated by others on an *inter*industry level as well as on the *intra*industry level. "Between 1953 and 1959 total productivity in the private sector of the United States economy increased at an average annual rate of 2.8 per cent. . . . It is clear that negotiated wage increases of 5, 6, or 7 per cent in important industries could only lead in time to a rise in the general price level. These wage increases were reflected in wage settlements in other less productive or less prosperous industries." (Fellner *et al.*, *op. cit.*, p. 488.)

71. See Appendix G-2.

72. This attempt at formalizing the vague concept of "key industry" approaches E. S. Redford's concept of "strategic sectors in the economy in which the exercise of market power might have the greatest inflationary potential." Such "strategic sectors" are determined by the size of "the direct effect on the costs to ultimate users . . . of the price increase of a particular product." A more indirect way of pinpointing the "strategic sectors" would be to "concentrate attention on those [price] increases which diffused cost and price increases widely throughout the economic system." *Potential Public Policies to Deal with Inflation Caused by Market Power* (Study Paper No. 10, Joint Economic Committee [Washington, D.C.: Government Printing Office, December, 1959]), p. 13. Dunlop singled out fifteen industries with the highest diffusion rating. (John T. Dunlop "Policy Problems: Choices and Proposals," in *Wages, Prices, Profits, and Productivity* [New York: The American Assembly, June, 1959], pp. 152–53.)

73. The strict logic of the national productivity-rate average as the criterion for a noninflationary wage policy was first pointed out explicitly in Alvin Hansen, *Economic Policy and Full Employment* (New York: McGraw-Hill, 1947), pp. 244–47.

74. A firm may have either an "unliquidated monopoly gain" (see Galbraith, "Market Structure and Stabilization Policy") or expect the government to "validate" higher prices through its monetary and fiscal policies, offsetting in that way the decline in demand due to higher prices. (See C. A. Zebot, "Economics of Affluence," *Review of Social Economy*, September, 1959, pp. 112–25; and Galloway, "The Wage-Push Inflation Thesis, 1950–1957," *The American Economic Review*, December, 1959, pp. 1033–37.)

75. In other words, the firm has not been maximizing its profits.

76. Weintraub, *op. cit.*; Moulton, *op. cit.*; S. Slichter, *American Economy* (New York: Alfred A. Knopf, 1948), pp. 42–44; "Wage Price Policy and

Employment," *The American Economic Review*, May, 1946; and the selection of his essays in John Dunlop (ed.), *Potentials of the American Economy*; Edward H. Chamberlin, *The Economic Analysis of Labor Union Power* (Washington, D.C.: American Enterprises Association, 1958); and Roy Harrod, *Policy Against Inflation*, are the most representative examples of the predominantly wage-pressure version of the cost-push theory.

77. See R. Harrod, "Inflation in Dynamic Theory," *Stabile Preise in wachsender Wirtschaft*, p. 175.

78. See n. 70 above and Appendix G-4.

79. Government is forced to act because of the Employment Act of 1946 and also because trade unions' influence on local and national elections has been important since World War II.

80. The wage settlement in the steel industry in March, 1962, and the ensuing failure of the steel industry to increase prices were unique exceptions. It is unlikely that the President could so directly and exceptionally intervene in wage-price cases in the future.

81. Fellner *et al., op. cit.*, p. 485.

82. According to Fellner (Fellner *et al., op. cit.*, pp. 460–62), the potential inflationary pressures due to collective bargaining are greater in the United Kingdom, where contracts are signed for indeterminate periods, and even in Germany, where contracts run for one year, than in the United States, where contracts are signed for definite time periods. In both cases, the British as well as the German one, the unions may ask for renegotiations and cluster them at the moment most advantageous for themselves.

83. The government's responsibility for maintaining full employment has already been mentioned in connection with the Employment Act of 1946.

84. There are, in fact, two criteria of what is meant by full employment. One runs in terms of the labor force and has not, as yet, been clearly defined in terms of the minimum percentage of the labor force employed. The other criterion runs in terms of plant and equipment capacity. See D. Hamberg, "Full Capacity vs. Full Employment Growth," *The Quarterly Journal of Economics*, September, 1952, pp. 444–49; and C. A. Zebot, "Toward an Integrated Theory of Inflation . . . ," p. 355.

85. See Appendix G-3.

86. A level of close to 5 per cent of unemployment consistent with maximum noninflationary aggregate demand was defended on empirical grounds by J. Aschheim, "Price-Level Stability and Employment Act Objectives," in *The Relationship of Prices to Economic Stability and Growth* (Compendium, Joint Economic Committee [Washington, D.C.: Government Printing Office, March 31, 1958]), pp. 25–28.

87. See H. Johnson, "The Wage Push Inflation Thesis," *The American Economic Review*, December, 1959, pp. 1033–37.

88. The change occurred by virtue of the Federal Reserve–Treasury Accord of March, 1951.

89. Gardiner C. Means asserted that "in the last three years [1956–58] we have lost . . . at least $70 billion of national production, which would have been available if demand had not been so curbed by the tight money policy. . . ." (U.S. Congress, Committee on Judiciary, *Hearings, Administered Prices* [Washington, D.C.: U.S. Government Printing Office, 1958], p. 4917.) Galbraith said that "monetary and fiscal policy can be a remedy for cost-push inflation only by severely cutting back output and employment" (*ibid.*, p. 4929).

90. Such "open-market operations" are today the major tool used by the Federal Reserve for regulating the total supply of money.

91. At the time of its introduction, the changing of the discount rate was meant to be the major tool in the hands of the Federal Reserve. This, however, has not been the case. For reasons, see W. Smith, "The Discount Rate as a Credit Control Weapon," *The Journal of Political Economy*, April, 1958, pp. 171–78.

92. See, for example, W. Patman, "High Interest Is a U.S. Sales Tax," in *Texas Observer*, January 15, 1960; *idem*, in *Congressional Record*, 86th Congress, Second Session, A2556–57, March 22, 1960.

93. See chap. 7, pp. 81–82.

94. See chap. 7, pp. 73–77.

95. Galbraith, "Market Structure and Stabilization Policy."

96. U.S. Congress, Committee on Judiciary, *Hearings, Administered Prices*, p. 39.

97. See Haberler, *Inflation*, pp. 44–45; O. Eckstein, "Inflation, the Wage-Price Spiral and Economic Growth," *The Relationship of Prices to Economic Stability and Growth* (Compendium, Joint Economic Committee [Washington, D.C.: Government Printing Office, 1958]), pp. 367–68; and Fellner *et al.*, *op. cit.*, pp. 69–72. See also Appendix G-4.

98. American steel prices between 1945–58 increased by much more than the wholesale price index and also by more than steel wages. It is not clear whether another price increase in steel in April, 1962, was prevented by the power of President Kennedy or by the weakness of the market for steel.

99. The attitude of the labor union as a social institution has been considered by many economists as an important cause of inflation: for example, J. Akerman, "An Institutional Approach to the Problem of Inflation," *Stabile Preise in wachsender Wirtschaft*, pp. 8 ff.; Gardner Ackley, *Macroeconomic Theory* (New York: The Macmillan Company, 1961), pp. 439–59; H. Aujac, *International Economic Papers*, No. 4, pp. 109–24; Fellner *et al.*, *op. cit.*, pp. 45–65 and 281–488. G. A. Briefs has formalized such labor-union behavior by terming the union an "independent variable of the contemporary pluralistic capitalism."

100. Baumol, *op. cit.*, pp. 50–52. See also Baumol, "The Theory of Expansion of the Firm," *The American Economic Review*, December, 1962, pp. 1078–87.

101. Baumol, *Business Behavior*, chap. 6.

102. Fellner *et al.*, *op. cit.*, p. 53; Dunlop, "The Task of Contemporary Wage Theory," pp. 16–20.

Chapter 8

1. The need to use various selective instruments was voiced by A. Smithies, "Price Policy and Economic Growth and Stability," and O. Eckstein, "Inflation: The Wage-Price Spiral and Economic Growth," in *The Relationship of Prices to Economic Stability and Growth* (Compendium, Joint Economic Committee [Washington, D.C.: Government Printing Office, 1958]), pp. 611–15 and 361–74, respectively.

2. See Joseph Davis, "The Consumer, the Economy and the Government," a paper presented at the Third Annual Conference of the Council on Consumer Information, St. Louis, Missouri, April 5, 1957, pp. 8 and 12 ff.

3. See A. Lerner, "Inflationary Depression and the Regulation of Administered Prices," *The Relationship of Prices to Economic Stability and Growth*, pp. 257–68; Galbraith, in *Hearings, Administered Prices*, pp. 4928 ff.; and Senator O'Mahoney's bill, in *Hearings, Administered Prices*, p. 102.

4. This does not mean that government fiscal and monetary policies can be conducted with such precision that aggregate demand will be of the exact size to achieve full employment of the labor force without inflation. See John R. Hicks, *A Contribution to the Theory of Trade Cycles* (Oxford: Clarendon Press, 1950), chaps. 7–8.

5. A characteristic example is the so-called Pigou effect, which is analytically valid but practically useless. See A. Pigou, "The Classical Stationary State," *Economic Journal*, December, 1943, and "Economic Progress in a Stable Environment," *Economica*, August, 1947. See also William Fellner, *Trends and Cycles in Economic Activity* (New York: Henry Holt, 1956), pp. 125, 203, 283, and 302.

6. For a detailed exposition of the purposes and working of monetary policy, see *United States Monetary Policy*, (New York: The American Assembly, December, 1958), and The Commission on Money and Credit, *Money and Credit* (Englewood, N.J.: Prentice-Hall, 1961).

7. See chap. 7, p. 72.

8. Some economists object to this on the ground that over the long-run period, the velocity of money, i.e., the frequency with which money is used for purchases, has been relatively constant or predictably decreasing. See a variety of papers in Milton Friedman (ed.) and R. Selden "Studies in the Quantity Theory of Money," *The Journal of Political Economy*, September, 1959.

9. See chap. 7, pp. 72–73; also Smith, "The Discount Rate as a Credit Control Weapon"; and D. A. Alkadeff, "Credit Controls and Financial Intermediaries," *The American Economic Review*, September, 1960, pp. 655–71.

10. See on this C. A. Zebot, "For Economic Controls," *The New York Times*, August 13, 1950, and *idem*, "Need for Economic Controls," *The New York Times*, January 25, 1951 (refuting the straight macro-policy approach to the Korean War inflation by S. Harris in *The New York Times*, January 22, 1951).

11. See chap. 7, pp. 86–89.

12. For a discussion of government–central bank relationship, see *Government and the Central Bank*, Federal Reserve Bank of Philadelphia, pp. 3–11.

13. See also Fellner *et al.*, *op. cit.*, p. 40.

14. See chap. 7, p. 78.

15. For the detailed argument between A. F. Burns and the Council of Economic Advisers, see A. F. Burns, "Examining the New 'Stagnation' Theory," *Morgan Guaranty Survey*, May, 1961, pp. 1–7; "The Council's View," *ibid.*, August, 1961, pp. 1–6; and A. F. Burns, "A Second Look at the Council's Economic Theory," *ibid.*, August, 1961, pp. 6–15.

16. Recently, however, a trend of opinion toward greater reliance on sales taxes, in order to avoid the growth-impairing effect of steeply progressive income-tax rates, has been noticed. See Galbraith, *The Affluent Society*, pp. 262, 315–20, 332; and Hansen, *Economic Issues of the 1960's*, pp. 104–12.

17. Representative of the growing consensus was a statement in favor of *Reducing Tax Rates for Production and Growth* by the Research and Policy Committee of the Committee for Economic Development, December, 1962.

18. See, on this, The Bank for International Settlements, Thirty-second *Annual Report*, June, 1962, pp. 12, 14, 23–24; OECD, Economic Surveys by the OECD, *United States*, November, 1962, pp. 18–33; *idem*, *Policies for Economic Growth*, November, 1962, pp. 27–42; *idem*, *Policies for Price Stability*, November, 1962, p. 15.

19. OECD, *United States*, p. 19; *idem*, *Policies for Economic Growth*, p. 28.

20. The proposed tax reduction was passed by Congress and, on February 26, 1964, President Johnson signed into law the new Revenue Act of 1964. The Administration calculated that in order to reduce unemployment to 4 per cent the aggregate demand for goods and services should be increased by at least $30 billion. The combined spending effect of the enacted tax reduction and the transitional federal budget deficit is expected to accomplish just that. See *Economic Report of the President*, January, 1964, pp. 37, 171–72, and 274; and A. Mokum, "Potential GNP: Its Measurement and Significance," *1962 Proceedings of the Business and Economic Statistics Section of the American Statistical Association*.

21. In repeating its strong suggestion for a full-employment fiscal policy in the United States, the 1963 annual report of the Bank for International Settlements, of June 1963, claims that despite the apparent deficits in recent Federal budgets, in terms of the economic impact of its revenues and expenditures on the size of the aggregate demand for goods and services, the Federal government has shown a "surplus position." The report states that the Federal budget has been a "continuing dampening factor" on the American economy. The report is critical also of the proposed Federal budget for 1964, stating that "while the budget . . . is aimed at . . . recovery, it is not designed to lift total demand to a full employment level over any specified time period." The report sees the reason for this basic shortcoming in that "for the wider public a consensus on effective full employment policy has been hampered by a belief in spontaneous private demand and by misunderstanding of fiscal policy." See "Europe's Bankers Assail U.S. Policy," *The New York Times*, June 11, 1963, p. 47.

22. See Appendix H-1.

23. See U.S. Congress, Joint Economic Committee, *Hearings on President's Economic Report* (Washington, D.C.: Government Printing Office, March, 1963), Part I; and U.S. Congress, Joint Economic Committee, *The Federal Budget as an Economic Document* (Washington, D.C.: Government Printing Office, 1963).

24. For attempted calculations of these effects, see *Hearings on President's Economic Report*, pp. 45–55.

25. See chap. 8, pp. 97–98.

26. See *Hearings on President's Economic Report*.

27. See Appendix H-2.

28. Although wholesale and consumer price indices since 1958 have been edging up almost imperceptibly, the rate of increase in GNP was a meager annual average of 2.5 per cent and unemployment moved between 4.5 and 7 per cent.

29. See on this chap. 7.

30. See chap. 7, p. 88.

31. See F. Holzman, "Inflation: Cost Push and Demand Pull," *The American Economic Review*, Maıch, 1960, pp. 20–43. In this article, Holzman distinguishes between "cost push" ("the change in prices and employment as a direct result of the cost effect of higher wage rates," p. 22); "direct cost pull" ("the change in prices and employment due to the change in spending which results from increasing wage rates at the expense of other factor incomes," p. 22); and "indirect cost pull" ("the change in prices and employment which results from changes in investment, exports and Government expenditures induced by the wage-rate increases," p. 22).

32. See chap. 7, pp. 88–89. Also see F. Holzman, "Creeping Inflation," *Review of Economics and Statistics*, August, 1959, pp. 324–29. In this article, Holzman shows that the increase in demand from the cost push will not be sufficient to offset fully its unemployment effects.

33. A deliberate increase of aggregate demand to "validate" cost-push inflation, will result in another measure of additional inflationary pressures on the demand side when all the cost-pushed income increases will have translated themselves into their delayed demand effects.

34. *Economic Report of the President*, January, 1962, pp. 185–90. See also *Economic Report of the President*, January, 1963, pp. 85–86.

35. See also Appendix G-1.

36. See Appendix G-1. The following discussion concerning the criteria for a noninflationary but full-employment-oriented wage-price behavior originated in C. A. Zebot, "President's Advisory Cimmittee on Labor-Management Policy," *Review of Social Economy*, September, 1961, pp. 114–32.

37. For cyclical fluctuation of the rate of productivity increase see S. Fabricant, *Basic Facts on Productivity Change* (New York: National Bureau of Economic Research, 1959), pp. 10–17.

38. J. Akerman ("An Institutional Approach to the Problem of Inflation," *Stabile Preise in wachsender Wirtschaft*, p. 13), however, seems to be leaning toward abiding by the cyclical influences on productivity.

39. J. B. Clark was the first economist systematically to introduce the marginal productivity concept into the analysis of income distribution. His approach was quickly accepted as a useful analytical tool. However, although incorporated into general economic theory, the concept of marginal productivity never became very meaningful operationally as a criterion for *income distribution* as distinct from its *employment effects*. But it should also be kept in mind that J. B. Clark dealt with the *microeconomic* question of distributing the total revenue of a *firm*, and not with the *macro-micro* problem of how to distribute additional *national* income generated by economy-wide productivity improvements.

40. Kendrick-Fabricant's new productivity concept implies joint, multiple causation of productivity improvements. However, they still recognize that separate labor and capital productivity concepts and statistics are useful for special purposes. See S. Fabricant, *op. cit.*, pp. 3–6. See also Appendix G-1.

41. A great many research grants from private and government sources have been given each year to universities and individuals throughout the country. In addition, productive efficiency can also be fostered by legal regulations. Thus, for example, the British Patent Act of 1949 and 1958, in Section 37 under the heading "Compulsory Licenses," states that if the patent were not used by its owner after the period of three years, an interested party could request permission to use it.

42. In the message announcing the establishment of the President's Advisory Committee on Labor-Management Policy, President Kennedy charged the new committee with the duty to advise him and the public "with respect to actions that may be taken by labor, management and the public which will promote free and responsible collective bargaining, industrial peace, sound wage policies, sound price policies and stability, a higher standard of living, increased productivity, and America's competitive position in world markets." *The New York Times*, February 2, 1961.

43. See a very good article by F. Holzman, "Income Determination in Open Inflation," *Review of Economics and Statistics*, May, 1950, pp. 150–58.

44. For an original approach to the problem of inflation resulting from the behavior of pluralistic groups, see H. Aujac, *International Economic Papers*, No. 4, pp. 109–24.

45. Some writers maintain that the basic distributional pattern will be followed even if there were a conscious attempt to level wage differentials. See Fellner *et al.*, *op. cit.*, p. 53, and John R. Hicks, *The Essays in World Economics* (Oxford: Clarendon Press, 1959), pp. 96–102.

46. See on this also Hicks, *op. cit.*, pp. 113–15; Fritz Machlup, in *Hearings, Administered Prices*, pp. 4953 and 4969.

47. See John W. Kendrick, *Productivity Trends in the United States* (New York: National Bureau of Economic Research, 1961), pp. 136–37.

48. See the Chase Manhattan Bank, *Business in Brief*, September–October, 1961, pp. 2–4.

49. The late Per Jacobsson of the International Monetary Fund suggested that, in line with Keynes' assumption of a constant "wage unit" in the short run, money wages in the United States be held constant or at least be kept below productivity increases, until full employment is re-established. This suggestion could also be inferred from the spirit of the "Guideposts" according to which unemployment, by reducing relative labor scarcity, would call for wage increases (if any) by less than productivity improvements. P. Jacobsson's suggestion was contained in a paper presented at a symposium on economic growth on February 25, 1963, and published as a special IMF press release.

50. This may be difficult to achieve until the rank and file in *labor and business* understand the necessary criteria for a fair and noninflationary wage-price policy. The difficulty points to an urgent need for a systematic economic education of citizens.

51. For a much needed clarification of *self-interest* (conforming to the nature of economic activity) as distinct from *selfishness* (morally objectionable antisocial behavior), see P. Danner, "A Justification of Self-Interest," *Review of Social Economy*, September, 1961, pp. 99–113.

52. The existing legal regulation of collective bargaining in the United States is minimal, to say the least. The Labor-Management Relations Act of 1947 contains only two general provisions concerning collective bargaining. The law requires employers to bargain "in good faith" with the corresponding certified union, and it stipulates a sixty days' notice whenever one of the two parties intends to press for contractual changes upon the termination of the existing collective agreement.

53. According to Wilson (*op. cit.*, pp. 261–631), collective bargaining has a built-in inflationary bias.

54. On the growing operational significance for developed Western economics of the concept and methods of consensus through dialogue, see "Les Con-

flits et les Dialogues," in the new *Encyclopédie Française, L'Univers Économique et Social*, F. Perroux, ed., Paris, 1960, pp. 9.58–3 to 9.66–2. See also J. Solterer's review of this work in *The American Economic Review*, June, 1961.

55. The need for such procedural improvement in the process of collective bargaining was at least implied in the report of the President's Commission on National Goals when it said that "government should provide appropriate guidance to the process of collective bargaining." *Goals for Americans* (Englewood, N.J.: Prentice-Hall, 1961), p. 152.

56. See G. Briefs, "The Roots of Totalism"; *idem*, "The Ethos Problem in the Present Pluralistic Society," *Review of Social Economy*, March, 1957, pp. 47–75; and *idem*, "Some Economic Aspects of the Pluralistic Society," in F. Vito *et al., Naturordnung* (Innsbruck, 1961), pp. 218–31.

57. It has been observed by a number of writers that the labor share of the national product has been relatively stable over a large number of years. For a good analysis on that subject, see G. Johnson, "The Functional Distribution of Income in the U.S., 1850–1952," *Review of Economics and Statistics*, May, 1954, pp. 175–83.

58. See Appendix H-2.

59. See Appendix H-3.

60. *Economic Report of the President*, January, 1962, pp. 185–90.

61. See chap. 8, pp. 108–11.

62. OECD, *Policies for Price Stability*.

63. On these developments in Western Europe, see "Trade Block Panel Urges Tariff Cuts," *The New York Times*, June 6, 1963, p. 47; and "Wages in Europe Defy Restraints," *ibid.*, June 23, 1963, p. 18. *The Economist* (London) of March 7, 1964, p. 919, reported the following comparative increases in consumer goods prices over the period 1962–63: U.S.A., 3 per cent; Great Britain, 5 per cent; Western Germany, 6.5 per cent; France, 10.5 per cent; and Italy, 13.5 per cent.

64. The problem of a more effective administration of fiscal policy was discussed recently in Fellner *et al., op. cit.*, pp. 40–41, and W. Baumol *et al., What Price Economic Growth?* (Englewood, N.J.: Prentice-Hall, 1961), pp. 30–61 and 147–49.

65. On the deeper meaning of this, see C. A. Zebot, "Economics of Affluence," *Review of Social Economy*, September, 1959, pp. 112–25, and chap. 5 of this book.

Chapter 9

1. On the interrelationship between economic growth and inflation in newly developing countries, see G. S. Dorrance, "The Effect of Inflation on Economic Development," *Staff Papers*, International Monetary Fund, March, 1963.

2. For a rigorous analysis of an appropriate investment policy based on the relationships between the available supply of human skills and saving at various stages of economic development, see J. M. Power, "Laborsaving in Economic Growth," *The American Economic Review*, May, 1961. See also Appendix B-1.

3. On the Soviet inflation during and immediately following World War II and how it was wiped out by a general but discriminatory confiscation of accumulated savings, see C. A. Zebot, "A Lesson in Soviet Economics," *America*, May 22, 1948, pp. 166–67.

4. On the spontaneous behavior of administered prices, see chaps. 7–8.

5. It is this aspect of Keynesian economics that Fellner called "cyclical Keynesianism," which virtually everyone accepts. See W. Fellner, "Keynesian Economics After Twenty Years: What is Surviving," *The American Economic Review*, May, 1957, pp. 67–76.

6. In the U.S.S.R., income taxes play a very limited role. "In 1958 . . . income tax levied on 'workers and employees' will be gradually abolished in the peroid 1960–65." See Alec Nove, *The Soviet Economy* (New York: Frederick A. Praeger, 1961), p. 102. Compulsory savings, on the other hand, represented for a long time an important source of government revenue. "The mass-subscription loan . . . was a compulsory deduction from wages to buy premium bonds. . . . In 1958, it was decided to abandon the practice while simultaneously suspending . . . repayments on already existing bonds." (*Ibid.*, p. 101.) It is obvious, therefore, that high rates of Soviet sales (turnover) taxes will assume an even greater importance as a source of government revenue. In 1960, legislation was introduced gradually to eliminate Soviet income taxes by 1965. However, in September, 1962, it was decided to postpone indefinitely the scheduled first reduction in personal income taxes. This may be interpreted as a measure counteracting the underlying inflationary pressures in Soviet consumer-goods markets.

7. See chap. 4, pp. 25–26.

8. Soviet housing, which is chronically short in the extreme, is, of course, subject to rigid and meticulous rationing.

9. See chap. 4.

10. G. Grossman, "Industrial Prices in the USSR," *The American Economic Review*, May, 1959, p. 52.

11. F. Holzman, "Soviet Inflationary Pressures, 1928–1957: Causes and Cures," *The Quarterly Journal of Economics*, May, 1960, p. 183.

12. See Th. Shabad, "Soviet Accuses 50 Kirghiz Aides," *The New York Times*, January 16, 1962, p. C-3. This report presents a fantastic case of "informal activities" carried on by Soviet officials. It was discovered in the Republic of Kirghizia that a number of very high officials and managers, including a former head of the State Planning Committee of the Kirghiz Republic, engaged in an embezzlement ring that amounted to a veritable private enterprise system.

13. See J. Berliner, "The Informal Organization of the Soviet Firm," *The Quarterly Journal of Economics*, August, 1952, p. 356.

Chapter 10

1. See "The Soviet Communist Party Draft Program," *The New York Times*, August 1, 1961, pp. 13–20.

2. *Ibid.*

3. See Appendix A-1.

4. The original Marshall Plan Organization for European Economic

Cooperation has been renamed and reorganized into the Organization for Economic Cooperation and Development, OECD, which now has twenty members, including the United States and Canada.

Chapter 11

1. Real choices are of course not simply reducible to self-evident calculations but require judgment and democratic consensus. This is because actual alternatives are in between the two theoretical limits, a more convenient solution being usually the costlier one, and vice versa.

2. The term "socialization," as used here, is taken from the text of the papal encyclical *Mater et Magistra,* where it means "the progressive multiplication of relations in society, with different forms of life and associated activity, and juridical institutionalism." So understood, "socialization" is said to be not a "product of natural forces working in a deterministic way" but "a creation of men." See text of the encyclical by Pope John XXIII on social problems of the modern world, *The New York Times,* July 15, 1961, pp. 5–6.

3. The reader is invited to direct his curiosity toward the almost unbelievable dimensions of luxury with which some dictatorial leaders of relatively underdeveloped countries surround themselves. Dictators such as Tito, Sukarno, Nkrumah, etc., more than match the variety of consumer goods and services enjoyed by the richest rulers and wealthy individuals in the "affluent societies" of the West.

4. See chap. 8.

5. The information is from the concluding address by President L. S. Senghor of Senegal, Chairman of the Lagos Conference, as reported in *The New York Times,* February 1, 1962, p. 7.

6. See *The New York Times,* "Africa's Unity Charter," May 27, 1963, p. 8.

7. For early public discussion of the problem, see W. Fellner, "Factors in Rising Prices," *The New York Times,* March 25, 1957; C. A. Zebot, "Diagnosing Inflation," *ibid.,* April 10, 1957; *idem,* "Wage-Price Relationship," *ibid.,* June 26, 1957.

8. See Appendix F-1.

9. *Economic Report of the President,* January, 1962, pp. 185–90.

10. See chap. 8.

11. In the United Kingdom, in July, 1961, the government called for a wage pause in order to give time to the National Economic Development Council to prepare long-range policies for economic growth and for limiting the rise in money incomes. For 1962, the government has recommended that increases in average earnings should not exceed 2–2½ per cent. In France, the government, employers, and the unions review together every autumn the wage claims in relation to the estimated growth of national income. A similar procedure has been adopted in Austria by the joint price-wage commission. Holland adopted a more complex formula. In each industry, wages should not exceed one quarter of the sum of thrice the average annual long-term (over nine years) productivity increase in that industry and the anticipated percentage increase in productivity for the economy as a whole in 1962 (2 per cent). See Economic Commission for Europe, *Economic Survey of Europe in 1961*

(Geneva, 1962), Part I. See also OECD, *Policies for Price Stability;* and *idem, Policies for Economic Growth.*

12. The "grammar" analogy was suggested by Professor Josef Solterer in our discussion of American economic goals on the TV program "Decade of Crisis," on Channel 4, Washington, D.C., February 4, 1962. The "style" comparison was added by the author.

13. *Opus Justitiae Pax* (peace is the work of justice) was the motto of Pope Pius XII.

SUBJECT INDEX

NAME INDEX

(*Italics indicate references in Notes.*)